Where to Wat

IRELAND

Where to Watch Birds in

IRELAND

Clive Hutchinson

Illustrated by David Daly

Gill & Macmillan

Published in Ireland by
Gill & Macmillan Ltd
Goldenbridge
Dublin 8

with associated companies throughout the world

© Clive Hutchinson 1994

0 7171 2204 2

Line illustrations by David Daly

Printed and bound by Biddles Limited, Guildford, Surrey

A catalogue record for this book is available from the British Library.

CONTENTS

v

ACKNOWLEDGEMENTS

This book has benefited from the assistance of a great many people all over Ireland, who have helped over the years with the provision of data for bird surveys and censuses, counting their own local site and ensuring that the results of their work appears in bird reports and survey papers. My own knowledge of the country's birdwatching sites originates from the early 1970s when I organised wildfowl and wader counts. My first car – a little Fiat – was in 30 of the 32 counties of Ireland in search of birds, and while subsequent cars were not quite so widely travelled, I have tried to visit all the major wetlands, seabird colonies and migration watchpoints whenever away from my home base in Cork.

It is really impossible to list all the people who have helped me visit sites over the years or who have accompanied me. They include many birdwatchers from all parts of Ireland, and if I list some I will certainly exclude others, so to all those who have watched and discussed Irish birds with me I express my sincere thanks for sharing your knowledge.

I must, however, single out those who responded to requests for information for this book and who kindly read sections of the text in draft and examined the maps. None of them is responsible for any errors which have slipped through the checking process, but they all helped to reduce the level of mistakes. Advice and helpful literature on reserves in Northern Ireland was received from Dave Allen (RSPB reserves in Northern Ireland), Sarah Anderson (Dundrum Bay), Shaun D'Arcy-Burt (Quoile Pondage), Phil Davidson (Oxford Island), Liam McFaul (Rathlin Island) and James Orr (Castle Espie). Jane Coman provided information on the IWC hide at the Little Brosna.

Texts were read and commented on by Declan McGrath and Paul Walsh (Waterford), Jim Wilson (Cork), Pat Smiddy (Ballymacoda, Ballycotton and Cork Harbour), Terry Carruthers and Peter McDermot (Kerry), Tony Mee (Limerick and Clare), Tony Whilde and Marianne ten Cate (Clare, Galway, Mayo, Sligo and Roscommon), Don Cotton (Sligo), Tom Cooney (Louth, Dublin, Meath, Wicklow), David Daly and Oran O'Sullivan (Wexford), Chris Wilson (North Slob), Oscar Merne (Offaly), Bruce Carrick (Westmeath), Dave Allen (Ulster), Ralph Sheppard (Donegal), Liam McFaul (Rathlin Island), David Thompson (Strangford Lough), James Orr (Strangford Lough and Castle Espie in particular), Shaun D'Arcy-Burt and Stephen Foster (Strangford Lough and Quoile Pondage in particular), Sarah Anderson (Dundrum Bay) and Phil Davidson, Bob Davidson and Brian Nelson (Lough Neagh sites).

Many of those who commented on earlier drafts suggested the inclusion of additional sites, but space has not permitted this. There remains an obvious demand, however, for detailed site guides covering many more sites in individual counties and I hope that some publications will appear shortly.

David Daly produced the line drawings which so enhance the text. I hope that the wider exposure that this book will give his work may lead readers to seek out more of his art. The stunning mural he has painted within the observation tower at the North Slob in Wexford should be seen by all visitors to that site.

The preparation of so many maps was a forbidding task but I received computing advice from Willie Kelly and technical suggestions on presentation from Tom Cooney, which removed a lot of the pain from the process.

Robert Kirk at Christopher Helm was a tolerant editor, always receptive to proposals on layout and quick to respond to queries.

Long evenings before a word processor could have a disruptive effect on some families. I have been fortunate in that much of the writing of the book was done while my sons were studying in the evening, so family activities did not suffer unduly. Indeed, I am grateful for the encouragement I have always had from Rachel, Andrew and Mark, and for the good company when seeking out new or little-known sites in the course of research.

INTRODUCTION

Ireland has a very distinct bird fauna, in some respects rather impoverished when compared with other European countries, but in other ways extraordinarily interesting. Compare Ireland to the neighbouring island to the east, and consider that only two-thirds of the species recorded in Britain have been recorded here; that only two-thirds of the number of breeding birds occur; that there are no woodpeckers; that some migrant birds, which pass through each spring and autumn and nest as close as west Wales, do not stay to breed.

Yet, on the other hand, Ireland has a small human population, a relatively unspoiled environment and a very tiny number of birdwatchers, so there are great opportunities for exploring places with potential for birds where other birdwatchers will not be found. Because of the location of the island right on the western fringe of Europe projecting far out into the Atlantic, the opportunities for seeking out migratory seabirds, waders and passerine vagrants from America are immense. The small size of the island, its climate and topography all contribute to the type of bird community it has.

Seabirds

There is an abundance of seabirds: Ireland projects into the Atlantic and is surrounded by rich and relatively shallow seas stretching to the edge of the Continental Shelf. Throughout much of the year, large numbers of shearwaters, auks and petrels are recorded on all coasts. These movements were first reported at Cape Clear, Co Cork, where birdwatchers were amazed in the early 1960s at the vast numbers of passing seabirds in summer and autumn and at the presence among the common species of rarer skuas from the north and of shearwaters from the south, including Great Shearwaters and Sooty Shearwaters from south of the equator and Cory's Shearwaters from the Mediterranean, the Canaries, Madeira or the Azores.

Since the discoveries at Cape Clear were made, birdwatchers have visited headlands and islands all around the coast and spent many hours in wet and windy weather measuring the extent of seabird passage. We now know that most south and west coast headlands can attract large number of seabirds in the right conditions. Passage on the south coast is predominantly westerly, on the west coast most birds pass south; on the north coast more pass west than east; on the east coast passage is largely southerly. Many of the movements observed involve feeding birds. For example, the late summer passage of Manx Shearwaters at Cape Clear clearly consists mainly of birds from the Kerry island breeding colonies. But the most remarkable movements, those in which southern shearwaters, northern skuas and rarities such as Sabine's Gulls and Leach's Petrels are sometimes seen, appear to result from weather conditions driving birds which are normally out of sight of land inshore. At Cape Clear, south-westerly winds and rain, usually associated with the passage of a front, provide the best conditions, as the birds are presumably pushed eastwards; at Brandon Point and Loop Head, westerlies and north-westerlies are optimal, funnelling the birds

1

into Tralee Bay and Galway Bay. Seabirds moving back out to sea appear to follow leading lines when they encounter barriers to their movement, so those species which are normally not visible from the mainland can be observed temporarily as they pass headlands or islands.

There are clearly large numbers of seabirds feeding well out to sea to be seen from the land only in exceptional weather conditions. Several trips have been made in small boats to observe seabirds at sea, and these have located high densities, higher than off much of the British coast, off south-west Ireland including many Great and Sooty Shearwaters, smaller numbers of Cory's Shearwaters and a very few Wilson's Petrels.

Winter Visitors

Wintering birds come from a wide geographical range of breeding areas. Being on the western fringe of Europe, Ireland provides winter quarters for birds from as far west as Arctic Canada, for a number of species breeding in Greenland and Iceland and for birds which breed in northern Europe east to Siberia. Brent Geese from northern Canada winter in Ireland. The wintering numbers of Great Northern Divers are far greater than the Icelandic population can account for, and may well include Canadian birds as well as Greenland breeders. From Greenland alone come Barnacle Geese and White-fronted Geese and several wader species. Ireland is the principal wintering area for a number of Icelandic species, particularly Whooper Swans, Golden Plovers, Black-tailed Godwits and Redshanks. From Scandinavia and the Baltic come many ducks, waders and finches and from as far east as Siberia come wintering Bewick's Swans, Grey Plovers and Bar-tailed Godwits.

Vagrants

Location is also the principal explanation for the pattern of vagrancy. Being on the western edge of Europe, Ireland is the first landfall for many vagrants from North America, but birds from as far east as Siberia such as Yellow-browed Warblers also occur every autumn. However, Ireland receives far fewer eastern or southern vagrants than Britain, which of course is not surprising, given the extra distance such birds have to travel.

Island Size

The area of Ireland is 84,421 km^2; the adjoining island of Great Britain is 2.8 times as large. There is little doubt from island biogeography theory that the smaller size of Ireland is the principal reason why it has only two-thirds of the number of breeding species found in Britain.

A small island is less likely to be landed on by a scarce bird than a large island, purely because the chances of the bird finding the larger island are greater. A smaller island is also more likely to have lower habitat diversity than a large island. There are some habitats in Britain which are not represented in Ireland: the lowland heath and chalk downland of southern England and the high mountains and Caledonian Scots pine woodland of Scotland have no Irish equivalent. The absence of these habitats may explain why Woodlarks, Dartford Warblers, Stone-curlews, Dotterels, Greenshanks and Crested Tits do not nest in Ireland.

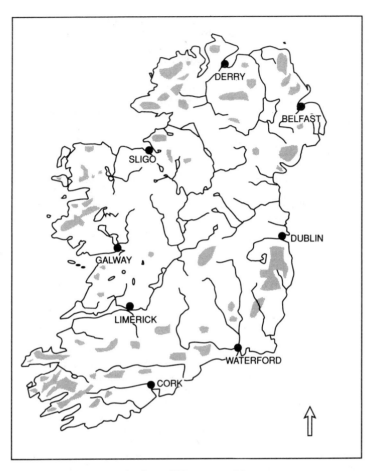

Ireland: land over 300 metres and river systems

Climate

The mild but extremely moist Irish climate also affects bird distribution, both indirectly and directly. The high Irish rainfall, for example, produces winter flooding which provides refuge for wildfowl. Ireland's climate does, however, affect bird distribution directly when the milder winter temperatures keep the ground soft and the lakes free of ice, thus ensuring their availability for feeding birds, when extreme winter conditions over Europe drive many birds westwards. In these circumstances, Teal, Lapwings and Redwings, to name just three species, flood into Ireland seeking exposed water or soft ground.

Topography

Topography, like climate, affects bird distribution by its influence on the habitats which cover the landscape. Geological history has formed the basis of the modern landscape, but climate, the effect of erosion by wind and water, and the pattern of plant and animal colonisation after the Ice Age, have all played parts in producing the habitats which cover the island nowadays. The principal habitats can conveniently

3

be divided up into the broad categories of coast, inland wetlands, mountain and bog, farmland, woodland and urban areas.

Coastline

The Irish coastline is varied. The cliffs support large populations of breeding seabirds, the estuaries and coastal lagoons hold many wintering and passage wildfowl and waders. More than 85% of the coast consists of rocky shore, but much of it is lowlying. Only about nine seabird colonies have more than 10,000 breeding pairs. Of these, only Lambay Island off the Dublin coast, Great Saltee off the south Wexford coast and Rathlin Island, Antrim, are away from the west coast. The largest colonies are in Kerry, where some tens of thousands of Manx Shearwaters, Storm Petrels, Gannets and Puffins breed on the Blaskets, the Skelligs and the appropriately named Puffin Island. These are the largest Storm Petrel colonies in the world. The colonies close to the Irish Sea have large numbers of Razorbills, Guillemots and gulls. Those species which feed farther out to sea are concentrated on the more exposed coasts.

Less than 15% of the coastline is sandy beach, mudflat or saltmarsh. These shores, however, incorporate a large inter-tidal zone and are important for wintering waders and wildfowl, though only six estuaries – the Shannon Estuary, Lough Foyle, Strangford Lough, Dundalk Bay, the North Bull and Cork Harbour – hold more than 20,000 waders regularly. These estuaries, as would be expected, have the largest areas of inter-tidal mudflat.

The sandy shores on the west coast are known to support quite large winter populations of Ringed Plovers and Sanderlings but their extent is not known. The sandy beaches are numerous and long and a co-ordinated count is not feasible at present.

As well as winter waders, sandy shores also support some breeding terns, though the colonies tend to be small and widely dispersed.

On the west coast, grassy islands are the main wintering ground for Barnacle Geese breeding in west Greenland. The Inishkea Islands, Mayo, hold nearly half the Irish winter population. Many of these islands also provide secure nesting sites for Arctic, Common and Sandwich Terns.

There is a small amount of sand dune machair in the west. Machair comprises stable dune grassland with sands enriched by calcareous shell fragments. It is heavily grazed and frequently includes wet pools and marshes. This habitat is thinly distributed in Donegal, Sligo, Mayo and Galway.

Inland Wetlands

In winter the open waters of the inland wetlands provide feeding and relative security from predation for ducks and geese, mainly from breeding areas to the north-west and north-east. The damp edges provide grazing for the wildfowl and also attract Lapwings, Golden Plovers and Curlews, which can locate food more easily on soft ground. In summer ducks and grebes nest on the larger waters, Little Grebes, Moorhens and Grey Wagtails on the rivers, and ducks and Snipe on the marshes.

The largest Irish lake is Lough Neagh which has a surface area of 387 km². In summer it holds well over 750 pairs of Great Crested Grebes, much the largest breeding concentration in the country, but in winter it is of European importance for the huge numbers of wintering waterfowl

4

it holds. Lough Corrib, Galway, with an area of some 170 km², is the second largest lake, and it too is shallow, with a large diving duck population in winter. These two lakes are much the most important for birds, principally because they are so shallow. The other large lakes – Loughs Derg, Lower Lough Erne and Conn – are deeper and of less importance in winter. However, a number of the midland lakes, especially Loughs Iron, Owel and Derravaragh, have sizeable winter duck populations.

In summer most of the lakes have breeding Great Crested Grebes, Mallard and Tufted Ducks. Common Scoters nest on the Lough Erne system, on Lough Conn and increasingly in small numbers on other lakes. The principal inland gull colonies are on the western lakes and Lough Neagh, and Common Terns breed on islands on a number of lakes as well. Arctic and Sandwich Terns also nest on islands away from the sea, though in small numbers.

The water table in the west of Ireland rises with winter rain, the slower flowing rivers flood and the few remaining turloughs fill with water. This flooding produces large areas of water where ducks, geese and swans can graze, relatively safe from predators; it drives invertebrates up to the surface, where Lapwings, Golden Plovers and Curlews search in the soft ground for prey; and it covers such large tracts of country that startled birds can find feeding again after a short flight.

The callows or flood meadows on both sides of the River Shannon between Athlone and Portumna, on either side of the River Suck in Roscommon and on either side of the Little Brosna in Offaly and Tipperary, are the finest examples, though the Blackwater callows in Waterford are also superb. Here Wigeon graze on the edge of the water in great flocks of several thousand birds, Whooper Swans graze out in the middle of the flood and large flocks of Golden Plovers wheel about. Black-tailed Godwits probe in the soft alluvium, while the more common Curlews and Lapwings can be seen in most fields. At some of these sites, White-fronted Geese winter in small numbers, feeding on the callows and usually roosting on the surrounding bogs. The feeding appears to be very rich in spring, for numbers of Wigeon and Black-tailed Godwits normally reach a peak in March on the Little Brosna, apparently because many birds of Icelandic origin assemble here before departing to their breeding grounds.

Because the central plain is so flat, most Irish rivers are slow and sluggish in their upper courses, but they tend to run much more rapidly as they come close to the sea. Moorhens are common on almost all rivers and Kingfishers, Dippers, Grey Wagtails and Reed Buntings breed on most. In recent years the spread of Mink on rivers has been seen as the cause of some reduction in bird numbers.

Mountains

The birds of high ground are little known. Golden Plovers once nested on high ground in the south, east and midlands but now only remain as breeding birds in the north and west. Ring Ouzels almost certainly continue to nest in small numbers in most of the mountain ranges in the country, though they are difficult to track down. Ravens were once true montane birds but have increased and spread into the lowlands. The principal birds of high ground are Meadow Pipits and, in winter, the highest hills hold Snow Buntings.

Woodland

About 5% of the land surface of Ireland consists of forest, most of which is planted coniferous woodland, but some oak woods remain and these tend to be rather richer in bird species. The most numerous species in oak woods are Chaffinch, Robin, Goldcrest, Blue Tit, Coal Tit and Wren, these six comprising 75%-85% of the breeding bird communities in studies carried out to date. Comparison with results from Welsh and Scottish oak woods which had a somewhat similar history of management and utilisation shows that Willow Warblers, Garden Warblers and Blackcaps, all of which breed in Welsh and Scottish woods, were absent from the Irish plots, though they breed in other parts of Ireland. It may be that the absence of Willow Warblers was due to the occupation of their niche by Goldcrests, or that the absence of pioneer growth in the Irish census plots, especially of birch, militated against Willow Warblers. Both explanations have been proposed.

The birdwatcher going into mature planted coniferous woodland in summer will be impressed by the high density of Goldcrests. Studies of Norway spruce and Sitka spruce woods found up to 180 pairs per ten hectares in the Norway spruce, of which 59 were Goldcrests. This is much the highest recorded density in any habitat in Britain or Ireland, but unfortunately only 14 species were found. The Sitka spruce wood had fewer birds and only eight species were found. Again, Goldcrests were the most numerous species, with Chaffinch and Robin in second and third place as in Norway spruce.

Urban Areas

The features of Irish towns, which have drawn most attention in the ornithological literature, have been the roosts of Pied Wagtails and the increase in urban Magpies.

The Irish Avifauna

The reasons for the differences between the Irish avifauna and that of Britain or other parts of Europe are obviously complex. Ecological factors arising from the small size of the island have been of great importance as have the location and climate of the country. The various habitats, which have evolved or been modified by man, have provided the conditions within which those bird communities which occupy the country must survive. Modification of these habitats can have a marked effect on their bird populations and man's activities are the principal cause of changes to the landscape or its vegetation. Conservation is mainly about the careful planning of the landscape, and the future of the Irish avifauna depends on the influence of conservationists in the years to come.

GENERAL NOTES FOR THE VISITOR

Political Systems

The Republic of Ireland is an independent Republic with its own legislature and administration. Northern Ireland is part of the United Kingdom of Great Britain and Northern Ireland and is administered by a Secretary of State appointed by the British Government.

Access to Ireland

As Ireland is an island, the visitor to the country must come by air or sea. The following airports have daily connections:

Dublin	Major UK cities, most European capitals and some US cities.
Shannon	Major UK cities and some US and Canadian cities. Via Dublin to most European capitals.
Cork	London and via Dublin to other UK cities, most European cities and the US.
Belfast	Major UK cities and some European capitals.

Services change from season to season, so a check should be made with a local travel agent for up to date schedules. In addition, there are regional airports at Derry, Galway, Sligo, Waterford, Enniskillen in Fermanagh, Knock in Mayo and Farranfore in Kerry. These airports are serviced mainly from Belfast (Derry and Enniskillen) or Dublin (others) but some flights are direct from London.

Ferries bring passengers by sea to the following ports:

Dublin	Daily from Holyhead via B & I Line.
Dun Laoghaire	Daily from Holyhead via Stena Sealink.
Rosslare	Daily from Pembroke via B & I Line and from Fishguard via Stena Sealink, several sailings per week from Le Havre and Cherbourg via Irish Ferries.
Cork	Several sailings per week from Swansea in summer via Swansea Cork Ferries. Several sailings per week in summer from Le Havre via Irish Continental Lines and from Roscoff via Brittany Ferries.
Belfast	Daily from Liverpool via Norse Irish Ferries.
Larne	Daily by fast catamaran from Stranraer via Hovercraft SeaCat and by boat from Cairnryan (via P & O European Ferries) and Stranraer (via Stena Sealink).

Public Transport within Ireland

The railway system links the major towns and cities: Dublin to Waterford, Cork, Tralee, Limerick, Westport, Ballina, Sligo and Belfast and Belfast to Bangor, Larne, Portrush and Derry.

There is an express bus system covering the other large towns. Local services operate throughout the country, north and south. Details of routes and times are available from bus offices in the large towns.

Driving in Ireland

Driving is on the left hand side in both Northern Ireland and the Republic. Cars can be brought on the car ferries or hired at the international airports.

Currency

The currency in the Republic of Ireland is the Irish pound, in Northern Ireland the pound sterling. The exchange rate between the two varies from time to time within a range of plus or minus 10%. Most currencies can be changed readily at banks, of which there are several in every major town.

Accommodation

There is an enormous variety of accommodation in the country, ranging from high quality, and very expensive, hotels through modest hotels, guest-houses and hostels to camp sites. The tourist boards can provide current lists of available accommodation in all areas. Booking is essential for the months of July and August but outside this season accommodation is usually available to the caller at the door. Some camp sites and hotels close for the winter.

Maps and Guides

A number of road maps are available at various scales, but the standard series are the half inch and 1:50,000 series (the latter of which is replacing the old 1 inch series). The Ordnance Survey of Ireland (OSI) publishes half inch maps covering the entire island except the vicinity of Belfast. The Ordnance Survey of Northern Ireland (OSNI) publishes four half inch maps covering the six counties of Northern Ireland and substantial parts of the adjoining counties in the Republic. All of Ireland is to be mapped on a 1:50,000 scale but so far all the Northern Ireland and only a handful of the Republic of Ireland maps have appeared.

Telephone System

The telephone systems in Northern Ireland and the Republic are different. However, direct dialling is available to most numbers. From the Republic use the prefix 08 before the Northern Ireland number quoted in this book. From Northern Ireland or Britain use the prefix 010–353 before numbers in the Republic and drop the first digit 0 of the local code.

To dial a British number from the Republic, dial 0044 followed by the local code, but omit the first digit 0.

Conservation

In Northern Ireland, the Department of the Environment (NI) is responsible for conservation, the establishment of nature reserves and the protection of Areas of Special Scientific Interest (ASSIs).

In the Republic, the National Parks and Wildlife Service of the Office of Public Works has this responsibility, except that there is as yet no statutory protection of Natural Heritage Areas, the new term for Areas of Scientific Interest, though legislation has been promised.

Voluntary bird conservation in Northern Ireland is spearheaded by the Royal Society for the Protection of Birds (RSPB) which has its own headquarters at Belvoir Park Forest, Belfast BT8 4QT, full-time staff, reserves and a number of wardens. Its telephone number is

0232–491547. The Irish Wildbird Conservancy (IWC) performs a similar function in the Republic, but has much more limited resources and does not employ any full-time wardens. Its address is Ruttledge House, 8 Longford Place, Monkstown, Co Dublin and its telephone number is 01–2804322.

The National Trust for Northern Ireland, Rowallane House, Saintfield, Ballynahinch, Co Down (telephone 0238–510721) operates the Strangford Lough Wildlife Scheme and Murlough Nature Reserve and employs its own wardens. The Wildfowl and Wetlands Trust operates a reserve at Castle Espie on Strangford Lough. The Department of the Environment operates several reserves and Craigavon Borough Council runs Oxford Island Nature Reserve.

Birdwatching

The IWC has a network of branches throughout the Republic. These organise both indoor meetings and organised outings each month in winter. Members receive *IWC News*, a quarterly newsletter.

In Northern Ireland, the RSPB has members' groups in the major towns, which have a similar programme. Members receive the RSPB magazine *Birds* and, in addition, a Northern Ireland newsletter.

The British Trust for Ornithology has a network of regional representatives in Northern Ireland who organise survey work. The IWC runs similar surveys in the Republic.

Up to date news of rare birds throughout Ireland is available to callers of telephone numbers in both Northern Ireland and Republic. The system in the Republic is charged at premium rates. The Northern Ireland number can be phoned from within Northern Ireland by dialling 0247–467408, from the Republic by the number 08–0247–467408. The Republic of Ireland number, only available from within the Republic, is 1551–111–700.

Journals, Reports and Magazines

The major Irish ornithological journal is *Irish Birds*, an annual journal available from the IWC, Ruttledge House, 8 Longford Place, Monkstown, Co Dublin and incorporating the Irish Bird Report and the Irish Ringing Report.

A quarterly magazine, *Irish Birding News*, is published by the promoters of the Birds in Ireland News Service (BINS), which operates the premium rate telephone news service in the Republic. It is available by subscription from Birds in Ireland News Service, 46 Claremont Court, Glasnevin, Dublin 11.

The Northern Ireland Birdwatchers' Association publishes the *Northern Ireland Bird Report*, which appears at intervals of several years. The report may be purchased from the RSPB, Belvoir Park Forest, Belfast BT8 4QT (telephone 0232–491547).

Annual bird reports and the addresses to write to for copies are as follows:

Irish East Coast Bird Report Tom Cooney, 42 All Saints Road, Raheny, Dublin 5.

Cork Bird Report Mark Shorten, Nirvana, Menloe Gardens, Cork.

Bird Observatories

There are two bird observatories. Visitors are welcome to stay at both. Cape Clear Bird Observatory, Skibbereen, Co Cork has accommodation for ten people in addition to the warden, who is in residence from March to the end of October. The observatory is open all year. The island is reached by daily mailboat from Baltimore. Bookings to Kieran Grace, 84 Dorney Court, Shankill, Co Dublin.

Copeland Bird Observatory, Donaghadee, Co Down has accommodation for up to 20. The island is reached by chartered boat from Donaghadee and the observatory is open most weekends and some weeks from April to October. Bookings to Neville McKee, 67 Temple Rise, Templepatrick, Co Antrim BT39 0AG (telephone 08494–33068) or to Dr Peter Munro, Bruichladdich, 8 Lismenary Road, Ballynure, Ballyclare, Co Antrim BT39 9UE (telephone 09603–23421).

Bird Recording

After your birdwatching trip, please send your records to the local bird recorder. Bird recorders tend to change so no addresses are given in this book. Records for Northern Ireland are best sent to the RSPB and, for the Republic, to the IWC. Both organisations will forward records to the relevant recorders.

Further Reading

The standard book on the status of Irish birds is:
Hutchinson, Clive D. *Birds in Ireland* (T & A D Poyser, Calton, 1988).

For an overview of what is distinctive about Irish natural history read:
Mills, Stephen. *Nature in its Place: the Habitats of Ireland* (The Bodley Head, London,1987).

To understand the cultural background to the study of Irish birds read the forthcoming:
Foster, John Wilson & Ross, Helena C.G. (editors). *Nature in Ireland: a Scientific and Cultural History* (Lilliput Press, Dublin, in press).

A good general guide to Ireland for the visitor is:
Bord Failte Irish Tourist Board 1993 *Ireland Guide* (Gill and Macmillan, Dublin).

SUGGESTED ONE-WEEK AND TWO-WEEK TRIPS

Visitors from outside Ireland, or Irish birders willing to travel around the country in search of diversity of species, frequently look for suggestions for brief trips. The following is a list of the more popular areas for visiting at different seasons. It is based largely on records of rarer birds over the past decade and is biased towards the autumn when most rarities turn up, but it should not be followed too rigidly. There are lots of good birding sites waiting to be found.

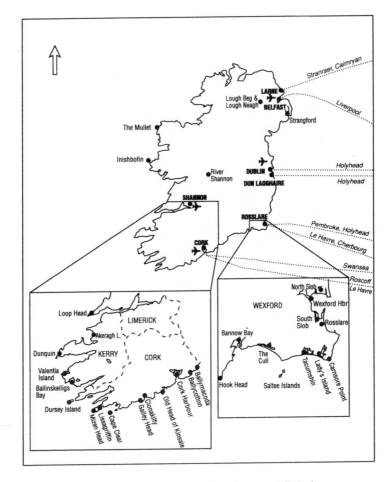

Ireland: suggested hotspots for short trips, especially in Autumn

Autumn

Wexford and Cork

Week-long trips to the south coast in August, September and October can be built around visits to headlands and islands for passage seabirds and migrant passerines and to estuaries and coastal lagoons for American waders and the possibility of other vagrants.

August is the peak month for passage seabirds. In Cork, the headlands which have recorded the largest movements have been the Old Head of Kinsale, Cape Clear and Mizen Head, though good numbers have also been seen from Galley Head. Expect Sooty Shearwaters and Great Shearwaters in conditions of south-westerly wind and rain, but Greats are erratic and not always seen in these conditions. Cory's Shearwaters are even more erratic, but these headlands are among the best places in Europe to see Great and Cory's side by side. Manx Shearwaters, Fulmars, Kittiwakes and auks are abundant and Great, Pomarine and Arctic Skua can all be seen on a good August day. Sabine's Gull and other rare species are less regular, but remember that almost everything from Black-browed Albatross to Frigatebird has appeared off these headlands.

An August trip along the south coast in search of seabirds can be mixed with visits to the estuaries and lagoons to look for waders and terns. Lady's Island Lake and Tacumshin in Wexford and Ballycotton, Clonakilty and Lissagriffin in Cork are all well worth covering daily. They have attracted rarities such as Pacific Golden Plover, Least Sandpiper and Caspian Tern at this time. Migrant passerines tend to be fewer, though Cape Clear has a good list of species recorded during the month. Melodious Warblers and Red-backed Shrike are almost an August speciality.

September is not so good a month for seabirds, though Great Shearwaters have appeared in thousands, but it is the best period for American waders. Any American species can occur on the coast, and not just the hot spots listed in this book turn them up. Many small lagoons and patches of mud at the head of estuaries produce Pectoral, White-rumped and Baird's Sandpipers. These estuaries are all easily accessible, and a three-day run from Wexford Harbour to Mizen Head will give sufficient time for adequate coverage.

September is also good for passerines. Cape Clear has received far more coverage than anywhere else but, in recent years, Dursey Island and the nearby mainland on the Beara peninsula have been watched for several weeks at a time. Rarities have been prolific: Dursey has had Ovenbird and Cape Clear has had Northern Waterthrush at this time. Other headlands such as Hook Head in Wexford and Helvick Head in Waterford are also worth visiting.

October is the month when most rarities are seen. A few late American waders turn up, and Sabine's Gulls can still be seen off the promontories, but the real action is in the little gardens, along the hedges and stone walls and in the small fields of the coastal headlands. Vagrants from Siberia can be seen in the same field of view as passerines which have just dropped from the sky after crossing the Atlantic. At Cape Clear, for example, Pallas's Grasshopper Warbler and Grey-cheeked Thrush were found within minutes of each other in the same garden. Working from east to west along this coast, Hook Head has had Radde's Warbler and Bobolink; the Old Head of Kinsale has held Dusky Warbler and Siberian Stonechat; Galley Head has had Paddyfield Warbler and

Philadelphia Vireo; Mizen Head and Crookhaven have had Isabelline Wheatear and Red-eyed Vireo; Dursey has had Parula Warbler and Olivaceous Warbler.

A one- or two-week trip along this coast could take the form of a leisurely drive from site to site or, alternatively, choosing one place as a base. If driving about, one could take Wexford, Cork city or west Cork as a base. If spending a week or more in one location, there are several obvious options. Tacumshin has sufficient turnover of birds to justify an extended stay and there are several other sites nearby which could be checked daily. Ballycotton has similar advantages and was once run as an observatory, with results that showed considerable turnover of birds. The Old Head of Kinsale and the Mizen Head can be very exciting when the winds are right, but when quiet they can appear extremely birdless. Cape Clear is the obvious choice for a week's stay. The Observatory has excellent facilities and, if it is full, there are a number of guest houses, a Youth Hostel and a camp site. More important, there is excellent company from other birders. Allihies, on the mainland opposite Dursey, is another place to spend a few days and it can be very rewarding.

Saltee

A stay on Saltee for a week in autumn can be very exciting, but it does require permission from the owner and some organisation as all food and cooking equipment must be brought out to the island. The island is not particularly good for seawatching, but it can be outstanding for passerine migration. In recent years it has not been covered regularly in autumn. The modern twitcher fears uninhabited islands because they are beyond the reach of telephone calls and news of nearby rare birds cannot get to them. Some of us might find this a very good reason for spending a week on Saltee looking for our own birds. Rarities seen in autumn include Siberian Stonechat, Bonelli's Warbler and Olive-backed Pipit. The island has been overshadowed by other sites to the west in recent autumns, but there is no reason why it should not be a very exciting place when the winds are from the south-east in October.

Kerry

The corner of Kerry, which runs from Lough Gill east to Tralee and north to Akeragh Lough, is where it was first discovered that many American waders are annual visitors to Ireland. Frank King, who put Akeragh Lough on the map in the late 1950s and 1960s, still watches the area regularly. Among his more remarkable records are flocks of 13 American Wigeon and 14 Pectoral Sandpipers as well as a list which includes the first Irish records of Least, Baird's, Stilt and Solitary Sandpiper and most other waders on the Irish list.

Drainage has led to a deterioration in habitat at Akeragh Lough in recent years, but it still attracts American waders. Tralee would be an excellent base for a stay in the area. When the wind turns north-westerly and rain comes, head immediately for Brandon Point at the west end of Tralee Bay. Some of the finest seawatching anywhere has been carried out from here: Sabine's Gulls are a particular speciality.

Kerry has possibilities for passerine migrants which have only been explored in the last few years. The tip of the Dingle peninsula has been shown to have similar species to the west Cork headlands, though in smaller numbers, and there must be further potential on Valencia Island and around Ballinskelligs.

Loop Head and Bridges of Ross

The western tip of the Clare coastline has very little cover as it runs out to the lighthouse at Loop Head. Yet an informal bird observatory and ringing station has operated here with great success for several years. A house is rented in autumn and made available to visiting birders and ringers, and this provides an excellent base for a week's holiday in September or October.

September tends to be the best time for seawatching, and north-westerly winds are essential. But, in these conditions, virtually anything can occur. Parties of Long-tailed Skuas and Sabine's Gulls and good numbers of Leach's Petrels and Grey Phalaropes are the main feature, but Wilson's Petrel has been reliably recorded and there has been an unpublished record of an all black petrel.

Passerine migration depends on quite different weather conditions of course, and numbers of birds are low, but the quality of birds seen is extraordinary: Rustic Bunting, Pied Wheatear and Yellow-rumped Warbler are among the highlights. Each year produces some new and exciting bird.

The area is thinly watched in autumn. Rarely are there more than four birdwatchers present, except when seawatching is good, and then the nearby Bridges of Ross can have 20 or more people on the cliff.

The Mullet

Many birdwatchers have looked at the map of Ireland and seen the westerly projection at the north-west corner of Mayo and realised that it has to be attractive to migrants in autumn. The area is a long drive from any of the major centres of population, and bird numbers and diversity can be low when weather conditions are unattractive for migrants.

There was a Bird Observatory here for a few years in the 1960s, and a few individuals have done some seawatching off the headlands. However, the real potential must be for American vagrants, and a number of waders have been seen. One American passerine, a Red-eyed Vireo, was found in a roadside garden by a visiting birder in 1990 so who knows what a lengthy visit in October would produce.

Other west coast sites

A number of other sites on the coast of Galway, Mayo and Donegal might repay an autumn stay. The island of Inishbofin off the Galway coast has had Yellow-browed Warbler in October and has excellent accommodation; Tory Island and Inishtrahull off the Donegal coast were both manned for long periods in the 1960s and produced a number of rare migrants. Tory is inhabited and has a hostel, but Inishtrahull has no human population. A visit to Malin Head – opposite Inishtrahull but on the Donegal mainland – would be easier to organise.

In recent years more adventurous birdwatchers have spent long periods on almost all the Cork headlands, on the Dingle peninsula in Kerry and at Loop Head in Clare, but the west coast north of Loop remains very much virgin territory. The surface was scratched by the observatory movement in the 1960s but there are many new finds to be made.

Winter

Wexford

Early in January, if the weather is crisp and dry, there are few better places to spend a few days birdwatching than the south-east corner of

Ireland. The climate in general is milder than elsewhere in the country and the concentration of geese on the Slobs provides a focal point. There are always lots of birds to see.

Accommodation is widely available in Wexford and a week's holiday, or even a long weekend, could be well filled by visiting the Slobs for geese, the shore at Curracloe for diving ducks and grebes, the lagoons at Lady's Island Lake and Tacumshin for ducks and the unexpected, and the harbour at Wexford and the coast at Kilmore Quay for gulls and other strays (Forster's Tern and Brünnich's Guillemot have both occurred).

The Slobs have nearly 10,000 Greenland White-fronted Geese, but they also hold Brent Geese and a few Canada (usually of one of the small races) and Pink-footed Geese. A white or blue-phase Snow Goose is present in most winters and other goose species can occur. There are lots of Bewick's Swans (and Whistling Swan has been seen among them) and most of the common duck species can be found.

On the coast, just north of the North Slob, the beach at Curracloe has long lines of Common Scoters offshore. Around the edges of the flocks are divers and grebes, and among the scoters are a few Velvet Scoters and, in some years, Surf Scoters. A telescope is essential to view the birds, but the sand dunes behind the strand provide a good vantage point. The strand is long and well worth working very thoroughly.

Wexford Harbour might seem rather unexciting from the town but birders have found Bonaparte's Gull and Forster's Tern just off the bridge, and there are lots of waders beside the road.

Lady's Island and Tacumshin are both well watched in autumn, but in January and February birders are far fewer and the chances of finding interesting birds for oneself increases.

Lough Neagh and Lough Beg

Lough Neagh is so enormous that it requires several days to cover it any way adequately, and Lough Beg requires a day to itself. Winter is one of the best times in the entire area, for then diving ducks are at their peak. One of the great unanswered bird survey questions is whether the wildfowl counts, which are carried out from the shoreline, are comprehensive, or whether there are large flocks of duck in the middle of the lake which cannot be seen from the edge and are missed. Whatever the truth of the matter, the numbers which can be seen are absolutely immense and are one of the great ornithological sights of the country.

A visit in December, January or February should catch the birds at their peak. At least two days should be spent in the south-east corner visiting Oxford Island and the smaller lakes nearby. Large numbers of wild swans and duck can be found at Oxford Island, but there is considerable movement between this site and Lurgan Park Lake and the Craigavon Lakes. The rare ducks, which turn up regularly in this area, include Ferruginous Duck, Ring-necked Duck, Ruddy Duck, Goosander and Smew, and in recent years the only Lesser Scaup recorded in Ireland has wintered here. This really is a very exciting place for the duck enthusiast to spend a few days.

This corner of Northern Ireland is close to Belfast Lough and Strangford Lough to the east, where large flocks of Brent Geese winter together with divers, grebes, wild swans, ducks and waders. It is also close to Lough Beg, a smaller lough at the north-west corner of Lough Neagh, where rare ducks and waders turn up with regularity.

Spring

Saltee

Without any question the prime place in Ireland for watching spring passerine migration is Great Saltee Island off the Wexford coast. Its location at the south-east corner of the country is right on the track which many migrants take on returning from Africa, and it has a lighthouse nearby at Tuskar Rock known to attract birds.

In late April and May, the best times on Saltee, falls of warblers can number hundreds of birds. Willow Warblers are usually the most numerous, but in the right conditions they are accompanied by Cuckoos, Turtle Doves, Redstarts, Grasshopper Warblers, Whinchats, and rarities such as Hoopoe, Golden Oriole, Woodchat Shrike and Tawny Pipit sometimes occur as well. Extreme rarities seen in spring include Lesser Grey Shrike, Dusky Warbler and Subalpine Warbler.

A trip for more than a day requires prior permission from the owner and considerable organisation as the island is uninhabited, but there are usually expeditions of ringers in May. The Warden at the Wexford Wildfowl Reserve can usually provide information on whether there are birdwatchers on the island.

Cape Clear

Many birdwatchers find it difficult to organise a trip to Saltee and are wary of the very real risk of being stranded there for an extra few days if the weather turns foul. Cape Clear, which does not attract anything like as many spring migrants as Saltee, has the advantages of ready accessibility, social life in the island's bars and the facilities of a Bird Observatory.

The birdwatching on Cape Clear in late April and May is much more dependent on weather than on Saltee where migrants trickle through in spring in most conditions. Cape Clear requires a period of south-easterly winds if it is to have a successful spring, and even then the numbers of migrants are small. Quality, however, can rival Saltee. In recent years rarities have included Stone-curlew, Red-footed Falcon, Bluethroat, Black-eared Wheatear and Scarlet Rosefinch. Even when the passerine movement is slow, there is reasonable seabird passage with parties of Pomarine Skuas perhaps the highlight.

Summer

Saltee

It is already evident that Saltee is a great place to spend a few days in spring and autumn. It is also a wonderful place in summer with its huge numbers of breeding seabirds. The Gannet colony is not the largest off the Irish coast but it is much the most accessible and the Puffins, Guillemots and Razorbills provide a wonderful sight. There are few better ways of spending a sunny summer day than sitting on the edge of the seabird colony on Saltee, watching the adult birds return from the sea with food for their young.

Bird photographers find the island irresistible and some visit it every summer. Not just seabirds can be approached closely, but also Oystercatchers and late migrant passerines.

A day trip is much easier than a visit for several days, but the longer visit does provide better opportunities for close observation.

Shannon

This account of places to visit for a week or so has emphasised coastal sites with the single exception of Lough Neagh in winter. One site, the River Shannon, provides unrivalled opportunities for mixing a leisurely holiday with good birdwatching, and hiring a boat is far and away the best way to enjoy it.

The stretch of river between Athlone and Portumna is surrounded by callows, which flood in winter and hold great hordes of wildfowl. In summer they have the largest concentrations of breeding Corncrakes left in Ireland and lots of breeding waders. Mute Swans, Teal, Mallard and Shoveler also nest, though the birds are hard to see from a boat. A boat provides access to several moorings, where the call of Corncrakes still reverberates at night. Even from the town of Banagher, Corncrakes can be heard from a boat after the restaurants and pubs close.

Farther north, on Lough Ree, there are breeding Common Scoters, gulls and terns. North again, there are lots of nesting ducks, but the river north of Lough Ree is surrounded by reedbeds where birds are very difficult to see.

Boats of various sizes can be hired at Killaloe, Williamstown, Portumna, Banagher and Carrick-on-Shannon. Rates are highest in July and August, but the overall cost appears more reasonable if a party of five or six share the boat.

HOW TO USE THIS BOOK

The Country

This book covers sites of importance for birds throughout the entire island of Ireland. Although the island is divided politically into the Republic of Ireland and Northern Ireland, the birds recognise no boundaries and birdwatchers from both parts see the island as a biogeographical unity. The text of the book is divided into sections, corresponding with the four provinces, and within these sections the site accounts are arranged within counties.

Criteria for Site Inclusion

As the country is quite large and a number of potentially exciting sites for birds have been little watched, the selection of sites for this book has been difficult. Firstly, those sites known to have a wide diversity of species, and to be attractive for uncommoner birds, have been included. Secondly, sites have been chosen which hold certain specialised birds (e.g. geese). Finally, care has been taken to ensure that most parts of the country are represented.

The authors of some of the companion volumes in this series have stressed that the listed sites are all open to the public. Not many of the sites in this book are nature reserves and very few have resident wardens, so the position is somewhat different. A number are on private land and, while most landowners do not mind birdwatching on their property, it is essential that permission be sought in advance before entering gardens or crossing fields.

A total of 143 sites has been included. These are divided into 62 major sites and 81 other sites worthy of attention. The major sites are dealt with in considerable detail and some have been broken down into sections which are dealt with separately. The lesser sites have been included as a guide to areas where interesting birds could be expected but which are less well watched.

Measurements

As distances shown on road signs are in the course of being changed from miles to kilometres, all measurements are given in metric units (see Metric Conversion Tables at the end of this chapter). The references to maps are all to those of the Ordnance Surveys of the Republic of Ireland (in general to the half inch series, but, where published, to the new 1:50,000 series) and of Northern Ireland (again to the half inch and the 1:50,000 series). Grid references are to the 10 km square or squares within which each site is situated.

Habitat

This section incorporates a brief description of the site or county, emphasising those features that are of particular importance for birds. A brief account is given of other aspects of the fauna and flora and the ownership or reserve status.

Species

This section outlines the most interesting aspects of the birdlife of each site. Breeding, migratory and winter birds are discussed, generally starting with the birds of the season which is best for birdwatching. Common and widespread birds are excluded unless there is a particular feature of interest, and rare vagrants are listed only where they occur with some regularity.

Timing

This section advises on the best season, time of day, weather conditions, state of tide etc. to see the birds mentioned for each site. Some places, such as the islands where seabirds nest, are better in summer than at any other time; others, such as estuaries, are best in autumn and winter. Early morning tends to be the best time for looking for autumn migrants, while seawatching requires quite precise weather conditions depending on where the site is located.

Access

This is one of the key parts of the book. Nearly all the major sites have an accompanying map showing the roads and paths from which birdwatching can be carried out. The text provides directions to the site, generally commencing from the nearest town or major road, and continuing with detailed instructions to ensure that the site can be located with ease. Most sites are accessible by road or public right of way, and where access is restricted at the time of writing this has been stated. For bird observatories booking information is given and for reserves the name and address of the warden is provided.

The text should be used in conjunction with the outline map accompanying it, and also with the relevant Ordnance Survey maps. References to the 10 km square within which the area is situated have been given for all sites, and the relevant sheets of the half inch Ordnance Survey of Ireland (OSI) and Ordnance Survey of Northern Ireland (OSI) and of the 1:50,000 maps are referred to at the head of each site account. Since many of the 1:50,000 maps have yet to be published, less than half the sites in this book are covered by the series.

Calendar

This section is for quick reference to check the most likely species to see at each season. It lists the more interesting species and, where rarities turn up frequently, those most likely to be seen are included as well. At sites good for seawatching, details of species likely to be seen are given here. This section should be used in conjunction with the more detailed Species account.

The Maps

The site maps scattered throughout the text are designed to help the visitor to find the best viewing points at the major sites. The location of all sites is shown in general terms on the maps of each province which preface the four main sections of the book.

Inter-tidal sand and mud is shown in a consistent pale tone on all the maps. Built-up areas are shown in a dark pattern of hatching and are named. Three categories of road are shown, each one thicker than the other. Narrow country roads are the thinnest, main roads the next and motorways the broadest. Road numbers are used more on maps of

19

Northern Ireland sites than in the Republic as the numbers are more widely shown on signposts there. Railways are indicated with a broad, dark (but not black) line.

Parking places and hides are indicated with a ringed letter P and H respectively. Particularly good places for viewing birds are given an asterisk.

At times other features are shaded. Where this is done, the map has a key or note to indicate what the feature is.

Metric Conversion Tables

For readers more familiar with the imperial system, the accompanying tables are designed to facilitate quick conversion to imperial units. Bold figures in the central columns can be read as either metric or imperial: e.g. 1 km = 0.62 miles or 1 mile = 1.61 km.

km		miles	ha		acres
1.61	1	0.62	0.40	1	2.47
3.22	2	1.24	0.81	2	4.94
4.83	3	1.86	1.21	3	7.41
6.44	4	2.48	1.62	4	9.88
8.05	5	3.11	2.02	5	12.36
9.65	6	3.73	2.43	6	14.83
11.26	7	4.35	2.83	7	17.30
12.87	8	4.97	3.24	8	19.77
14.48	9	5.59	3.64	9	22.24

CODE OF CONDUCT FOR
BIRDWATCHERS

Today's birdwatchers are a poweful force for nature conservation. The number of those of us interested in birds rises continually and it is vital that we take seriously our responsibility to avoid any harm to birds.

We must present a responsible image to non-birdwatchers who may be affected by our activities and particularly those on whose sympathy and support the future of birds may rest.

There are ten points to bear in mind:
1. The welfare of birds must come first.
2. Habitat must be protected.
3. Keep disturbance to birds and their habitat to a minimum.
4. When you do find a rare bird think carefully about whom you should tell.
5. Do not harass migrants.
6. Abide by the bird protection laws at all times.
7. Respect the rights of landowners.
8. Respect the rights of other people in the countryside.
9. Make your records available to the local bird recorder.
10. Behave abroad as you would when birdwatching at home.

A shortened version of *The Birdwatcher's Code of Conduct* (RSPB *et al.*).

MUNSTER

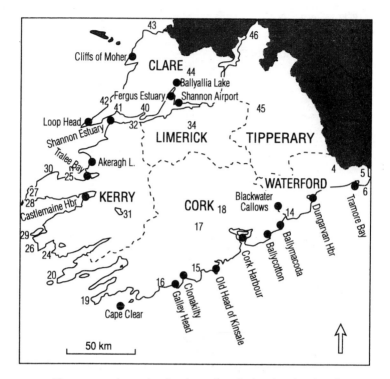

Munster: counties, major sites (named) and other sites (numbered)

Waterford
1. TRAMORE BAY AND BROWNSTOWN HEAD
2. DUNGARVAN BAY AND HELVICK HEAD
3. BLACKWATER CALLOWS
4. River Suir at Coolfin
5. Waterford Harbour
6. Dunmore East

Cork
7. BALLYMACODA AND KNOCKADOON HEAD
8. BALLYCOTTON
9. CORK HARBOUR
10. OLD HEAD OF KINSALE AND KINSALE MARSH
11. CLONAKILTY
12. GALLEY HEAD AND KILKERRAN LAKE
13. CAPE CLEAR
14. Youghal
15. Courtmacsherry
16. Roscarberry
17. Lee Reservoirs
18. Kilcolman
19. Lissagriffin and Mizen Head
20. Dursey Island and Allihies

Kerry
21. CASTLEMAINE HARBOUR
22. TRALEE BAY AND BARROW HARBOUR
23. AKERAGH LOUGH
24. Ballinskelligs Bay
25. Lough Gill
26. Skelligs
27. Dunquin
28. Blasket Islands
29. Puffin Island
30. Brandon Point
31. Killarney National Park
32. Ballylongford and Tarbert

Limerick

33. SOUTH SHORE OF SHANNON
ESTUARY
34. Lough Gur
Clare
35. SHANNON AIRPORT LAGOON
36. FERGUS ESTUARY
37. BALLYALLIA LAKE
38. CLIFFS OF MOHER
39. LOOP HEAD AND BRIDGES OF
ROSS

40. Clonderalaw Bay
41. Poulnasherry Bay
42. Mutton Island and Lurga Point
43. Ballyvagham
44. Lough Atedaun
Tipperary
45. Gortdrum Mine
46. Lough Avan

WATERFORD

Introduction

Waterford comprises a coastal plateau with a row of high mountains behind. The coastline has four estuaries: Waterford Harbour, Dungarvan, Tramore and Youghal (partly in Cork and dealt with under that county). These are interesting for wintering wildfowl and waders. Between the estuaries are long stretches of cliff with colonies of breeding seabirds and Choughs. Some of these lead out to headlands, which provide sites for watching seabird passage.

The major rivers, the Suir and the Blackwater, enter the sea at the eastern and western ends of the county respectively. Both have callows (flood meadows), which hold wildfowl, particularly after heavy rainfall.

The lower slopes of the mountains are afforested but certainly hold interesting breeding birds. In recent years, both Golden Plover and Nightjar have been found nesting here.

Sites

1 TRAMORE BAY AND BROWNSTOWN HEAD
Estuary; seawatching; passerine migrants.
2 DUNGARVAN BAY AND HELVICK HEAD
Estuary; seabird colony; seawatching; passerine migrants.
3 BLACKWATER CALLOWS *Flood meadows; wild swans and Black-tailed Godwits.*

Other sites:

4 River Suir at Coolfin *Wintering Greylag Goose site.*
5 Waterford Harbour *Estuary.*
6 Dunmore East *Breeding Kittiwake colony.*

Reference

McGrath, D. and Walsh, P. *Where to Watch Birds in Waterford* (IWC, Waterford, 1990).

1 TRAMORE BAY AND BROWNSTOWN HEAD

OSI ½" map: sheet 23
S60 X69

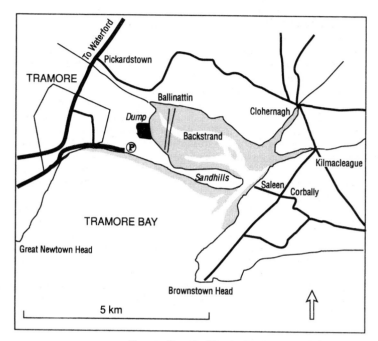

Tramore Bay, Co Waterford

Habitat

Tramore Bay and Backstrand comprise a sandy outer bay and a muddy estuarine system impounded by sand dunes. The town of Tramore is a popular tourist destination and large numbers of people frequent the strand in summer. The best bird areas are the Backstrand and the Sandhills.

Birdwatching at the Backstrand is rather difficult at low tide because of the width of the estuary. There are beds of *Zostera* or eelgrass on the north side providing excellent feeding for wildfowl, especially Brent Geese, and *Spartina* is well established on the western side. The town dump, located at the western end, provides feeding for gulls. Two embankments crossing the mud to the east of the dump provide high tide roosts for waders. There is reclaimed land to the north, behind a seawall, and at the eastern end there are lowlying fields which are protected from the tide by raised ditches. At the south-eastern corner of the bay, Brownstown Head projects well out to sea and is an excellent seawatching site.

The inner bay is protected from the open sea by an extensive sand dune system. Privet *Ligustrum vulgare* and dewberry *Rubus caesius* bushes are found here. On the seaward side, a sandy beach provides views of the open bay.

25

Species

The bay is very much a winter birdwatching site. In autumn the most favoured place for Brent Geese is on the *Zostera*, but in early winter the geese move to the eastern end of the Backstrand. By mid-winter they are scattered all across the mud. Several hundred are present each winter, all being usually of the Pale-bellied race, though in recent years single Black Brant, the Pacific subspecies, have been seen occasionally. Some Shelduck, Mallard, Wigeon and Teal also feed here. A few Red-breasted Mergansers can usually be seen in the channel. The mudflats hold a diverse wader population. Oystercatchers, Grey Plovers, Black-tailed Godwits, Bar-tailed Godwits, Redshanks, Greenshanks and Dunlin feed on the mud but can best be seen at their roosts on the embankments or at the north-eastern corner of the Backstrand. A few Turnstones and Ringed Plover can be seen here as well. Golden Plovers, Lapwings and Curlews favour the fields at Clohernagh throughout the winter. The Clohernagh inlet itself is always worth looking at. Kingfishers are regular and autumn migrant waders such as Spotted Redshanks and Green Sandpipers are occasional. The beach and the shingle area usually hold a small feeding flock of Sanderlings and sometimes a few Ringed Plovers in winter. In summer Ringed Plovers nest in small numbers.

Gulls are best sought for at the town dump where Herring, Great Black-backed and Lesser Black-backed Gulls occur in good numbers. Glaucous and Iceland Gulls are not infrequent in winter. Off the beach, Gannets can be seen fishing throughout most of the year and both Red-throated and Great Northern Divers are regular in winter. In autumn, Sandwich Terns feed off the beach and roost on the sand. Sometimes other tern species occur with them, and skuas, mostly Arctic, occasionally follow them into the outer bay. Large numbers of Kittiwakes can be seen at times in winter.

The Sandhills have nesting Stonechats, Skylarks and Meadow Pipits and, in winter, Short-eared Owls are not infrequent. Choughs are often to be seen feeding here and Kestrels are usually present.

Brownstown Head to the south-east is an excellent seawatching and passerine migration watchpoint. Manx Shearwaters, Gannets, Kittiwakes, skuas, Guillemots and Razorbills pass in spring, summer and autumn and divers and rarer shearwaters in autumn. Passerine migrants can be found in autumn in gardens and hedges: the large garden at the south end of the road to Brownstown Head has produced many scarce migrants in the past, including Bonelli's Warbler and Red-eyed Vireo. The hedges along the narrow lanes and bordering the fields are also productive.

Timing

The Backstrand is best visited between August and the end of March when wildfowl and wader numbers are at their highest. A rising tide bunches the birds and makes viewing easier. The route along one side of the Sandhills and back on the other is a very popular walk.

For seawatching at Brownstown Head, the best conditions are a combination of south-west to south-east winds, mist and rain. Falls of passerine migrants can occur from late March to May and from August to mid-November. South-easterly winds are best for scarcer species.

Access

Tramore town is best approached by the main road from Waterford.
The Backstrand can be viewed from several locations. To see the

south-western end drive east from Tramore to the carpark at the end of the promenade near the dump. Walk out along the embankment, which crosses the mudflats, then follow the Sandhills to the tip. The beach can be viewed from the south side and the mudflats from the north.

The turn off the Tramore-Waterford road at Pickardstown leads after 1 km to Ballinattin. A side road provides space for parking and the Backstrand embankment can be reached by following the lane directly opposite this point. Turn right just before the gate at the end of the lane rather than cross through.

Great Black-backed Gull

Clohernagh inlet can be viewed from Clohernagh on the main road or by turning south-west at Kilmacleague, just before Corbally Church.

Saleen in the south-east has a carpark from which the mudflats can be scanned or the eastern side walked.

Brownstown Head is approached from Tramore by turning off the Tramore-Waterford road at Pickardstown, following the narrow road to Corbally Church, then forking right to follow that road to the headland. A car can be parked near ruined farmyard buildings and the head approached on foot.

Calendar

All year: Cormorant, Shag, Grey Heron, Shelduck, Oystercatcher, Ringed Plover, Rock Pipit

Spring: Divers, Gannet, waders including Whimbrels and Sanderlings, Kittiwakes, terns, skuas, passerine migrants.

Summer: Summer migrants including Sedge Warbler.

Autumn: Fulmar, Gannet, Brent Geese and wildfowl, occasional Curlew Sandpiper and Spotted Redshank, terns and occasional Little Gull, Arctic Skua. Seawatching and passerine migrants at Brownstown. Possible rarities at Brownstown.

Winter: Divers, occasional Common and Velvet Scoters, Long-tailed Ducks, wildfowl including Brent Geese, waders, gulls including Glaucous and Iceland, occasional Short-eared Owl and Snow Bunting.

2 DUNGARVAN BAY AND HELVICK HEAD

OSI ½" map: sheet 22
X28 X29 X38 X39

Habitat
Dungarvan Bay is a broad, shallow bay fed by three small rivers. The inner part of the bay is impounded by a long, narrow, sandy spit named the Cunnigar. On the seaward side of the Cunnigar is an extensive sandy beach with large tracts of eelgrass *Zostera*. The inner bay has a wide expanse of mudflats with smaller *Zostera* beds.

Helvick Head to the south projects well out to sea and has high cliffs. The coastline to the north as far as Ballyvoile Head is lowlying.

Species
The inner bay provides good views in winter of Wigeon, Shelduck, Oystercatchers, Curlews, Black-tailed Godwits, Redshanks and Dunlin. From the old swimming baths in the town most wader species can be seen close to the road and small numbers of Great Northern Divers, Great Crested Grebes, Cormorants, Shags, Goldeneyes and Red-breasted Mergansers are present in the channel. When the tide is out in spring, Brent Geese feed close to the swimming baths.

The main Dungarvan-Cork road also provides a ready viewing place for Brent Geese, Shelduck and Wigeon as well as Black-tailed Godwits and Redshanks.

Killongford Bridge on the main Cork road crosses the river Brickey. Upstream, Green Sandpipers can be seen frequently by the observer ready to walk along the embankment.

The Cunnigar is perhaps the best place in the estuary for large numbers of birds, especially at high tide. As well as large flocks of Brent Geese, Wigeon, Oystercatchers and Black-tailed Godwits, there are Grey Plovers, Turnstones, Bar-tailed Godwits and Knots. In autumn, Curlew Sandpipers and Little Stints occur here, and there are usually terns, especially Sandwich Terns. The sandy area at the base of the Cunnigar often holds very accessible parties of Ringed Plover, Dunlin and Sanderling.

Ballyneety Bridge provides excellent viewing of waders at close range, especially when near to high tide. The town dump, just above the bridge, has large numbers of gulls.

On the east side, the road to the Gold Coast provides a number of vantage points for looking out over the bay for grebes and diving ducks. There are good numbers of Great Crested Grebes and usually a few Great Northern Divers and Slavonian Grebes. Red-breasted Mergansers are dotted around the bay. Ballynacourty Pier, at the end of the road, is

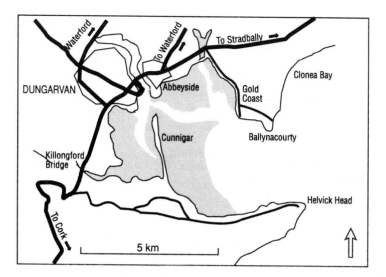

Dungarvan Harbour, County Waterford

one of the best places from which to scan the area.

Helvick Head is another few kilometres on from the Cunnigar and, as a fishing port, is a good site for Glaucous or Iceland Gulls. In autumn, good sea passage of Manx Shearwaters occurs and Great, Cory's and Sooty Shearwaters have all been seen. In the same season the gardens and hedges often hold common migrants and there have been records of rarities, including Radde's Warbler. The headland has breeding Shags, Fulmars, Kittiwakes, Guillemots, Razorbills and Black Guillemots as well as Ravens and Choughs.

As with other south coast headlands, there is always the chance of seeing porpoises or dolphins and there are often migrant butterflies and moths in autumn.

Timing

The estuary is best from August to early April. Most areas are best on a rising tide when the birds come closest. The Cunnigar should be walked at or close to high tide.

Helvick Head is worth a look at any time of the year, but the seabird colony is occupied chiefly in summer and migrant seabirds and passerines are most likely in May or from August to October. As elsewhere on this coast, south-westerly or southerly wind and mist provide the best seawatching conditions.

Access

The town of Dungarvan is easily approached by main road from all directions. In the town, cars can be parked at the old swimming baths and the walk around the quays can produce an interesting variety of species.

To the south of the town, the estuary can be watched from the Stafford Miller factory on the main Cork road. About 4 km on is Killongford Bridge, where recent road widening has taken place, located just before the left turn for Helvick Head.

The Cunnigar is reached by turning left at the junction for Helvick

Head, then taking a left turn after 1.5 km and continuing for about 2 km, where a sharp left turn at a farmhouse leads to the base of the Cunnigar where cars can be parked.

Helvick Head is reached by taking the Dungarvan-Cork road and turning off to the east where signposted about 5 km from the town. The pier is suitable for carparking.

The north side of Dungarvan Bay is readily viewed from the coast road at Abbeyside. Leave the main Dungarvan-Waterford road at the signpost for Clonea and follow the coast road to Kilminnin Bridge.

Calendar

All year: Cormorant, Shag, Mute Swan, Mallard, Oystercatcher, Curlew, Redshank, Kingfisher.

Summer: Seabirds on Helvick Head.

Spring: Whimbrel, terns.

Autumn: Sea passage. Waders including Green Sandpiper, Curlew Sandpiper and, in most years, Little Stint. Passerine migrants.

Winter: Great Northern Diver, Great Crested Grebe, Slavonian Grebe, Brent Goose, Wigeon, Teal, Pintail, Shoveler, Goldeneye, Red-breasted Merganser, Ringed Plover, Golden Plover, Grey Plover, Lapwing, Knot, Black-tailed Godwit, Bar-tailed Godwit, Greenshank, Green Sandpiper, Dunlin, Sanderling. Rarities include regular Dark-bellied Brent Goose.

3 BLACKWATER CALLOWS   OSI ½″ map: sheet 22 W89 W99 X09

Habitat

The lowlying fields along the river valley of the River Blackwater between Fermoy and Cappoquin are prone to flooding in winter when large shallow pools form. There are deciduous woods on the hilly slopes to the north and south. Lismore Castle, owned by the Duke of Devonshire and available for rental if you prefer a change from hotel life, provides a glorious backdrop at Lismore Bridge.

Species

Several hundred Whooper and Bewick's Swans graze in the fields in winter and large flocks of Wigeon and Black-tailed Godwits (often over 1,000) occur on floods at times. Greylag Geese, Pintail, Shelduck and Goldeneye are irregular visitors. Mallard, Teal, Shoveler, Tufted Duck, Pochard, Lapwing, Snipe and Curlew winter in small numbers.

The largest numbers of duck and waders are to be found on the road between Lismore and Ballyduff. The swans are often found

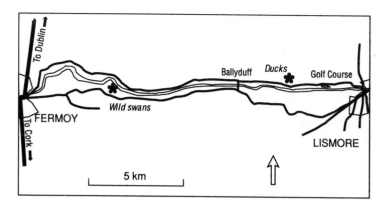

River Blackwater Callows, Co Waterford

between Ballyduff and Fermoy. The southern road is usually the best. At times, there are large numbers of birds between Lismore and Cappoquin so the whole area from Fermoy to Cappoquin deserves investigation.

Large numbers of Redwings and Fieldfares feed on the hedges in winter and the woodlands hold Jays, Woodcock and Siskins.

Dippers and Grey Wagtails can usually be seen on the fast-flowing river about 100 m to the north-east of Lismore Bridge.

Timing

Wild swans are usually present throughout most of the winter, but numbers of Wigeon and Black-tailed Godwits are very dependent on the level of flooding. If there has been little flooding, then bird numbers are low, and when the callows are frozen over most of the waterfowl move to the coast.

Access

Lismore is a good starting point. The river from Lismore to Cappoquin can be seen by taking the northern road to Cappoquin and returning by the southern arm. The north road from Lismore Bridge to Ballyduff provides a number of excellent viewing places commencing at the marshy area just beyond the golf course.

The south road from Ballyduff to Fermoy usually gives better views of swans than the north road, but at times the birds are on the other side. In all cases, they can be well seen from the road and a car acts as an excellent hide.

Calendar

All year: Grey Heron, Cormorant, Mute Swan, Mallard, Dipper, Grey Wagtail, Kingfisher, Jay.

Winter: Whooper and Bewick's Swan, Wigeon, Teal, Shoveler, Tufted Duck, Pochard, Curlew, Black-tailed Godwit, Lapwing.

OTHER WATERFORD SITES

4 RIVER SUIR AT COOLFIN

OSI ½" map: sheet 22
S41

Habitat and Species

Coolfin is a wildfowl sanctuary protected by the National Parks and Wildlife Service. It is an area of grassy fields between the Suir and Clodiagh rivers and the Waterford-Carrick-on-Suir road.

The site holds between 300 and 600 Greylag Geese from October to April, one of the largest flocks in Ireland. Whooper Swans also winter here and small numbers of Greenland White-fronted Geese sometimes occur. Duck, mostly Teal and Tufted Ducks, are usually found on the river itself. Lapwings, Golden Plover, Snipe and Curlews feed in the fields and Green Sandpipers winter regularly.

Kestrels, Peregrines and Sparrowhawks are regular throughout the year.

Access

Coolfin is best approached from the Waterford-Cork road. Take the right turn where signposted for Portlaw just beyond Kilmeadan, about 11 km from Waterford town. After 5 km a fork is reached: turn right for Carrick-on-Suir, rather than left for Portlaw, and Coolfin is reached on the right hand side just after the first bridge. The geese can be seen easily from the road, but care should be taken to avoid disturbance.

5 WATERFORD HARBOUR

OSI ½" map: sheet 22
S60 S78 X69 S61 S71

Habitat and Species

Waterford Harbour has inter-tidal mudflats on the west side at intervals from Passage East south to Creadan Head. A couple of thousand waders winter here, including Oystercatchers, Ringed Plovers, Curlews, Bar-tailed Godwits, Redshanks and Turnstones, and many Common Gulls roost. Small numbers of Great Crested Grebes, Brent Geese, Wigeon and Red-breasted Mergansers occur.

Access

Passage East is approached from Waterford by taking the turn for Dunmore East at the Tower Hotel. Turn left at the petrol filling station 3 km south of Ardkeen Regional Hospital. A ferry crosses the harbour at this point and provides convenient access to south Wexford without the necessity to drive north to New Ross. There are some exposed mudflats here.

Follow the road from Passage East south for Woodstown and stop the car just over 3 km from Passage East. Walk down the narrow lane to the left to Geneva Strand where grebes and waders can be seen.

Woodstown is another 2 km south by road and Creadan Strand is farther south again. Take the Dunmore East road from Woodstown, take the next turn left, then the next left again and drive down to the strand. Both these sites afford access to the mudflats.

6 DUNMORE EAST

Habitat and Species

The small town is an attractive fishing port famous for its cliffs, which hold about 900 pairs of nesting Kittiwakes. The birds are present between November and August. Fulmars also breed on the cliffs. A number of Herring Gulls nest on buildings in the town.

Turnstones and Purple Sandpipers feed outside the seawall in winter. Oystercatchers are present there throughout the year.

Large numbers of gulls winter in the harbour and Glaucous and Iceland Gulls are both regular.

Access

Dunmore East is 17 km from Waterford city. Take the road to the south at the Tower Hotel and follow the signposts.

CORK

Introduction

Cork is the largest county in Ireland and it almost certainly has the longest bird list as well. The coast stretches from Youghal in the east, roughly the mid-point of the southern Irish coastline, to Dursey Island in the west and around the corner into Kenmare Bay. The coast is broken by a number of muddy estuaries, most of which hold good numbers of wildfowl and waders, though geese are scarce in the county.

There are several islands and mainland cliffs on which seabirds nest, but the headlands and islands are attractive to the birdwatcher principally because of the opportunities for seeing wind-blown seabirds and passerines. This is the best county for seeing American passerine vagrants. Inland, there are several mountain ridges and a string of lakes in the valley of the River Lee, some of which hold large numbers of duck.

Sites

7 BALLYMACODA AND KNOCKADOON HEAD
   Estuary; passerine migrants.
8 BALLYCOTTON *Brackish lagoons; possibility of rare waders; seawatching; passerine migrants.*
9 CORK HARBOUR *Estuary.*
10 OLD HEAD OF KINSALE AND KINSALE MARSH
   Seabird breeding colony; seawatching; passerine migrants.
11 CLONAKILTY *Estuary.*
12 GALLEY HEAD AND KILKERRAN LAKE
   Seawatching; passerine migrants.
13 CAPE CLEAR *Bird observatory; seawatching; passerine migrants.*

Other sites:

14   Youghal *Estuary; reedbeds.*
15   Courtmacsherry *Estuary.*

16	Rosscarbery	*Estuary.*
17	Lee Reservoirs	*Reservoirs with wintering wildfowl.*
18	Kilcolman	*Nature refuge; marsh with wintering wild-fowl.*
19	Lissagriffin and Mizen Head	
		Scarce waders; seawatching; passerine migrants.
20	Dursey Island and Allihies	
		Seawatching; passerine migrants.

References

Cape Clear Bird Observatory Reports.
Cork Bird Reports.
Hutchinson, C.D. & O'Halloran. J. The Waterfowl of Cork Harbour (*Irish Birds* 2: 445–456, 1984).
Hutchinson, C.D. & Ridgway, M. *The Natural History of Kilcolman* (Kilcolman Wildfowl Refuge, Buttevant, 1990).
Sharrock, J.T.R. *The Natural History of Cape Clear Island* (T & A.D. Poyser, Berkhamsted, 1972).
Smiddy, P. The Waterfowl of Ballymacoda, Co. Cork (*Irish Birds* 4: 525–548, 1992).

7 BALLYMACODA AND KNOCKADOON HEAD

OSI ½" map: sheets 22, 25
X07

Habitat

The estuary of the Womanagh river at Ballymacoda is a broad area of inter-tidal mudflats surrounded by lowlying farmland. A ridge of sandstone to the south extends out to Knockadoon Head and Capel Island offshore. As with so many other south coast estuaries, a sand spit impounds the bay. Many of the fields surrounding the bay are marshy and provide feeding for ducks and waders.

Species

The estuary has more waders in winter than any other in Cork apart from Cork Harbour (a far larger area). Diversity, however, is rather disappointing and despite being well watched fewer rare species have been seen than at some of the other Cork sites. There are good numbers of Wigeon, Teal, Mallard, Shelduck, Oystercatcher, Curlew, Black-tailed Godwit, Bar-tailed Godwit, Redshank and Dunlin. But the speciality of the estuary is its huge flocks of Lapwings and Golden Plovers, at times among the largest in Ireland, and its gathering of over 300 Grey Plovers in spring.

Curlew Sandpipers, Ruffs and Green Sandpipers are seen in most years; Little Stints and Wood Sandpipers occur in some autumns; Amer-

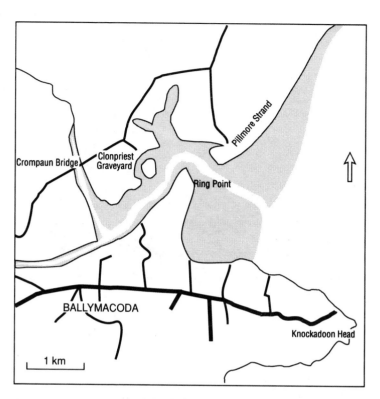

Ballymacoda, Co Cork

ican vagrants have included Killdeer, Spotted Sandpiper, Baird's Sandpiper and Long-billed Dowitcher.

A small flock of Brent Geese has wintered in recent years.

In autumn passage migrants can be found in the hedgerows on Knockadoon Head. Goldcrests and Chiffchaffs are particularly common in late autumn and Turtle Doves, Pied Flycatchers and Black Redstarts probably occur in most years. Yellow-browed Warbler, Firecrests, Red-breasted Flycatcher, Pied Wheatear and Woodchat Shrike have been seen. The headland is very much underwatched.

The entire area is good for raptors in winter. Sparrowhawk, Kestrel, Merlin, Peregrine and Hen Harrier are all regular and Short-eared Owls are seen in most winters.

Timing
This is very much a winter estuarine site. It is probably best watched on a rising tide when the waders are pushed in from the extensive mudflats. Knockadoon Head is best in late autumn.

Access
Ballymacoda estuary can be approached from various aspects. The west and north sides can be approached from the road between Ballymacoda and Youghal. This road crosses the estuary at Crompaun Bridge and an energetic visitor can walk south along the bank of the Womanagh river

Peregrine

until the estuary opens out. A less energetic birdwatcher can drive about 500 m to Clonpriest graveyard where the car can be parked. The estuary can be approached on foot by taking a track to the shore about 100 m past the old graveyard. This approach provides access to much of the estuary.

The north-east corner is approached by driving east beyond Clonpriest and turning right for Pillmore strand, where the main road turns sharply left for Youghal, about 2 km beyond Clonpriest. The car can be parked at the beach and the estuary scanned from here.

The south side can be seen by taking the second left turn after passing through the village of Ballymacoda. This narrow road leads down to the edge of the estuary. The third and fourth roads to the left lead down to Ring strand.

To search for passerines in autumn, take the road out to Knockadoon Head and work backwards, looking at the hedgerows. The area around the caravan park has been productive in the past but the whole area has great and relatively untapped potential.

Calendar

All year: Peregrine and Chough at Knockadoon Head.

Winter: Wildfowl and waders, especially large flocks of Golden Plover and Lapwing. Divers off Knockadoon Head. Small flock of Brent Geese.

Autumn: Passage migrants on the headland. Terns on the beach, especially Sandwich Terns.

8 BALLYCOTTON

Habitat

Ballycotton Bay is a shallow, sandy, eastward facing bay with three shallow lagoons isolated from the sea behind sand bars and a gravel bank. Ballycotton Lake, the largest of these lagoons, was formerly completely open to the sea and nineteenth-century Ordnance Survey maps show it appearing like an estuary. It is now completely enclosed by a shingle bank, the result of wave action which is also steadily eroding the sand cliffs at the southern end of the bay close to the town. The shingle bank is breached at the request of farmers interested in draining the lake, but the gap in the past was usually closed by south-easterly gales. At the time of writing, however, the gap is open and the lake very dry. Reedbeds *Phragmites australis* are spreading steadily across the lake, and the area of open water and muddy edge has perceptibly declined in the past 20 years.

Farther north, there are two pools at Shanagarry which remain tidal, although a sand spit separates all except the main channel from the sea. Drainage has taken place at one pool and there is evidence of silting.

The muddy surfaces of these lagoons are extremely attractive to wading birds both for feeding and roosting. Out on the open beach, the extensive inter-tidal and rather muddy sands provide feeding for some species, but the combination of brackish lagoon and inter-tidal flats is what holds such a diversity of wader species in the Ballycotton area.

To the west of the road which crosses the top of Ballycotton Lake from Shanagarry village is a large area of *Phragmites* known as Ballycotton bog. This is an excellent breeding area for duck but is completely impenetrable.

The town of Ballycotton has many gardens and hedges providing feeding for grounded passerine migrants in spring and autumn. At the end of the town, the pier projects out into the bay and provides a view of two small islands, one of which has a lighthouse.

Species

This is an autumn migration site *par excellence*. The lagoons and inter-tidal sands hold a great diversity of waders including parties of Black-tailed Godwits, Bar-tailed Godwits, Redshanks, Greenshanks, Ringed Plover and Sanderling, but also small numbers of Spotted Redshanks, Ruffs, Curlew Sandpipers, Little Stints and occasional Wood and Green Sandpipers. American waders occur every year. Pectoral Sandpiper is the most regular but most species on the Irish list have been seen including up to three Semipalmated Sandpipers together, near annual White-rumped and Baird's Sandpipers and records of such extreme rarities as Stilt Sandpiper, Killdeer and Greater Yellowlegs. Wintering wader numbers are low and usually much less exciting, but there is always the chance of a surprise wintering vagrant. Dowitcher and Lesser Yellowlegs have both wintered in the past.

The diversity of wildfowl is less marked, but there are usually Whooper Swan, Bewick's Swan, Mute Swan, Wigeon, Teal, Gadwall, Mallard, Shoveler, Tufted Duck, Pochard, Red-breasted Merganser and occasional

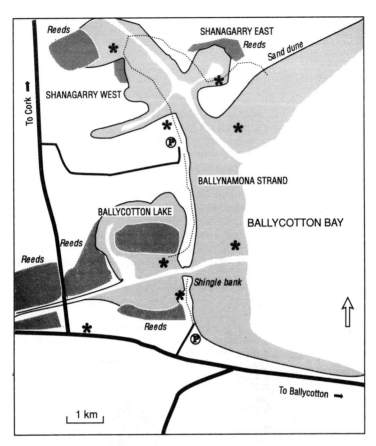

Ballycotton, Co Cork

Pintail and Goldeneye. American Wigeon and Green-winged Teal should both be looked for.

Over the pools, gulls and terns hawk for insects. Look for Mediterranean or Little Gulls at the lagoons; on the beach or at the pier check for Glaucous and Iceland Gulls. Both species are recorded every winter. Many other gull species have been recorded including Ring-billed and Ivory Gull.

The bay is always worth checking from the pier. Seabirds drift in at times, especially if fishing boats are arriving, and can include Sabine's Gull, near annual in autumn, as well as three species of skua and both Manx and Sooty Shearwater. If conditions are good for seawatching, it can be worth taking the road up to the clifftop carpark and watching out to sea. Unfortunately, the cliffs are well in from the two islands and seabirds usually pass rather far out, but good shearwater passage can sometimes be seen.

Interesting passerines can be found throughout the area. Larks and pipits abound in the fields. Wheatears are common on the beach in spring and autumn. The reedbeds hold large numbers of breeding Sedge Warblers (and many more in autumn) and a small population of breeding Reed Warblers. Ballycotton was where Reed Warblers were first proved breeding in Ireland in 1981 after a very long absence (the only previous record was in 1935 in Down). Reed Buntings are also common in the reedbeds. The gardens in the village have had Icterine, Melodious and Yellow-browed Warblers. Pied Flycatchers occur every autumn.

The reedbeds are hunted over by a number of species of bird of prey. Sparrowhawks and Kestrels can be seen almost every day. Peregrines are regular and Merlins are frequent in winter. Hen Harriers can be regular in winter in some years and have been known to roost in the bog above Ballycotton Lake. Short-eared Owls are elusive, but probably winter at the bog. Rare birds of prey recorded here have included Red Kite and Marsh Harrier.

In summer, Ringed Plovers struggle to raise their young as the beach is taken over by holidaying humans. Common Terns nested in the recent past and Little Terns before that, but the level of disturbance is now too great. Mute Swan, Shelduck and Mallard nest and Pochard, Shoveler, Teal and Gadwall probably breed in most summers.

The cliffs to the west of the town have some breeding Fulmars and several small colonies of cliff-nesting House Martins.

Sedge Warbler

Timing

Ballycotton is best in spring and autumn, but interesting birds can be found at any time of year. Hot summer days, with crowds on the beach and uncontrolled dogs criss-crossing the marshy areas, are probably best avoided. The state of the tide makes very little difference, though waders are usually seen most closely when the tide is high.

Access

The lagoons can be approached by taking the left turn for Ballynamona about 1 km beyond Shanagarry on the road for Ballycotton. This narrow road leads to a carpark by the beach. Ballycotton Lake can be seen by walking south along the path at the top of the beach and the Shanagarry lagoons can be watched from the path which runs to the north. All the fields here are private and the landowners do not permit birdwatchers on their land so keep outside the fences.

The western end of Ballycotton Lake can be viewed from the Shanagarry-Ballycotton road. Leave Ballynamona strand and turn left when the Ballycotton-Shanagarry road is reached. At the next junction turn left and park your car about 200 m onwards. The lake can be viewed through gateways from this road.

Drive on to the village and park your car at the end of the pier. Check the bay for seabirds and then, if weather conditions are encouraging, walk back through the village watching for passerine migrants.

To get to the cliffs, turn sharp left after coming up from the pier and drive to the carpark at the end of the road.

Calendar

All year: Cormorant, Mute Swan, Shelduck, Gadwall, Mallard, Oyster-catcher, Ringed Plover, Curlew, Redshank, Reed Bunting.

Autumn: Shearwaters, skuas, waders including Curlew Sandpiper, Little Stint, Spotted Redshank, Ruff, rare vagrants from North America. Terns and passerine migrants.

Winter: Whooper Swan, Bewick's Swan, Wigeon, Teal, Shoveler, Pochard, Tufted Duck, Glaucous and Iceland Gulls.

Spring: Waders including Whimbrel, Common Sandpiper and Sanderling. Hirundines, Wheatears, other passerine migrants.

Summer: Terns, Sedge Warbler, Reed Warbler.

9 CORK HARBOUR

OSI ½" map: sheet 25
W76 W77 W86 W87

Habitat

With over 5,000 wildfowl and 20,000 waders in winter, Cork Harbour is much the most important estuarine area in Cork county. It is also by far the largest. The area is famous as one of the finest natural harbours in the world and was the departure point for most Irish emigrants to the United States up to the late 1950s. The outer harbour and channels surrounding Great Island are very deep, but there are extensive mudflats around Lough Mahon, the Douglas Estuary and the North Channel on the northern side of the harbour, Lough Beg on the west and around Saleen, Rostellan and Whitegate on the eastern side. These mudflats support sizeable duck and wader populations.

The shallow waters of Lough Mahon, the eastern end of the North Channel and off Rostellan provide feeding for grebes and diving ducks. A lagoon at Lough Beg on the west side has brackish water and a soft edge which attracts migrant waders. There is a small lake at Rostellan and a brackish lagoon at Cuskinny on the south side of Great Island.

There are industrial complexes at Little Island, Ringaskiddy and Whitegate, and there has been much local controversy over the potential for pollution by some of the pharmaceutical factories located here. Because of awareness of the need to collect baseline biological data to support the conservation case, bird numbers have been counted at intervals over the past 20 years so the main concentrations are well known.

Species

The harbour is at its best for birds in winter and the largest numbers are present from October to March. Great Crested Grebes concentrate at Lough Mahon and off Aghada, in both of which areas over 50 can be seen. Little Grebes occur at Douglas Estuary, Rostellan Lake and Cuskinny. Ducks scatter throughout the harbour. Most Shelducks are found in the North Channel and near Carrigaline. Wigeon, Teal and Mallard are widely scattered but Pintail and Shoveler are scarce. Some diving ducks occur, especially Tufted Duck, Goldeneye and Red-breasted Merganser at the Douglas Estuary. The Tufted Ducks tend to assemble around the sewage outfall pipe off the old railway bridge at Rochestown. Red-breasted Mergansers and Goldeneyes are also found across Lough Mahon, the North Channel and south-east to Whitegate.

There are concentrations of waders at Douglas, Lough Mahon, Glounthaune and the North Channel. Flocks of up to 5,000 Golden Plover, 2,000–5,000 Lapwings, 1,000–2,500 Dunlins and 500–1,500 Black-tailed Godwits can be seen at each of these locations in winter. Smaller numbers of Oystercatchers, Curlews and Redshanks feed throughout the muddy areas of the harbour. Greenshanks can be found feeding in the deep channels or on stonier shores and Grey Plovers are found at Douglas, on the North Channel and east of Carrigaline. Lough Beg, near Ringaskiddy, is particularly well worth a visit in autumn when Wood Sandpiper and Ruff are regular. American waders occur at this lagoon in most autumns.

The stony, weed-covered edges of the estuary all support Turnstones. In autumn, numbers of waders are not so high as in winter but Curlew Sandpipers should be looked for at Lough Mahon and Douglas. In spring, one of the most spectacular sights of the harbour is the return migration of Whimbrel. Over 2,000 fly north over Cobh each year, usually between mid-April and the first few days of May.

The entire harbour is good for gulls. During the week the largest concentrations are at the Cork City dump (entry prohibited). However, many of the birds which feed at the dump fly across to The Lough to wash and preen. Iceland and Glaucous Gulls can be seen here each winter and Ring-billed and Mediterranean Gulls are almost always to be found between late October and the end of March. Rarer gulls seen here include Laughing Gull, Kumlien's Gull, the American race of Herring Gull and Thayer's Gull. As well as the gulls, there is a wildfowl collection to be admired and, amongst the pinioned birds, parties of wild Shoveler, Teal and Pochard.

Many of the gulls move between the dump in Cork city, Cobh farther down the harbour and Kinsale to the south-west. The quays at Cobh are excellent for gull watching and have attracted Ross's and Laughing Gulls in the past.

In summer Common Terns nest in a small colony on barges near Marino Point. Kingfishers breed near the old railway bridge at the Douglas Estuary, near Passage West, downstream from Carrigaline and close to the Pfizer factory at Ringaskiddy.

Timing

Cork Harbour is at its best for the birdwatcher from September to the end of March when wildfowl, wader and gull numbers are highest. Most sites are best visited within two hours of high tide when the ducks and waders are closest to the observer. At high tide some of the wader roosts in particular can be difficult to study without putting the birds to flight.

Access

All parts of the harbour deserve visiting in winter. Start at Cork and visit the lough. From the city centre take the road for Douglas and Carriga-line past the City Hall. At the junction beyond City General hospital take the right turn up Summerhill South. At the traffic lights turn left for Turner's Cross. Drive to the next major junction, beyond the modern Church of Christ the King, and turn right. Bear right again at the next major right turn and drive past Musgrave Park rugby ground (on the left) until you see a lake in front of you. This is The Lough. Cars can be parked on the perimeter and the birds watched from the footpath around the lake.

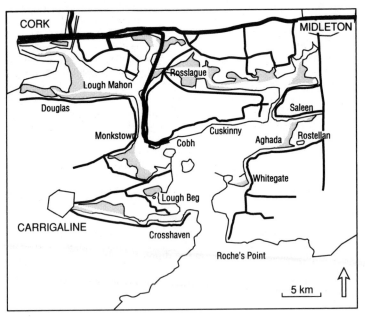

Cork Harbour, County Cork

42

To see the birds of the north part of the harbour, drive east from Cork for Midleton. At Cobh Cross, about 7 km from Cork, turn right onto Fota Island, following the signposts for Cobh. The first bridge you reach is worth checking for godwits and ducks. After this, drive on to Belvelly bridge (where a martello tower faces you). Turn left and left again to drive along the edge of the North Channel where waders and duck, especially diving duck, can be seen well. Keep on the road, passing the left turns for East Ferry and the yacht marina, and you will eventually reach the shore at Cuskinny where the lake should be checked for gulls. This is an IWC reserve. After working the area, travel on westwards to Cobh where the town jetties should be searched for gulls.

Drive back to Belvelly Bridge by taking the western route. A large flock of Shelducks feed on the open mud just before Belvelly Bridge from December to February.

The north side of the North Channel can be accessed at various points. Turn right on Fota Island, on the way back from Cobh, between the two bridges and take the right hand laneway about 1 km after leaving Fota. There is room to park a car at the entrance to a quarry. A laneway leads down beside the quarry to the estuary and to a large high tide wader roost. The North Channel can also be viewed at Ballintubbrid and Ahanesk.

The eastern side of the harbour can all be seen from the road from Midleton to Whitegate. Turn right, just over 1 km beyond Ballinacurra on the Whitegate road, for Rathcoursey and East Ferry. The road passes some excellent spots for duck and, near Saleen, a good viewing spot for checking through the grebes and ducks. The road for Whitegate passes Rostellan, a small lake on the right, and there are several stopping places on the way to Whitegate.

The inner harbour is also very accessible. Lough Mahon can be watched from the road from Blackrock Castle around to the old railway bridge at Rochestown. The Douglas Estuary can be seen well from this bridge.

The best spots on the west side are at Lough Beg, an IWC reserve, and along the Owenaboy estuary between Carrigaline and Crosshaven. To view Lough Beg, take the left turn for Currabinny at the large church in Carrigaline village. Follow the road for 3 km until a sign is reached at a right turn, signposted for Currabinny (just beyond the new Sandoz factory on the left). Follow the road to the Penn Chemicals factory and the attractive lagoon in front of it. Cars may be driven across the causeway to the small carpark at the hide outside the Penn security gates.

Calendar

All year: Mute Swan, Mallard, Oystercatcher, Curlew, Kingfisher.

Autumn: Waders, including Common Sandpiper, Curlew Sandpiper and Ruff. Terns.

Winter: Great Crested Grebe, a few Slavonian Grebes and perhaps Black-necked or Red-necked Grebe at Aghada, ducks, waders, especially Golden Plover, Lapwing and Black-tailed Godwit. Gulls, including Glaucous, Iceland and Ring-billed.

Spring: Whimbrel, terns.

Summer: Breeding Ringed Plover and Common Tern.

10 OLD HEAD OF KINSALE AND KINSALE MARSH

OSI ½" map: sheet 25
W63 W64

Habitat

The strangely named Old Head of Kinsale is the most obviously projecting of the headlands between Hook Head in Wexford and Cape Clear far to the west. It is a sandstone and mudstone promontory with sheer cliffs on the western side. There is a lighthouse at the tip and a tarred road extends from a carpark located beside an old tower fort. Just before the tip of the Old Head are ruins of an old lighthouse and an old coastguard station.

A number of gardens are scattered over the headland between the village of Old Head and the carpark. To the west, Garretstown strand is a sandy beach with extensive damp fields behind it and small areas of *Phragmites*. There are large areas of brambles at the western end of the beach which provide more cover for passerines.

Construction of a golf course is currently in progress on the tip of the Old Head.

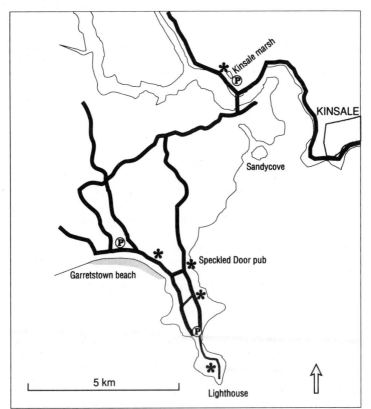

Old Head of Kinsale, Co Cork

Species

A large seabird colony is the principal ornithological feature of the Old Head in summer. On the west side, and visible by walking about 50 m to the cliff edge from the car park, is a colony of several thousand Kittiwakes and Guillemots and smaller numbers of Shags, Fulmars and Black Guillemots.

The tip of the Old Head is an excellent seawatching point. In south-westerlies in autumn, Great Shearwaters, Cory's Shearwaters and Sooty Shearwaters appear in numbers surpassed only by Cape Clear. Rarities have included Black-browed Albatross, Soft-plumaged Petrel and Little Shearwater. Leathery turtles have been seen several times and dolphins and small whales are frequent. Manx Shearwaters, Great Skuas, Arctic Skuas, Guillemots, Razorbills, Kittiwakes and Gannets are to be expected on any autumn day.

There is very little cover on the tip, so it tends not to be good for passerines, though Choughs find the open pasture to their liking. Bird-watchers in autumn tend to spend more time searching the hedges and gardens from the carpark back to the Speckled Door bar. These have all proved to be excellent habitat for warblers and flycatchers. Pied Fly-catchers, Chiffchaffs, Blackcaps and other common migrants are seen here every autumn along with a leavening of rarer species including near annual Yellow-browed Warbler. Particular rarities here have included Dusky Warbler, Radde's Warbler, Subalpine Warbler and Siberian Stonechat.

Behind Garretstown beach the fields are excellent habitat for pipits and buntings. The nearby reedbeds are hunted over by Hen Harriers and occasional Marsh Harriers as well as the more frequent Spar-rowhawks and, in winter, Merlins. Rarities recorded here include Purple Heron and Red-throated Pipit.

Most visitors to the Old Head check Kinsale marsh, a brackish pond near the bridge at Kinsale, for waders. This is an excellent place for scarce wader species, especially at high tide. Spotted Redshank, Ruff and Wood Sandpiper are regular and American waders almost annual.

Timing

Seawatching is best in August and September, though it should also be good in May when Pomarine Skuas can be expected. The numbers of seabirds passing are very dependent on weather. In north-westerlies very few are seen, but when south-westerlies are blowing hard and fronts are passing through with mist and rain the Old Head can be one of the most exciting seawatching spots anywhere.

Unfortunately, the best seawatching conditions tend to be among the worst for passerine migrants. A period of south-easterly winds is usually best for eastern migrants, though a spell of calm weather can also be good.

Access

The Old Head of Kinsale is approached from Kinsale by driving west through the town, crossing the modern bridge and following the sign-posts for the Old Head. About 1.5 km from the bridge, take the signposted sharp left turn for the Old Head and follow the road straight to the carpark near the tip. There is a locked gate at the old tower fort where the road ends but access on foot has been permitted by the owners. A golf course is currently being developed, but the promoters have given undertakings that birdwatching will continue to be permitted.

Kinsale marsh can be seen by keeping straight on for 600 m instead of turning left across the bridge west of the town. The small lagoon is on the right hand side of the road. Most of the birds can be seen easily from the road, thus minimising disturbance.

Calendar

All year: Cormorant, Shag, Peregrine, Rock Dove, Chough, Raven.

Autumn: Passage seabirds, passage passerine migrants, possibility of rare seabirds or passerines. Scarce waders at Kinsale marsh.

Winter: Red-throated and Great Northern Diver, Fulmar, Gannet, Kittiwake, Guillemot, Hen Harrier.

Spring: Terns, breeding and passage seabirds.

Summer: Breeding Shag, Fulmar, Kittiwake, Guillemot, Razorbill, Black Guillemot. Passage Manx Shearwater, Sooty Shearwater, Gannet, Great Skua.

11 CLONAKILTY
OSI ½" map: sheet 25
W33 W34 W43 W44

Habitat

The principal bird habitats at Clonakilty Bay comprise two estuaries, a shallow bay and a series of lagoons. At one time there was one estuary with an island in the middle. In the nineteenth century, Inchydoney Island was connected to the mainland by two embankments and the marshy land in between was drained.

Nowadays there is a rich, muddy zone from Clonakilty town downstream to Ring on the eastern side and to the turn for Inchydoney on the western side. From these points to the sea, the inter-tidal zone is sandy and of less interest for birds.

At Inchydoney Bay, the south-western estuary, there is similar muddy habitat with sandier strata nearer the sea. Inchydoney Island has sand dunes.

Species

The estuary has about 400 Wigeon and smaller numbers of other duck species in winter, almost all at Inchydoney. A large flock of up to 600 Black-tailed Godwits feeds on the mud at Clonakilty, most of the birds preferring the area close to the town. Up to 100 Bar-tailed Godwits join them in mid-winter and there are good numbers of Oystercatchers, Curlews, Redshanks and Dunlin. Small numbers of Grey Plover, Ringed

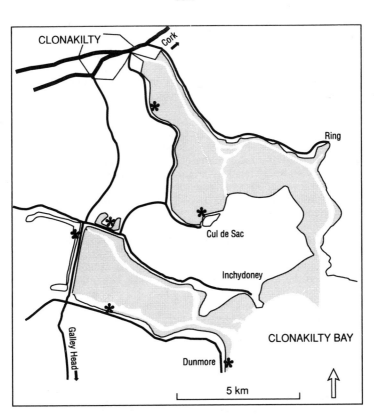

Clonakilty Bay, Co Cork

Plover, Greenshanks and Knots are also to be found, again mostly at Clonakilty. One or two Spotted Redshanks winter, usually at Inchydoney.

In autumn, scarcer species sometimes occur, usually at the muddy lagoons. Ruffs, Curlew Sandpipers and Little Stints are seen in most years and American waders are almost annual.

Out in the bay in winter, Red-throated and Great Northern Divers feed. They are best seen from Dunmore or from the high ground behind the Inchydoney Hotel. In autumn Arctic Skuas come in close to the beach after terns. No tern species breed in the bay, but Sandwich, Common and Arctic are frequent in autumn.

There is an enormous nocturnal gull roost in the bay, mostly of Black-headed and Common Gulls. They begin to assemble an hour or so before dusk and scarcer species can sometimes be seen. Ring-billed Gulls have been seen close to the town in most winters and Iceland and Mediterranean Gulls less frequently.

This estuary is hunted over by several species of bird of prey. The sudden eruption of large clouds of waders is usually a sign of the presence of a Peregrine. Sparrowhawks and Kestrels are common, but rarely have the same effect as a Peregrine. Hen Harriers are sometimes seen over the marshy fields behind the Inchydoney arm of the bay. Short-eared Owls winter here as well, but are rarely seen, unless the area is walked.

Timing

The first Black-tailed Godwits appear in July and are a magnificent sight in their rich red summer plumage. From then until the end of February the estuary has a good variety of waders. Numbers are very low in March, and from then until July only a handful of birds occur. The state of the tide matters little, except that roosts move about and birds can be hard to find at high tide.

Access

This is a most accessible estuary as a road runs around almost the entire shoreline. There is a road on the eastern side from Clonakilty town to Ring and then from Clonakilty around to Inchydoney and Dunmore.

The shallow lagoons should be thoroughly investigated. The nearest pool to Clonakilty is reached by taking the road from Clonakilty town along the west side of the estuary. After 3 km, the road swings right and away from the estuary. At this point, take the narrow road to the left sign-posted as a 'cul de sac' and drive about 300 m to the small lagoon at the end. To find the other pools, return from the cul de sac, turn left at the junction and drive on to the next arm of the bay at Inchydoney. Turn right when the estuary is reached rather than continuing straight on down the north-east side. There are brackish pools on the right hand side and migrant waders frequently feed on the muddy edge. At high tide large numbers of waders roost here.

Dunmore at the south-western end of Inchydoney estuary is an excellent vantage point for searching for divers.

Calendar

All year: Cormorant, Mute Swan, Shelduck, Mallard, Oystercatcher, Curlew.

Autumn: Wigeon, Teal, Ringed Plover, Golden Plover, Dunlin, Curlew Sandpiper, Ruff, Black-tailed Godwit, Spotted Redshank, Redshank, Greenshank, terns. Possibility of American waders.

Winter: Wigeon, Teal, Ringed Plover, Golden Plover, Grey Plover, Lapwing, Knot, Dunlin, Spotted Redshank, Greenshank, Kingfisher. Occasional Brent Goose.

Spring: Wigeon, Teal, Dunlin, Redshank, Greenshank.

Summer: Occasional terns.

12 GALLEY HEAD AND KILKERRAN LAKE

OSI ½" map: sheets 24, 25
W33

Habitat

Galley Head projects well out into the Atlantic and has a lighthouse at its tip. As a result, it is the best migration watchpoint (for both seabirds and passerine migrants) between the Old Head of Kinsale and Cape Clear. The tip of the head is private property and clearly indicated as such. It should not be entered upon without permission.

The principal bird areas are farther back. Sands Cove and Dirk Bay on the eastern side are coastal bays with deciduous trees providing cover for autumn passerine migrants. To the north of Dirk Bay is Red Strand, a sandy beach with a small reedbed and damp fields behind with potential for pipits and buntings. On the road across Galley Head from Dirk Bay to the west are several gardens and an area of hedgerows which also attract migrants. At the western side of the headland is Kilkerran Lake, a shallow, freshwater lake which attracts duck and waders. Out beyond the lake is the Long Strand, as the name suggests a long stretch of sandy beach, and the surf provides excellent feeding for divers.

Species

Off the Long Strand and Red Strand divers feed in winter. Sometimes sea-ducks are seen: Red-breasted Mergansers are occasional, Common Scoter and Long-tailed Duck rarer. Galley Head is a good watchpoint for shearwaters, skuas and petrels when the conditions are right (invariably south-westerlies, rain or mist).

Sands Cove, Dirk Bay and the gardens at Galley Head all attract a rich mix of passerine migrants in autumn. They may well be productive in spring as well, but they have never been watched at this season. Each autumn they produce Yellow-browed Warblers, Firecrests and at least one major rarity. In the recent past they have had Pallas's Warbler, Philadelphia Vireo, American Redstart and Desert Wheatear (the last at Red Strand). Because of all the cover, passerines can be difficult to find and patience is required.

Kilkerran Lake should be looked at whenever the area is visited. Normally it holds a handful of Little Grebes, Mallard and Tufted Ducks but occasionally rarer birds are seen. Cattle Egret, Ring-necked Duck and Smew have occurred.

Timing

Most of these sites are best in autumn, but they have been little watched in spring, so they may well repay visits at other seasons.

Access

From Clonakilty take the road along the west side of the estuary and drive on to the causeway at Inchydoney Bay. Keep the estuary on your left until you reach the junction where the road turns left for Dunmore and goes straight on for Ardfield. Take the road for Ardfield and follow the signposts for Red Strand. On the way you will see a signpost to Sands Cove on your left. Follow the narrow road down to a small parking area

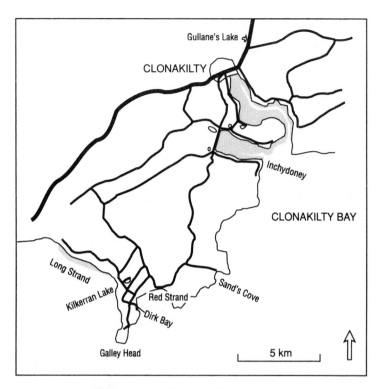

Clonakilty Bay, Galley Head and Kilkerran Lake, Co Cork

at the end. There is plenty of cover here to be explored for migrants. Return and turn left at the junction for Red Strand.

After leaving Red Strand, take the next left turn (signposted for Galley Head) about 1 km beyond the beach. The next left, marked as a cul de sac, takes you down to Dirk Bay. There is a small space for parking a car at the end.

Coming up from Dirk Bay, turn left for Galley Head or drive across the junction for an excellent area of gardens and, after about 2 km, Long Strand and Kilkerran Lake are clearly visible on the right. A sharp right turn leads down to the shore of the lake.

Calendar

All year: Shag, Gannet, Kittiwake, gulls in the bay, Rock Dove, Chough.

Autumn: Manx Shearwater, Sooty Shearwater, Arctic Skua, Great Skua, occasional Pomarine Skua, warblers, flycatchers, scarce migrants.

Winter: Red-throated Diver, Great Northern Diver, Tufted Duck, Red-breasted Merganser.

Spring: Terns in the bay.

Summer: Breeding Fulmar.

13 CAPE CLEAR

Habitat

This is, apart from the Fastnet Rock, the most southerly point of Ireland. Cape Clear is a hilly, sandstone island of about 300 hectares, which is almost cut in two by the North Harbour and the South Harbour. It is sharply indented at the south-west end by wave action and has some cliffs on the east and south-west sides. Much of the island is covered by heath with bracken and gorse, but there are large areas of cultivation and some areas of marshland.

Between 150 and 200 people live on the island and there are a number of small gardens with conifers and shrubs. A Bird Observatory was started in 1959 and has functioned successfully ever since. It is located at the North Harbour and provides accommodation for up to ten people. There is a warden resident from March to early November.

Species

The island is famous for its seabirds and rare passerine migrants. Seawatching from the Irish coastline really started here and systematic recording continues. No years are quite the same, so the birds to be seen vary each year. However, Manx Shearwaters, Sooty Shearwaters, Fulmars, Gannets, Arctic Skuas, Great Skuas, Kittiwakes, Guillemots and Razorbills are seen on most days in autumn. Great Shearwaters tend to

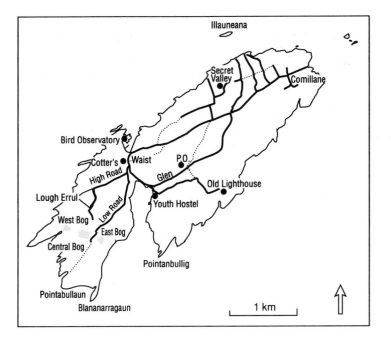

Cape Clear, Co Cork

be seen mostly in August, are almost annual, and can sometimes be seen in large numbers. Cory's Shearwaters are a great rarity, but can sometimes be seen in hundreds. Other species recorded over the years include Black-browed Albatross, Soft-plumaged Petrel, Bulwer's Petrel, Frigatebird and Long-tailed Skua.

Although the number and variety of seabird species vary, there are almost always large numbers of passing birds in late July and August. The numbers of Manx Shearwaters alone at this time of year can be up to 30,000 per hour.

The best seawatching spots are at the southern headlands. Blananarragaun, or Blanan' for short, is much the best in poor visibility. Seabirds come very close indeed, close enough for an observer some years ago to notice that Guillemots fly with their bills partly open, whereas Razorbills fly with theirs closed. Skuas sometimes come right overhead and shearwaters come within 100 m.

In summer there are nesting Guillemots, Black Guillemots, a handful of Puffins, Great Black-backed Gulls, Lesser Black-backed Gulls and Herring Gulls. A few pairs of Ravens and Choughs breed and Peregrines also nest. The commonest land birds are Meadow Pipits.

For autumn passerine migration Cape Clear is famous and the island seems taken over by birdwatchers in October, when vagrants from both North America and Siberia have come to be expected. Rarities such as Yellow-bellied Sapsucker and Indigo Bunting from America have been matched by birds such as Olive-backed Pipit and Pallas's Grasshopper Warbler from the east. It is not necessary to visit Cape Clear in autumn to see rarities, however. Needle-tailed Swift and Little Swift were both seen in summer and Alpine Swift and Stone-curlew in spring.

Passerines should be searched for in all parts of the island, but the best spots tend to be the gardens and hedges in Ballyieragh, Cotter's garden near the North Harbour and the area of bracken and small gardens north-west of the two windmills which are used for electricity generation.

The list of species recorded had reached 277 by the end of 1990, a very high percentage of the total of just over 400 species on the Irish list.

As well as birds, there are ample opportunities for watching cetacea and, in August, turtles. Many species of whale have been seen, though minke whale is perhaps the most regular.

Timing
Autumn is the best time for seeing seabirds and passerine migrants. The largest numbers of seabirds occur from late July to mid September. The most exciting passerine watching in recent years has been in the month of October. However, the number of birdwatchers is much the greatest in October, and a visitor wanting to enjoy a more relaxed atmosphere might prefer September or indeed May, when Cape Clear can be exceptionally beautiful and tranquil. And the birds can also be exciting.

Access
To stay at the observatory write to the Booking Secretary, Kieran Grace, 84 Dorney Court, Shankhill, Co Dublin. If the observatory is full there is a youth hostel and a number of guest houses on the island.

The ferry leaves Baltimore (south-west of Skibbereen) at 2.15 p.m. daily except on Sunday when there are special times. It leaves Cape Clear at 9.00 a.m. each morning, again excepting Sundays. In the summer months of July and August there are additional sailings. Sailing times

Female Red-backed Shrike

can be checked with Cape Clear Co-Operative (telephone 028–39119).

Calendar

All year: Cormorant, Shag, Gannet, Peregrine, Sparrowhawk, Kestrel, Guillemot, Razorbill, Black Guillemot, gulls, Rock Dove, Stonechat, Meadow Pipit, Chough, Raven.

Autumn: Seabird passage, passerine migrants, rarities.

Winter: Red-throated Diver, Great Northern Diver, Little Auks at sea, Great Skua, occasional Mediterranean Shearwater, Redwing, Fieldfare.

Spring: Turtle Dove, other spring migrants, Pomarine Skua.

Summer: Breeding seabirds, possibility of rarities.

OTHER CORK SITES

14 YOUGHAL

OSI ½" map: sheets 22, 25
X08 X17

Habitat and Species

Youghal Bay is the tidal estuary of the Blackwater river. Muddy inlets on the eastern bank, at Kinsalebeg (in Co Waterford), and, on the western bank, between Youghal town and the bridge carrying the main Cork-Waterford road across the bay (in Co Cork), provide wildfowl and wader feeding habitat. The flooded field on the eastern side of the main road, about 1 km on the Youghal side of the bridge, is a particularly good wader roost at high tide.

Shelduck, Mallard, Wigeon, Teal, Oystercatcher, Redshank, Curlew, Black-tailed Godwit and Dunlin can all be seen well in winter, and migrant waders can be seen in autumn. Great Northern Divers and, sometimes, Red-throated Divers can be seen below the town of Youghal. Little Egrets, Curlew Sandpiper and Lesser Yellowlegs have all been seen from the road at the flooded field to the south of Youghal bridge.

The reedbeds between Youghal and Ballyvergan to the south-west are the largest beds of *Phragmites* on the Cork coast and hold breeding Mallard, Moorhens, Water Rails, Sedge Warblers and about 20 pairs of Reed Warblers. In winter Hen Harriers roost in the marsh and Short-eared Owls are probably annual.

Rarities seen here include Marsh Harrier, Savi's Warbler and Lapland Bunting.

Access

Kinsalebeg at the eastern side of the bay can be approached by turning south off the main Youghal-Waterford road about 3 km from Youghal at a crossroads signposted for Clashmore (to the north). At the next junction turn right to Ferry Point pier from where the inlet and mudflats can readily be accessed.

The best place for watching on the western side is at the flooded field on the side of the road about 1 km from the bridge on the road to Youghal. There is space to park a car and, if the tide is out, the mudflats can be searched by walking back towards the bridge and looking out into the bay.

The reedbeds can be seen from the main road from Youghal to Cork about 1 km from the town. More of the marsh can be seen by taking the narrow road towards the beach.

15 COURTMACSHERRY

OSI ½" map: sheet 25
W44 W54

Habitat and Species

Courtmacsherry is another estuary with a sizeable wader population. This is the estuary of the Argideen river and runs from Timoleague to the sea past Courtmacsherry village. There is some *Spartina* on the upper reaches of the estuary, especially on the south side. A large flock of Golden Plover is the principal feature, but there are over 100 Black-tailed Godwits and good numbers of Redshanks, Dunlin and other wader species. This is a good site for Mediterranean Gulls, which are often to be seen on the mudflats below the old Franciscan friary at Timoleague.

Off the town of Courtmacsherry excellent close views may be had of Great Northern Divers in winter.

Access

Drive from Timoleague along the coast road to Courtmacsherry. Stop at intervals to look at waders and gulls. Take the road beyond the hotel to the parking space where the road ends. This is the best spot for divers.

16 ROSSCARBERY

OSI ½" map: sheet 24
W23

Habitat and Species

Rosscarbery Bay is on the main road from Cork to Skibbereen and so is well known to birdwatchers travelling to Cape Clear Bird Observatory. The bay comprises a lagoon north of the causeway, across which the main road runs, and an estuary to the south. The lagoon holds small numbers of Mallard and Red-breasted Mergansers. The estuary has wintering Golden Plovers, Lapwings, Dunlins, Black-tailed and Bar-tailed Godwits, Redshanks and Greenshanks. Small muddy pools on the side of the roads which run to the sea on both the east and west side of the estuary often hold a Spotted Redshank in autumn and winter. The pier at the end of the road on the western side provides good views of divers in winter.

Access

The estuary is crossed by anyone travelling between Clonakilty and Skibbereen. A road runs around the entire estuary so viewing opportunities are excellent.

17 LEE RESERVOIRS

OSI ½"' map: sheets 21, 25
W36 W37 W47 W57

Habitat and Species

The Lee Reservoirs were created by the construction of dams at Inniscarra and Carrigadrohid for the generation of electricity. The Gearagh, the section west of Macroom, is much the most interesting botanically. The upper part has woodland cover of oak, birch, willow, ash and hazel which was formerly much more extensive as the blackened stumps of dead trees rising from the water indicate. What remains is of great importance in that it represents an ungrazed natural habitat which is very rare in Ireland. However, it is not of great ornithological significance.

Nowadays, the open water is what attracts the birdwatcher. At the Gearagh, at Carrigadrohid and at other points along the reservoir in winter one can see large numbers of wintering wildfowl including Whooper and Bewick's Swans, up to 4,000 Wigeon, 1,000 Teal and small numbers of Mallard, Shoveler, Tufted Duck, Pochard and Goldeneye. Scarcer species such as Goosander, Smew and Ring-necked Duck can occur at times.

There are some Greylag Geese in the area, but they are feral.

Access

The reservoirs can be watched from either the northern or southern sides, though the road does not run along the entire shoreline. The northern road from Cork to Coachford provides the best view of the eastern section. Take the road from Cork for Dripsey and follow the reservoir to Macroom, stopping when birds are seen. The section below the town of Macroom is usually good. Instead of driving into Macroom, turn left on the Cork road and take the first right turn (signposted for Bantry) after about 800 m. This road leads directly to the Gearagh which can be viewed from either the south or the north. There are also footpaths leading into the Gearagh which can be used when the water level is low.

The main Macroom-Cork road, about 5 km from Macroom, provides good views of the southern part of the Carrigadrohid reservoir.

18 KILCOLMAN

OSI ½″ map: sheet 21
R51

Habitat and Species

Kilcolman bog is a limestone marsh occupying a glacially-eroded hollow. The marsh floods in winter and, at this time of year, has a small population of Greenland White-fronted Geese and Whooper Swans and a large number of duck. The most numerous ducks are Wigeon, Mallard and Teal, but Shoveler, Gadwall, Tufted Duck and Pochard are usually present. Birds of prey include regular Peregrine, Merlin and Hen Harrier in winter.

A castle occupied by the poet Edmund Spenser in the sixteenth century overlooks the marsh.

A refuge was established here by Richard and Margaret Ridgway in 1969 when they purchased a section of the site. They planted trees, dug out channels, built up islands, constructed hides and an observatory and maintained meticulous records of weather, water-level, bird numbers and bird behaviour. Much of the data they collected has been analysed and is in the course of being published. Since Richard Ridgway died in 1985, Margaret Ridgway has continued to develop the reserve in liaison with the state and local landowners.

The refuge is a wonderful place for watching geese, swans and ducks at close quarters. However, because it is private and Mrs Ridgway lives at the marsh, advance reservation is essential.

Access

To visit Kilcolman, first phone Mrs Ridgway on 022–24200 and seek permission. When this is obtained, follow the directions below to get to the site. Mallow is the nearest large town to start from. Leave Mallow on the main Limerick road; at New Twopothouse village, about 3.5 km from Mallow, take the right turn for Doneraile. Drive through Doneraile and keep straight on for about 1.5 km to a crossroads. Turn left following the sign for Rathluirc, and drive on for about 2.5 km until a crossroads is reached. There is a signpost to the right marked Heatherside Hospital. Take the left turn and drive down the narrow road for about 500 m until you reach a gate on the right marked 'Kilcolman Wildfowl Refuge'. This is the entrance to the reserve. Please ensure that you close the gate each time you pass through.

19 LISSAGRIFFIN AND MIZEN HEAD

Habitat and Species

Lissagriffin Lake is a shallow, brackish lake impounded by sand hills which have developed behind the strand at Barleycove. It has a sandy edge and some growth of reeds and sedges.

The lake has a small winter population of Bewick's and Whooper Swans, Teal and Wigeon, and Mute Swans and Mallard occur throughout the year. Although wader numbers are small, this is one of the best sites in Ireland for American waders. Pectoral Sandpipers are virtually annual in September, and a long list of other species has been seen. Because the shoreline is so limited in extent, the birds are usually easy to see well.

Choughs feed on the sand dunes and Peregrines are frequent visitors.

To the south-west, Mizen Head is a bleak promontory with a lighthouse at the tip. It is an excellent seawatching site, probably as good as Cape Clear, which is just across the bay. Sooty and Great Shearwaters, Great and Arctic Skuas are usual in autumn, together with large numbers of Manx Shearwaters, Gannets, Fulmars, Kittiwakes and auks. As is usual with seawatching, optimal weather conditions are essential. This site requires south-westerly winds and mist or rain for its best performance.

There are some small seabird colonies on the cliffs.

Ireland's first Isabelline Wheatear was seen on the cliff-top in autumn 1992, and the gardens at Crookhaven village nearby attract passerine migrants. Rarities recorded here include Red-eyed Vireo and Bonelli's Warbler.

Access

From Skibbereen follow the signposts to Schull and thence for Goleen. At Goleen, drive straight on for Barleycove. After about 8 km you will reach a fork where the left turn runs on to Crookhaven village and the right turn to Barleycove past a large caravan park. Follow the road to the right, passing the caravan park, and after about 2 km you will see Lissagriffin Lake below you. The road runs across a causeway through the middle of the lake. A car can be parked here and the lake edge explored on foot.

Mizen Head is reached by turning left after crossing the causeway, then taking the next left turn past the Barleycove Hotel and continuing for about 4 km until the small carpark at Mizen Head is reached.

Crookhaven village is reached by forking left after Goleen rather than bearing right for Barleycove. The village has a number of well vegetated gardens and all should be watched from the narrow roadways.

20 DURSEY ISLAND AND ALLIHIES

Habitat and Species

Dursey Island is a high sandstone island, about 7 km long and 1.5 km wide, located off the tip of the Beara peninsula. It has been known as a prime location for rare passerines since the late 1970s when it was first worked regularly. Dr Derek Scott, an English birdwatcher who had come to live locally, found Ireland's second Olivaceous Warbler on his first visit to the island in 1977. He paid many visits to the island over about two years but then left the area. The island was unwatched again until 1983 when two English visitors found a Parula Warbler and a Rose-breasted Grosbeak in the little glen at Firkeel on the mainland. Since then, visits have been made each autumn to Dursey and the adjoining mainland, and a number of excellent birdwatching sites identified. The island is long and has rather little cover, so birds can be found almost anywhere. On the mainland there are a few small gardens, some areas of brambles and a glen with steep banks with lots of cover at Firkeel.

Passerine migrants tend to be found on Dursey itself, in Firkeel Glen or in the area around Garinish.

There are rarely large falls of any species in the area, but the diversity of species is remarkable. Scarlet Rosefinch, Lesser Whitethroat and Melodious Warbler are regular in autumn, and major rarities in recent years have included Upland Sandpiper, Great Snipe, Olive-backed Pipit, Ovenbird and Scarlet Tanager.

Seawatching is quite good from the tip. The species to be seen are similar to those at Cape Clear, but numbers are lower.

Access

Dursey is at the tip of the Beara peninsula. Drive from Glengarriff to Castletownbere, and take the road west. After 15 km of winding road, a junction is reached. The right turn is for Ballydonegan and Allihies; keep straight on for Dursey Sound. Firkeel Glen is reached after another 5 km. A turn to the left runs down to a small slipway and the glen can be seen on the left hand side. There is a path across the fields into the glen.

Take the road on for another 3 km and you will reach Dursey Sound. Access to the island is by cable car. Ask the operator for the times of crossing and, particularly, return. A roadway runs most of the length of the island. Make sure to walk right to the end of the island as the grassy area at the south-west tip can hold waders or pipits.

Garinish is approached by taking the first left turn after leaving Dursey Sound.

KERRY

Introduction

The Kerry landscape is dominated by the magnificence of the Macgillicuddy Reeks which tower over Killarney, and by the bays which eat into the heart of the county. Kenmare Bay is disappointing for birds as there is little inter-tidal edge, but both Castlemaine Harbour and Tralee Bay are rich with wildfowl, especially Brent Geese in winter. Off the peninsulas are several groups of rocky islands which provide nest sites for tens of thousands of Gannets, Storm Petrels, Manx Shearwaters and Puffins, certainly the finest seabird colonies in the country. Passage seabirds are fewer than off the Cork coast, but several headlands present opportunities.

Being situated so far west, Kerry is one of the first landfalls for American waders and ducks. Most have been recorded at Akeragh Lough but many other good sites must be awaiting discovery. There has been very little exploration of the potential for autumn passerine migrants.

The mountains have a thinly distributed avifauna, but breeding birds include Peregrine, Chough and Ring Ouzel and there may well be surprises awaiting the birdwatcher prepared to explore them in summer or winter.

Sites

21	CASTLEMAINE HARBOUR	*Estuary; Brent Geese.*
22	TRALEE BAY AND BARROW HARBOUR	
		Estuary; Brent Geese.
23	AKERAGH LOUGH	*Brackish lagoons; possibility of rare waders.*

Other sites:

24	Ballinskelligs Bay	*Shallow bay; Scoters.*
25	Lough Gill	*Lake; wintering wildfowl.*
26	Skelligs	*Breeding seabird colony.*
27	Dunquin	*Seawatching; passerine migrants.*
28	Blasket Islands	*Breeding seabird colony.*
29	Puffin Island	*Breeding seabird colony.*
30	Brandon Point	*Seawatching.*
31	Killarney National Park	*Breeding woodland birds.*
32	Ballylongford and Tarbert	*Estuary.*

References

McDermott, P. Site guide: Akeragh Lough and Tralee Bay, Co. Kerry (*Irish Birding News* 2: 121–129, 1992).

O'Clery, Michael, 1991. Site guide: Dunquin, Co. Kerry (*Irish Birding News* 2: 29–36, 1991).

21 CASTLEMAINE HARBOUR

OSI ½" map: sheet 20/
1:50,000 map: sheets 71, 78
Q30 Q60 V69 V79

Habitat

This wide, sprawling bay is the estuary of Rivers Maine and Laune at the head of Dingle Bay. It comprises a series of interlocking sand spits with broad saltmarshes behind them. There are also extensive inter-tidal mudflats and poorly drained agricultural land surrounds the estuary, especially at its eastern end. The strata in the outer bay are sandy; the inner bay is much muddier. There are broad sandy beaches on the seaward side of the sand spits on both sides of the mouth of the estuary.

At the north-west corner near Inch there are extensive beds of eelgrass or *Zostera*. *Spartina* is present as well, and there are reedbeds at the eastern end.

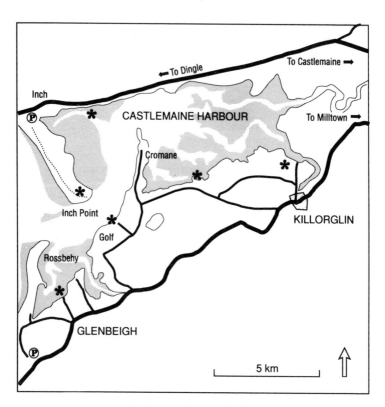

Castlemaine Harbour, Co Kerry

The mountains on both sides of the bay make this a magnificent site for birdwatching even if birds are few.

Shooting is prohibited over most of the estuary and there are signs to indicate this around much of the area.

Species

This is one of the major wintering sites of Brent Geese in Ireland and is also a major duck wintering area. Brent Geese arrive in late August, earlier than at most Irish sites, and remain until April. They can be found on both sides of the bay, from Rossbehy around to Inch, but the largest flocks are usually at Inch. Wigeon arrive early here as well, and the largest numbers are found in autumn. Up to 6,500 have been seen in autumn, but the mid-winter numbers are much reduced. The flock of Wigeon off Inch promontory is one of the great Irish ornithological sights.

Castlemaine Harbour has a flock of up to 100 Pintail. Why this should be, when there are so few elsewhere on the south coast, is a mystery. Nevertheless, they are a magnificent sight as they concentrate behind the sand dunes at Inch. Shelduck, Mallard, Teal and Shoveler also occur on the mudflats.

In the upper reaches of the estuary Scaup and Goldeneye can be found in flocks of varying size. Sometimes, there can be over 100 Scaup on the southern side.

Great Northern Divers and occasional Long-tailed Ducks frequent the deeper channels. The best place for Long-tailed Ducks is off Dooks Golf Links. There are a few small parties of Red-breasted Mergansers. Off the beaches on both southern and northern sides flocks of Common Scoters winter. The flock off Rossbehy numbers up to 2,000 birds.

The numbers of waders are not so spectacular as the flocks of ducks and geese. Oystercatchers, Dunlins, Curlews, Bar-tailed Godwits and Redshanks scatter over the mudflats in small parties. There are some solitary Greenshanks and a few Ringed Plovers and Grey Plovers. On the beach at Inch, Sanderlings can be seen. Flocks of Golden Plover and Lapwing sometimes occur.

The estuary is regularly hunted over by Peregrines. Being so far west it looks the ideal location for an American vagrant duck or wader, but very few rarities have been recorded. Perhaps more frequent visits by birdwatchers could improve this record.

Timing
This is very much a winter site, at its best from September to the end of March, though the first Brent Geese and Wigeon appear in late August. The area is best visited when the tide is rising so that birds can be seen at their closest. The mudflats are very extensive and a telescope is essential.

Access
On the southern side, Rossbehy Creek is approached by driving through Glenbeigh, past the Towers Hotel, and turning right on the turn signposted for Rossbeigh strand. The road leads to a carpark and provides views over mudflats and saltmarsh where geese and Wigeon can be seen.

Drive back towards Glenbeigh, but before reaching the bridge over the River Behy, turn left down a narrow road alongside the fastflowing river. Dippers can be seen here. Park the car at the end of the tarmac and walk down a short track to the estuary.

For superb views of the scoter flocks, take the narrow road which runs west from the carpark at Rossbeigh strand. A lay-by half way up the hill is an ideal vantage point for viewing the duck.

Returning to Glenbeigh take the road for Killorglin and turn left 500m outside the village. This narrow road leads down to the estuary and provides good views of the outer part of Rossbehy creek.

Drive back to the main Glenbeigh-Killorglin road again and drive towards Killorglin. Turn left after about 1 km, just after the road crosses the River Caragh where signposts indicate Dooks Golf Links. Follow the road for 4 km to a fork. Turn left for Cromane, though bird numbers here are relatively low; turn right to follow the southern shore of Castlemaine Harbour. Stop after about 1 km and look at the estuary. Scaup and Goldeneye can be seen in the channels here in winter and Brent Geese are usual.

To see the northern shore of Castlemaine, drive to Killorglin, then to Castlemaine and, at Castlemaine, take the turn for Dingle. It is about 19 km to Inch strand and there are a couple of left turnings which provide direct access to the inner mudflats. But the mudflats behind Inch strand are the highlight of this bay. Many of the birds can be seen from the main road and the extra height of the road provides a vantage point. However, a walk along the 4 km of sand dune at Inch will present opportunities for magnificent views of great flocks of Brent Geese,

Shelduck, Wigeon and Pintail and should be taken.

Calendar

All year: Mallard, Oystercatcher, Curlew.

Autumn: Great Northern Diver, Brent Goose, Wigeon, Teal, Shoveler, Red-breasted Merganser, Lapwing, Golden Plover, Ringed Plover, Dunlin, Bar-tailed Godwit, Redshank, terns.

Winter: Great Northern Diver, Brent Goose, Wigeon, Teal, Shoveler, Goldeneye, Scaup, Long-tailed Duck, Common Scoter, Red-breasted Merganser, Ringed Plover, Golden Plover, Lapwing, Dunlin, Sanderling, Bar-tailed Godwit, Redshank, Greenshank.

Spring: Brent Geese and lingering ducks and waders.

Summer: Visiting terns.

22 TRALEE BAY AND BARROW HARBOUR

OSI ½" map: sheet 20/
1:50,000 map: sheet 71
Q71 Q81

Habitat

Tralee Bay is rather like a small scale Castlemaine Harbour and shares many of the same bird species. It stretches from Blennerville west to Derrymore Island on the southern side, to Fenit on the northern side, and includes Barrow Harbour to the north. There are extensive inter-tidal mudflats to the east of Derrymore Island and saltmarsh above the inter-tidal zone on the southern side. Barrow Harbour also has mudflats, these having built up behind a sand bar. There are beds of eelgrass *Zostera* which provide feeding for Brent Geese.

Species

Like Castlemaine Harbour, this bay holds large wintering flocks of Brent Geese, Wigeon and Teal, and smaller numbers of Shelduck, Mallard, Pintail, Shoveler, Scaup and Red-breasted Merganser. Up to 3,000 Brent Geese have been counted, but there is frequent interchange between this bay and Castlemaine, only 10 km away over the Slieve Mish mountains. In Barrow Harbour, Whooper Swans join the Brent Geese on the *Zostera* in early winter.

Outside the bay there is a wintering flock of Common Scoters and scattered Great Northern and Red-throated Divers.

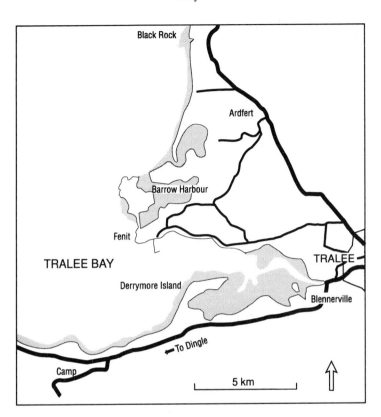

Tralee Bay, Co Kerry

Wader numbers are lower than at Castlemaine but there appears to be more diversity of species. Oystercatchers, Lapwings, Curlews, Bar-tailed Godwits, Redshanks and Dunlin are all found on the mudflats as in the neighbouring bay, but there appear to be more Grey Plovers, Black-tailed Godwits and autumn migrants such as Spotted Redshank at Tralee Bay. This bay has been much better watched than Castlemaine because it is so much closer to the town of Tralee where several bird-watchers live, but whether this is the reason for the apparently greater species diversity is not known.

In autumn Curlew Sandpipers, Little Stints and Ruffs are recorded most years at Blennerville and some American waders have been seen. Spotted Redshanks winter each year. The pier at Fenit has wintering Purple Sandpipers as well as the more ubiquitous Turnstones.

The dump in Blennerville is a good place for Glaucous, Iceland and Ring-billed Gulls (regular) in winter.

In winter Hen Harriers, Merlins and Peregrines hunt over the saltmarshes.

Timing

In autumn look for waders at Blennerville as well as checking the first arrivals among the wildfowl. Winter is good for wildfowl and waders. The town dump is at its best for gulls at this time of year as well. In spring numbers of birds are lower, but the area is well worth a visit.

A rising tide is the best for visiting. At high tide the wildfowl and waders are almost inaccessible at their roosts. A telescope is almost essential.

Access

The estuary is difficult to survey thoroughly because the surrounding road runs at some distance from the shoreline for most of its length. The southern side can be watched from the Tralee-Dingle road. The road crosses the river at Blennerville by a large white windmill and the estuary can be scanned from several points. A telescope is essential and it may also be necessary to explore the saltmarsh.

The northern side can be approached at several points by road. From Blennerville, having travelled north across the river take the first left turn and drive to the exit of the disused canal. This provides one vantage point. Another can be reached by driving from Tralee towards Fenit and stopping the car at Spa where there are further views of the bay.

Barrow Harbour can be watched by taking the road on through Fenit until the shoreline is reached, or by turning right just before the village and driving for about 1.5 km until the estuary is reached. There are a number of narrow roads here which give access to different sides of Barrow Harbour.

Redshank

Calendar

All year: Mute Swan, Mallard, Oystercatcher, Curlew.

Autumn: Red-throated Diver, Great Northern Diver, Brent Goose, Wigeon, Teal, Shoveler, Common Scoter, Red-breasted Merganser, Ringed Plover, Golden Plover, Lapwing, Dunlin, occasional Curlew Sandpiper and Little Stint, Ruff, Bar-tailed Godwit, Redshank.

Winter: Red-throated Diver, Great Northern Diver, Whooper Swan, Brent Goose, Wigeon, Teal, Shoveler, Goldeneye, Scaup, Common Scoter, Red-breasted Merganser, Ringed Plover, Golden Plover, Lapwing, Dunlin, Sanderling, Bar-tailed Godwit, Greenshank, Redshank, occasional Spotted Redshank, Glaucous and Iceland Gulls, Ring-billed Gull.

Spring: Brent Geese and lingering ducks and waders.

23 AKERAGH LOUGH

OSI ½″ map: sheets 17,20/
1:50,000 map: sheet 71
Q72

Habitat

Akeragh Lough is a brackish lagoon behind a line of sand dunes in the northern corner of Ballyheige Bay north of Tralee. In summer the lough consists of three ponds connected by dykes; in winter the surrounding meadows flood and the area becomes a large shallow lake. There is a strand on the seaward side of the dunes. In recent years the lake has suffered from varying water levels and the beach offshore has tended to attract most waders.

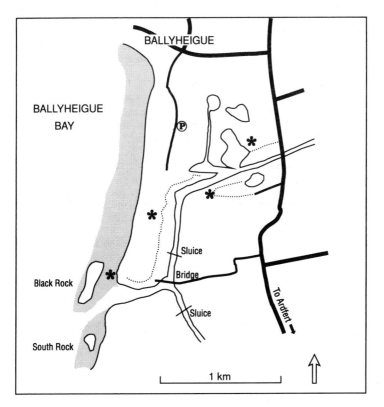

Akeragh Lough, Co Kerry

Species

The lough has been famous for over 30 years for the American ducks and waders which occur regularly. There is some evidence that the site does not attract as many rarities now as it did in the past, but it is still a premier location for seeking out unusual birds.

Highlights have included flocks of 13 American Wigeon and 14

Pectoral Sandpipers and records of most of the American wader species on the Irish list. The first Irish records of Baird's, Least, Solitary and Stilt Sandpiper were all at this lough. Rare birds come not just from the west: species such as Temminck's Stint and White-winged Black Tern have also been seen here.

As well as being a site with the potential for rarities, Akeragh Lough also has wintering Whooper Swans, Mallard, Wigeon, Teal, Gadwall, Pintail, Shoveler and small numbers of diving ducks. The numbers of wildfowl vary depending on the water level. Wader species in autumn include Spotted Redshank, Ruff, Little Stint, Curlew Sandpiper, Green Sandpiper and Wood Sandpiper in most years as well as the more common species. Again, the number of waders depends very much on the condition of the lough. Many of the waders feed on the beach when the lough is unsuitable.

Choughs can be seen in the surrounding fields. Peregrines, Merlins and Hen Harriers hunt over the surrounding area.

Timing
From autumn through winter to spring this is a superb area. In summer it is less likely to be exciting, but is often worth a visit.

Access
Akeragh Lough is best approached from Ballyheigue. Drive south from the centre of the village for 1.5 km along a rough track past caravans. The car should be parked at the open area beside the track and the ponds on the left explored on foot and with care. A new farmhouse at the end of this road is strictly private.

The lough can also be watched from the main road between Ardfert and Ballyheigue, but great care should be taken as the road is busy.

To reach the southernmost pond, take the minor road leading west from the main road about 0.5 km south of the bridge over the stream draining the lough. This minor road degenerates into a track leading to the pond.

Every visitor to Akeragh should take the southerly road which provides access to Black Rock and to the southern side of the lough. Driving from Ballyheigue south for Ardfert, cross the bridge over the river and take the right turn about 1 km south of the Ranch House guest house. This road leads to a sluice. From here, the lough to the north can be explored and the beach offshore can be walked. The small islet, Black Rock, joined to the beach at low tide has waders and gulls.

Calendar
All year: Mute Swan, Mallard, Oystercatcher, Ringed Plover, Curlew.

Autumn: Wigeon, Teal, Shoveler, Red-breasted Merganser, diving ducks, Golden Plover, Lapwing, Dunlin, Curlew Sandpiper, Litle Stint, Ruff, Black-tailed Godwit, Bar-tailed Godwit, Redshank, Greenshank, Green Sandpiper, Wood Sandpiper, American waders.

Winter: Whooper Swan, Bewick's Swan, Wigeon, Teal, Shoveler, Red-breasted Merganser, diving ducks, Golden Plover, Lapwing, Dunlin, Sanderling, Bar-tailed Godwit, Greenshank, Redshank, Dunlin, Sanderling.

Spring: Ducks and late waders.

OTHER KERRY SITES

24 BALLINSKELLIGS BAY

OSI ½″ map: sheets 20, 24
V46

Habitat and Species

The shallow bay from Hog's Head around to Ballinskelligs is a wintering area for Common Scoters. Velvet and Surf Scoters have been found here in the past and the location of the site, so far west, suggests that it should be worth investigating regularly for Surf Scoters. Great Northern and Red-throated Divers are also present in winter and Slavonian Grebes turn up regularly.

Access

From Kenmare take the Sneem road. After passing through Sneem, follow the signposts for Waterville. The bay can be seen well from Waterville or the road around to Ballinskelligs. Reenroe Point is the best place for seeing Slavonian Grebes.

25 LOUGH GILL

OSI ½″ map: sheet 20/
1:50,000 map: sheet 71
Q51 Q61

Habitat and Species

Lough Gill is a shallow lake of 1,800 hectares, with rough pasture on its inland side and sand dunes protecting it from the sea. Beds of *Phragmites* surround most of the lake. The outlet from the lake to the sea is a narrow stream at the eastern end and the water level is controlled by a sluice. The entire area is subject to a no-shooting Order.

This is a wonderfully productive lake with great numbers of wintering wildfowl.

The lake has varying numbers of swans and ducks throughout the winter. At times there are large flocks of Whooper and Bewick's Swans (up to 200 of each species) and large numbers of Mallard, Teal, Wigeon and Scaup. Smaller numbers of Gadwall, Shoveler, Tufted Ducks, Pochard and Coots can also be seen.

The lake is quite large and many ducks conceal themselves in the reedbeds so they can be difficult to see.

As well as being a good bird area, this is also the centre of the Irish population of natterjack toad.

Access

Drive from Tralee to Castlegregory. At Castlegregory bear left rather than taking either of the two right turns in the village, and drive straight on for about 200 m. Take the right turn marked Lough Gill and drive to a small parking area where a pier projects into the lake. Much of the lake, especially the eastern end, can be surveyed from here.

To see the eastern end, drive back onto the road out of Castlegregory and turn right (rather than returning to the village). Drive on for about 800 m and you will have a good view across fields of the western end of the lake. Many duck can be seen best from here.

26 SKELLIGS

Habitat and Species

The Skelligs are two towering rocks projecting out of the Atlantic about 13 km off Valentia Island. The islands are red sandstone and slate. Skellig Michael, much the larger of the two islands at 48 hectares, has a lighthouse which was manned from 1826 up to the very recent past. The Little Skellig is smaller, only 7 hectares in extent, with sheer cliffs and no room for human habitation. It holds over 20,000 pairs of nesting Gannets.

The Great Skellig has no Gannets but holds several thousand nesting pairs of Puffins, Storm Petrels and Manx Shearwaters, and smaller numbers of Fulmars, Kittiwakes, Razorbills and Guillemots. It is a unique experience to stand in front of the beehive huts on the Great Skellig, built by monks over 1,000 years ago, and to hear Manx Shearwaters groaning on their nest scrapes in crevices in the walls.

The Little Skellig is leased by the Irish Wildbird Conservancy.

Access

Boats travel to the Great Skellig in summer from Valentia, Caherciveen, Portmagee and Derrynane. Timetables are available in local hotels and guesthouses. If possible, negotiate a trip which will take you close to the Little Skellig for a good view of the Gannet colony. Landing on the Little Skellig is prohibited.

27 DUNQUIN

Habitat and Species

Dunquin is at the western tip of the Dingle peninsula, a spectacularly beautiful part of west Kerry. The village of Dunquin, with plenty of cover, and the fields and valleys around it have been shown in recent years to attract rare migrants in autumn. Red-eyed Vireo has been seen, and Crossbill, Yellow-browed Warbler, Icterine Warbler and Red-throated Pipit have also been recorded. The area has obvious potential for American passerine vagrants.

Seawatching can be carried out from Clogher Head, to the north of Dunquin, and in west or north-west winds good numbers of Sooty Shearwaters have been seen and smaller numbers of Great Shearwaters, Great Skuas, Arctic Skuas, Pomarine Skuas and Grey Phalaropes. Rarer seabirds seen include Long-tailed Skua and Sabine's Gull.

Access

Dunquin is reached by driving from Dingle to Ventry and then following the road around Slea Head until the village is reached. There is a Youth Hostel in the village and numerous guest houses in the vicinity.

28 BLASKET ISLANDS

Habitat and Species

The Blasket Islands are a group of islands off the Dingle peninsula with substantial colonies of breeding seabirds. Some thousands of pairs of

Manx Shearwater and Puffins and several tens of thousands of pairs of Storm Petrels nest on the small islands of Inishtearaght, Inishvickillane, Inishnabro and Inishtooskert, together with small numbers of Fulmars, Guillemots, Razorbills and gulls. Leach's Petrels have been seen in the surrounding waters during summer and several have been caught at night on the islands, so a small number probably breed.

A proposal to reintroduce White-tailed Eagles to Ireland is centred around the release of birds at Inishvickillane.

Cover on the islands is almost non-existent, and very few passerine migrants have been recorded. There are old records of migrants striking the lighthouses, and a few autumn migrants have been seen on the Great Blasket so a visit to that island at least might be productive in autumn.

Access

Unfortunately, the islands, apart from Inishvickillane which is owned by Mr Charles Haughey, former Irish Taoiseach, are uninhabited and access is only possible by negotiating with local fishermen and bringing camping equipment. Permission is required to land on Inishvickillane.

While the Great Blasket is visited regularly in summer by organised boat trips from Dunquin Pier (details in Kruger's pub in Dunquin), there are very few trips in autumn when the potential for seeing migrants should be highest.

29 PUFFIN ISLAND

OSI ½" map: sheet 20
V36

Habitat and Species

Puffin Island is an Irish Wildbird Conservancy reserve located on a small island to the south of Valentia Island and separated from the mainland by a narrow sound. It holds some thousands of pairs of Manx Shearwaters, Storm Petrels and Puffins and smaller numbers of other breeding seabirds.

Access

The island may only be landed upon with the consent of the IWC which tends to withhold permission from all except those carrying out bona fide research on the birds. Fishing boats can be chartered in Portmagee.

The island can be seen quite well from the sea by the visitor who takes a boat trip to the Skelligs from Portmagee.

30 BRANDON POINT

OSI ½" map: sheet 20/
1:50,000 map: sheet 70
Q51

Habitat and Species

Brandon Point is a classic seawatching point in north-west winds. It is located at the western end of a north facing bay and seabirds which are funnelled into the bay by strong gales exit almost below the feet of the observer at Brandon.

As well as Manx Shearwaters, Gannets, Fulmars, auks and skuas, large numbers of Great and Sooty Shearwaters have been seen, though not usually in such numbers as at Cape Clear. This site gets a somewhat different mix of species, reflecting its much more westerly location. The west coast of Ireland appears to have many more Sabine's Gulls, Leach's Petrels and phalaropes offshore than the south coast, and this has been reflected on days when small flocks of all three species have been seen.

Access

Follow the road from Tralee to Castlegregory and, at the fork for Dingle some 10 km beyond Castlegregory, turn right for Cloghane and drive out to the end of the road at Brandon Point. Remember, however, that this site requires north-west winds. If short of time, stop at Fermoyle, signposted just after the turn for Cloghane, and check the beach. Skuas and Sabine's Gulls can be seen assembling off here when the winds are suitable.

31 KILLARNEY NATIONAL PARK

OSI ½″ map: sheet 21/
1:50,000 map: sheet 78
V88 V98

Habitat and Species

The Killarney National Park covers 10,000 hectares of lake, mountain and woodland, principally of sessile oak, but with extensive coniferous wood, wet alder swamp and a fine yew wood. The old woodland holds a rich diversity of breeding species. The commonest birds are Chaffinches, Robins, Goldcrests, Blue Tits, Coal Tits and Wrens, but there are also Jays, Long-eared Owls, Blackcaps, probably a few Redstarts and perhaps a few Wood Warblers. Garden Warblers are also regular breeders.

Goldcrest

The lakes attract occasional rarities including Ring-necked Duck, Garganey and Osprey. The best area is on Lough Leane from Ross Castle around to Killarney Golf Club.

Access

There are several large tracts of deciduous woodland in the Killarney vicinity.

Ross Island has woodland close to the town. Follow the signposts for Ross Bay and park your car in the carpark.

Tomies Wood is on the far side of Lough Leane from Killarney town. Drive out on the Killorglin road and turn left after 5 km; turn left after a further 2 km and the road leads down to the lake shore. A path leads along the lake shore to the wood.

There is more woodland on the southern shore of the upper lake. Take the road for Kenmare and explore the various tracts of woodland within 15 km of Killarney. Even if birds are few, the views are justly famous.

32 BALLYLONGFORD AND TARBERT

OSI ½″ map: sheet 17
Q94 R04

Habitat and Species

The mudflats on the Shannon Estuary at Ballylongford and Tarbert are two small sections of an enormous complex which holds large numbers of wildfowl and waders. These two bays each hold up to 1,500 ducks (and Tarbert has had 3,000) and 3,000 waders. The main duck species are Wigeon, Teal and Mallard, with some Shelducks, Pintail and Shovelers and a few Red-breasted Mergansers off the mudflats. There are usually some wintering Scaup in both bays. Waders include Oystercatcher, Lapwing, Golden Plover, Grey Plover, Curlew, Bar-tailed Godwit, Redshank, Greenshank and Dunlin.

Access

Ballylongford Bay is easily watched by taking the road from Ballylongford west towards Ballybunion. Turn right 1 km after leaving Ballylongford and follow the narrow road down to Carrig Island.

The Tarbert mudflats can be viewed from the road leading from Tarbert village to the pier and ferry terminal. The road runs right alongside the estuary. Cars can be parked at the ferry terminal. The best time is when slightly more than half the mud has been covered by a rising tide.

LIMERICK

Introduction

Limerick is a rich and rather lowlying agricultural county, with its only coastline the south shore of the Shannon estuary. As a result, there are no seabird colonies to see, and the chances of finding unusual passerine migrants are slim.

The Shannon estuary runs from the city of Limerick to the border with Kerry and beyond and, while difficult of access, has a great deal of variety in its winter bird species. It has certainly been very much under-watched.

Sites

33 SOUTH SHORE OF SHANNON
    ESTUARY   *Estuary.*
Other sites:
34 Lough Gur   *Lake with wintering wildfowl.*

References

Brennan, P. and Jones, E. *Birds of North Munster* (IWC, Limerick, 1982).

33 SOUTH SHORE OF SHANNON ESTUARY

OSI ½″ map: sheet 17
R25 R35 R45

Habitat

The Shannon Estuary is approximately 80 km from Limerick to the open sea, and has numerous bays, many of which hold flocks of wintering wildfowl and waders. On the southern side, the stretch from the Maigue Estuary to Aughinish Island is unquestionably the most productive for birds. There are a number of inlets and the coastline around Greenish Island is particularly indented. The tide recedes for nearly 2 km in places. Behind the inter-tidal zone is an extensive area of saltmarsh and poor agricultural land with a number of drains. The road does not run alongside the mudflats and access is therefore difficult.

This is a wild and attractive estuary, but one for the enthusiast. The visual impact of the enormous alumina extraction factory at Aughinish Island detracts somewhat from the experience of birdwatching on the saltmarsh, but the relative inaccessibility of the best birdwatching sites means that the visitor is highly unlikely to come across another birder. This also means that if you simply want to see the species which occur here, you can probably get closer and better views at a number of other sites.

Species

The wintering wildfowl and waders of the Shannon estuary have not really been thoroughly surveyed since the 1970s when regular aerial surveys were carried out. These ceased when the aircraft ditched into the Shannon estuary close to the islands north of this shoreline. Fortunately, both pilot and ornithologist were able to scramble to safety. The counts, however, showed that between 3,500 and 6,000 wildfowl and between 5,000 and 11,000 waders used this area in winter.

Some wader ringing was also carried out near Greenish Island in the

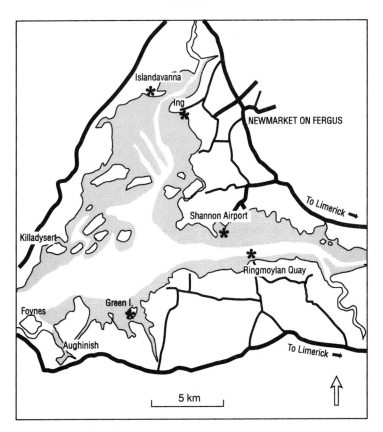

Shannon Estuary, Cos Clare and Limerick

1970s, but little birdwatching has been carried on here since.

The principal wildfowl species are Shelduck, Wigeon, Teal, Mallard and Scaup. Small numbers of Shoveler and Red-breasted Merganser also occur. There are small populations of both Greylag Geese and Greenland White-fronted Geese in the area, but the birds are very mobile and difficult to find. The Greylag Geese usually frequent the Maigue Estuary and the Greenland White-fronts are further downstream between Beagh Castle and Aughinish. The best section for duck is to the east of Aughinish Island and around Greenish Island.

Most of the waders are further east, from Beagh Castle to the mouth of the River Maigue. The principal species are Lapwing, Golden Plover, Curlew, Black-tailed Godwit, Redshank, Greenshank and Dunlin. Some Grey Plover, Ringed Plover and Knot occur. Robertstown Creek is a haunt of Spotted Redshanks in autumn, winter and spring.

Timing

The estuary is very quiet from spring to early autumn, so the best time for visiting is between early September and the middle of March. Numbers of some wader species are higher in autumn, but duck numbers are certainly highest from November to February. The area is shot over in winter.

Access

Access is difficult and requires serious commitment. From Limerick take the road for Mungret and Askeaton. This is well signposted.

After passing Mungret keep on the main road for about 12 km until you reach a right turn for Pallaskenry. Take the road to Pallaskenry and drive straight through the village. At a junction about 400 m past the village bear left; drive for nearly 2 km to another junction; then turn right and immediately afterwards turn left and drive down to Ringmoylan Quay. There are good views of the mudflats here.

Drive back to Pallaskenry and turn right. Drive straight for 5 km and then take the right turn for Beagh Castle. This road leads right onto the edge of the mudflats again.

Return from Beagh Castle and turn right. Follow this road into Askeaton. There are several stopping places where the saltmarsh and estuary can be approached on your right, but remember that the land here is all privately owned. The only access by road is on the narrow road to the right at Ballysteen.

To see Robertstown Creek drive on through Askeaton and turn right at Robertstown church. This road provides access to the western arm of the creek; the eastern arm can best be seen from the main road.

Calendar

All year: Cormorant, Grey Heron, Mute Swan, Mallard, Curlew.

Autumn: Greylag Goose, Greenland White-fronted Goose, Shelduck, Wigeon, Teal, Shoveler, Red-breasted Merganser, Oystercatcher, Lapwing, Golden Plover, Ringed Plover, Black-tailed Godwit, Redshank, Greenshank, Spotted Redshank, Dunlin.

Winter: Great Crested Grebe, Greylag Goose, Greenland White-fronted Goose, Shelduck, Wigeon, Teal, Shoveler, Scaup, Red-breasted Merganser, Oystercatcher, Ringed Plover, Golden Plover, Grey Plover, Lapwing, Knot, Dunlin, Black-tailed Godwit, Redshank, Greenshank.

Spring: Lingering geese, ducks and waders.

OTHER LIMERICK SITES

34 LOUGH GUR

Habitat and Species

This shallow lake is better known for its archaeological remains than its birds. There is an ancient lake dwelling or crannog in the lake which when excavated produced many artifacts, which can be seen in the National Museum in Dublin. The lake holds between 1,000 and 2,000 duck in winter. Wigeon and Tufted Duck are most numerous, but up to

200 Shoveler and smaller numbers of Mallard, Gadwall and Teal also occur.

At night up to 50 Whooper Swans roost on the lake, having travelled from their daytime feeding site on pasture fields at Rathcannon, Bruff.

Several rare duck species have been recorded, including Ring-necked and Ferruginous Duck. There is very little standing water in the vicinity so it is not altogether surprising that this lake has attracted rarities.

Access
Lough Gur is close to Kilmallock. Driving from Cork to Limerick on the main road between these two cities, turn off at Charleville for Kilmallock. Drive through Kilmallock on the road for Bruff and Holycross. Turn right at Holycross and view from the layby beyond the cemetery or from the main carpark at the northern end of the lake.

To get to Rathcannon, where the Whooper Swans feed, drive from Lough Gur to Bruff. Turn right just beyond the main bridge. The swans can be seen from November to April on fields to the right about 1.5 km from Bruff.

CLARE

Introduction
Clare is bordered on the east and south sides by the River Shannon and its estuary. To the west lies the Atlantic and to the north is Galway Bay and a stretch of limestone between the sea and the Slieve Aughty hills. The limestone pavement of the Burren dominates north Clare and the visitor in spring or summer should certainly explore this habitat for its flowers and butterflies.

The county has large numbers of wintering wildfowl on the Shannon estuary and the many lakes scattered across the county. Waders are most numerous on the Shannon estuary.

To the west there are breeding seabird colonies on the Cliffs of Moher and a good seabird and passerine migration watchpoint at Loop Head in the extreme south-west of the county.

Sites
35	SHANNON AIRPORT LAGOON	*Brackish lagoon; estuary.*
36	FERGUS ESTUARY	*Estuary.*
37	BALLYALLIA LAKE	*Lake with wintering wildfowl.*
38	CLIFFS OF MOHER	*Breeding seabird colony.*
39	LOOP HEAD AND BRIDGES OF ROSS	
		Seawatching; passerine migrants.

Other sites:
40	Clonderalaw Bay	*Estuary.*
41	Poulnasherry Bay	*Estuary.*
42	Mutton Island and Lurga Point	*Rocky shore; Purple Sandpipers; Barnacle Geese.*
43	Ballyvaghan	*Shallow coastline; divers.*
44	Lough Atedaun	*Shallow lake; winter wildfowl.*

References
Brennan, P. and Jones, E. *Birds of North Munster* (IWC, Limerick, 1982).
Whilde, Tony. *Pocket Guide to the Cliffs of Moher* (Appletree Press, Belfast, 1987).

35 SHANNON AIRPORT LAGOON

OSI ½″ map: sheet 17
R36

Habitat
The area described as the lagoon at Shannon Airport comprises three habitats. The lagoon proper is a shallow brackish lake created when two embankments were built between Dernish Island and the mainland. A sluice gate controls the water level. Sometimes the water level drops and a muddy shoreline is exposed.

There are reedbeds alongside the lagoon and these have been heavily mist-netted as part of a study of Sedge Warblers. The principal species is *Phragmites*. Around the reedbed is an area of marsh with stands of rushes and some invading willows *Salix*.

Outside the lake, the estuarine mudflat stretches into the distance beyond Rineanna in the west. However, the mudflat close to where the causeway around the eastern rim of the lagoon partially encloses the inter-tidal mud is one of the last areas to flood when the tide rises and is a particularly attractive area for large numbers of waders. Unfortunately, *Spartina* is spreading in the area.

Species
Mute Swans and sometimes Whooper Swans assemble on the lagoon proper, as do wintering flocks of up to 300 Mallard, 400 Wigeon, 630

Coots

Teal, 230 Shoveler, 200 Pintail, 40 Gadwall, 150 Pochard and 500 Coots. Flocks of Mallard, Wigeon and Shoveler also occur on the estuary, as do Shelduck and, in the channels, parties of Scaup.

Numbers of waders vary greatly, but have reached 20,000 at the mudflats off the lagoon. Up to 5,000 Dunlins, 4,000 Knots, 3,500 Golden Plover, 2,000 Redshanks, 2,000 Bar-tailed Godwits, 1,500 Black-tailed Godwits and smaller numbers of Grey Plover, Ringed Plover, Turnstone, Greenshank and Spotted Redshank winter here. In autumn, Ruffs, Curlew Sandpipers and Little Stints all occur. Rarities recorded in recent years include White-rumped Sandpiper, Wilson's Phalarope and Laughing Gull.

The lagoon holds breeding Water Rails, large numbers of Sedge Warblers and a few pairs of Grasshopper Warblers. In autumn, a few Reed Warblers have been caught among the migrant Sedge Warblers and rarer species trapped include Savi's Warbler and Bluethroat.

Timing

The area is worth visiting at any time of the year, but visits should ideally be made when the tide is rising and the mudflats are partially inundated. When the tide is fully out waders are difficult to see owing to the extent of the mudflats.

Access

The lagoon proper is owned by Aer Rianta, the airport authority, and is subject to patrols by security staff sympathetic to birdwatching. Park in the Airport Hotel carpark (just before the Airport on the left hand side) and walk out onto the lagoon causeway which commences just beyond the rear of the hotel. A hide, built by Aer Rianta, on the western side of the lagoon can be reached by driving past the main terminal building and taking the first left turn for the golf clubhouse. Walk through the gate at the far end of the clubhouse car park and follow the track to the wooden hide. The key to the hide can be collected at the Airport Fire Station.

The mudflats can easily be watched from the public road. Follow the signposts to Shannon Airport. Drive right to the airport itself, park your car in one of the public carparks and walk over to the edge of the estuary.

Calendar

All year: Little Grebe, Mute Swan, Shelduck, Mallard, Coot, Moorhen, Water Rail, Curlew, Black-tailed Godwit, Reed Bunting.

Autumn: Wigeon, Teal, Shoveler, Pintail, Pochard, Oystercatcher, Ringed Plover, Golden Plover, Turnstone, Lapwing, Knot, Dunlin, Curlew Sandpiper, Little Stint, Ruff, Bar-tailed Godwit, Spotted Redshank, Redshank, Greenshank, Swallow and Starling roosts, Sedge Warbler, Reed Warbler, Wheatear, White Wagtail.

Winter: Whooper Swan, Wigeon, Teal, Shoveler, Pintail, Pochard, Scaup, Oystercatcher, Ringed Plover, Golden Plover, Grey Plover, Lapwing, Knot, Dunlin, Bar-tailed Godwit, Spotted Redshank, Redshank, Greenshank, Turnstone, Merlin.

Spring: Late ducks and waders. Sedge Warbler, Willow Warbler, Whitethroat, Swallow, Wheatear, White Wagtail.

Summer: Sedge Warbler, Grasshopper Warbler.

36 FERGUS ESTUARY

Habitat

The Fergus is an enormous and daunting estuary, shaped rather like an inverted 'V' with its apex at Clarecastle and broadening out to Shannon in the east and Killadysert in the west. Both sides have extensive saltmarshes and, while access is possible at intervals on both sides, no road providing an opportunity for continuous views runs around the edge of the estuary. The mudflats, which cover many square kilometres, stretch right to the Shannon and birds interchange freely between this estuary, the Limerick shore of the Shannon, and the area around the Airport (see map on page 73).

Species

This is an exceptionally important wildfowl and wader wintering area, but a very frustrating place to watch birds because of the distances involved. Islandavanna on the west side often holds a small flock of Greenland White-fronted Geese and some Whooper Swans. The entire estuary holds several thousand wintering Wigeon and smaller numbers of Shelduck, Mallard, Teal, Shoveler and Scaup.

Wader numbers are also enormous, with similar species to Shannon Airport Lagoon. This area, however, is renowned as a spring staging point for Black-tailed Godwits returning to Iceland. Several thousand, sometimes over 6,000, have been seen here in March and April. They are a magnificent sight, as most are in full summer plumage. Islandavanna, Ing and Clenagh are the best places for them

This estuary also holds flocks of Grey Plover in spring.

Timing

The best time for the Fergus Estuary is between September and early April. It is essential to visit it on a rising tide if reasonable views of the birds are to be had.

Access

Ing on the eastern side has a small hillock from which good views can be had over the estuary with a telescope. Drive from Limerick on the Ennis road and pass through Newmarket-on-Fergus. About 1 km on the Ennis side of the village, take the next left turn and turn right at the junction reached after 2 km. Take the next left turn after 1.5 km and drive to the estuary at Ing.

Further south on the eastern side is Clenagh, which is approached from the same left turn just beyond Newmarket-on-Fergus. At the junction reached after 2 km turn left (instead of right for Ing) and follow the road to the estuary, by keeping to the right.

The western side is best watched from Islandmagrath and Islandavanna. To get to Islandmagrath, keep straight on after crossing the River Fergus at Clarecastle rather than going into the town proper. After less than 1 km take the left fork and drive on to Islandmagrath. The saltmarsh and estuary can be explored from here.

Islandavanna is reached by taking the Killadysert road out of Clarecastle and driving for 6 km. A narrow road on the left leads to Islanda-vanna.

Calendar

All year: Shelduck, Mallard, Black-tailed Godwit, Curlew, Reed Bunting.

Autumn: Wigeon, Teal, Shoveler, Pintail, Oystercatcher, Ringed Plover, Golden Plover, Turnstone, Lapwing, Knot, Dunlin, Bar-tailed Godwit, Redshank, Greenshank.

Winter: Whooper Swan, Greenland White-fronted Goose, Wigeon, Teal, Shoveler, Pintail, Scaup, Oystercatcher, Ringed Plover, Golden Plover, Grey Plover, Lapwing, Knot, Dunlin, Bar-tailed Godwit, Redshank, Greenshank, Turnstone.

Spring: Late ducks and waders. Large flocks of migrating Black-tailed Godwits.

37 BALLYALLIA LAKE

OSI ½" map: sheet 17
R38

Habitat

Ballyallia is a small lake on the River Fergus situated in a limestone depression in undulating countryside. It is surrounded by cattle pasture and there are woodlands around Ballyallia House to the north. Shooting is prohibited and there is a small public car park at the eastern side.

This is a particularly attractive place to see large numbers of wildfowl because they can be approached more readily than on the Shannon estuary or at the other nearby lakes.

Species

All three species of swans can be found on the lake, usually concentrating at its western arm. Whooper and Bewick's Swans are more numerous than Mute in most winters. Large flocks of Wigeon and Teal can be seen, often more than 1,500 of each species. Smaller numbers of Pintail, Tufted Duck and Pochard occur, but the lake is chiefly famous for its large numbers of Gadwall. Up to 200 or so have been recorded, making this one of the most important sites for the species in the country. There is also a large Coot population.

Waders occur on the pasture around the water's edge. Curlews, Lapwings, Black-tailed Godwits, Dunlin and occasional Ruffs are the principal species.

Rarities recorded here include American Wigeon, Blue-winged Teal, Little Gull and Black Tern.

Timing

Ballyallia is best between October and March.

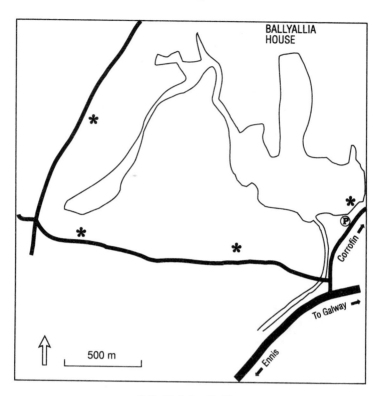

Ballyallia Lake, Co Clare

Access

The carpark is the first place from which to look at the lake. Driving north from Ennis on the Galway road, take the first left turn, about 1.5 km outside the town. Drive straight for a couple of hundred metres until the lake and car park appear. Gadwall are usually easily seen from here.

To see the rest of the lake, turn the car and take the narrow road to the right just before the main road. The road crosses a small stream and runs within sight of the lake for about 1 km. The lake is briefly lost to view and then reappears as a long, narrow channel. This part is usually good for swans.

Calendar

All year: Mute Swan, Coot, Mallard, Tufted Duck.

Autumn: Wigeon, Gadwall, Teal, Shoveler, Pintail, Pochard, Lapwing, Dunlin, Ruff, Black-tailed Godwit, Curlew.

Winter: Whooper Swan, Bewick's Swan, ducks and waders.

Spring: Late wildfowl and waders.

38 CLIFFS OF MOHER

Habitat
The Cliffs of Moher comprise 10 km of cliffs stretching from Fisherstreet to Cancregga Point. The cliffs rise sheer from the sea to just over 200 m and are one of the most popular tourist destinations in County Clare. The cliffs have several rock strata: beds of black shale at sea level alternate with layers of sandstone and flagstones. This layering of rock has led to the development of narrow horizontal ledges which provide excellent nest sites for seabirds.

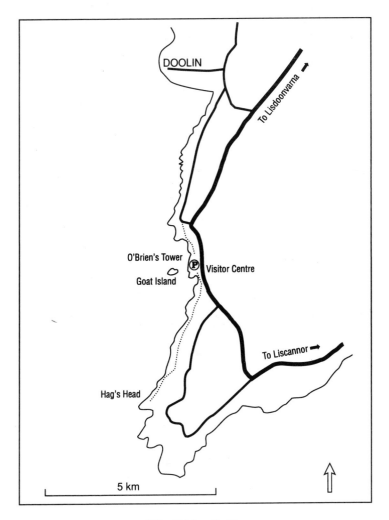

Cliffs of Moher, Co Clare

Species

The most numerous seabirds breeding on the cliffs are Fulmars, Kitti-wakes, Guillemots, Razorbills and Puffins. This is probably the most accessible breeding site of Puffins in the country and over 1,000 pairs nest here. They can be seen easily from the Visitor Centre at O'Brien's Tower as they wheel in to land on the grassy slopes of Goat Island. Over 2,000 pairs of Fulmars nest on the cliffs and they can be seen on ledges to the south of the Visitor Centre. Below them are scattered Razorbills, crouched in nooks and crannies in the rock; further down the cliff are rows of Guillemots and Kittiwakes on ledges. There are in the region of 3,000 sites where Razorbills nest, 5,000 Kittiwake nests and over 10,000 Guillemots occupying ledges.

Small numbers of Shags, Great Black-backed Gulls and Herring Gulls also breed here.

Ravens and Choughs usually attract attention with their characteristic calls, and Peregrines should be seen on a summer visit. Jackdaws and Rock Doves are also common on the cliffs. Above the cliffs Wheatears are easily seen, but the handful of pairs of breeding Twites are more difficult to find.

Timing

The best time to see seabirds at the Cliffs of Moher is at the height of the breeding season, from early May to the end of July. Some species are on the cliffs throughout much of the year, but they cannot be depended upon in autumn and winter.

Access

The Cliffs of Moher are well signposted from the surrounding villages of west Clare. From Lisdoonvarna or Ennistimon follow the signposts west and park in the public carpark. This is a very popular tourist centre so do not be surprised by large numbers of buses.

Puffins

There are walks along the clifftop north to Fisherstreet and south to Cancregga.

Calendar

Summer: Fulmar, Shag, Peregrine, Kestrel, Herring Gull, Great Black-backed Gull, Kittiwake, Razorbill, Guillemot, Puffin, Rock Dove, Wheatear, Jackdaw, Chough, Raven, Twite.

39 LOOP HEAD AND BRIDGES OF ROSS

OSI ½" map: sheet 17
Q64 Q74 Q75

Habitat

Loop Head is at the western extremity of Clare. To the north of the peninsula is a seawatching site, the Bridges of Ross, and to the south are some patches of cover on the road from Kilbaha village to the lighthouse. The clifftop around the lighthouse is very exposed. The cliffs on the northern side are quite steep and provide nesting sites for seabirds.

Species

The area has nesting Fulmars, Shags, Herring Gulls, Great Black-backed Gulls, Kittiwakes, Razorbills and Guillemots, breeding mainly on the northern side, but the Loop is chiefly known for the marvellous

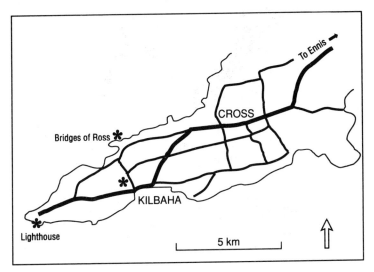

Loop Head, Co Clare

seawatching from the Bridges of Ross. In west and north-west gales in autumn, Sabine's Gulls, Leach's Petrels and Grey Phalaropes are regular. As many as 57 Sabine's Gulls have been seen in a season. Long-tailed Skuas are seen in most autumns. Wilson's Petrel has been recorded twice. Manx Shearwaters are numerous as one would expect and Sooty Shearwaters are common in some years, but Great and Cory's Shearwaters are not as frequent as on the south coast. The three regular skua species are common.

The variety of passerines recorded here in the past five years has been quite remarkable for a site so far west. They include Pied Wheatear, Rustic Bunting, Black-headed Bunting, Little Bunting, Red-rumped Swallow, Arctic Warbler, Serin and Yellow-rumped Warbler as well as regular Yellow-browed Warbler. Migrant numbers are generally low, but the unexpected frequently turns up. The road from Kilbaha to the north and the area around the lighthouse are the best places.

The area has been seriously watched only in autumn. Spring visits might be very worthwhile.

Winter seawatching, which has only been carried out on a handful of occasions, has shown that large numbers of Little Auks occur in west or north-westerly gales.

Timing

Breeding seabirds can be seen in summer, but this is a long way to travel to see species which are much more accessible on the Cliffs of Moher to the north-east. The autumn is the time to visit this site.

Good seawatching can be had from early August to the middle of October and sometimes later. Make sure, however, that the wind is from the north-west or west. Passerines are unlikely in these conditions, so look for them in south-easterlies or calm conditions. Early morning is much the best for passerines, as they move inland rapidly after dawn.

Access

To get to Loop Head from Limerick, drive north-west for Ennis, then south-west for Kilrush and then Kilkee. At Kilkee, follow the signposts for Loop Head. The Bridges of Ross are on the north side about 5 km before the lighthouse. There is a small carpark.

The lighthouse is at the end of the headland. Kilbaha village is on the southern side of the head, about 5 km back.

A rented house at Kilbaha has formed a base for an unofficial bird observatory since 1987. For details of access, contact Phil Brennan, The Crag, Stonehall, Newmarket-on-Fergus, Co Clare (telephone 061–472924).

Calendar

All year: Peregrine, Chough, Raven, Tree Sparrow.

Autumn: Seawatching, passerine migrants. Good chance of Sabine's Gull, Leach's Petrel, Grey Phalarope.

Winter: Little Auks on seawatches in suitable conditions.

Spring: Possibly good seawatching and passerine migration.

Summer: Breeding seabirds. Wheatears.

OTHER CLARE SITES

40 CLONDERALAW BAY

OSI ½" map: sheet 17
R05 R15

Habitat and Species

This deep inlet faces the south-west so is heavily exposed to the prevailing winds. It holds a winter duck population of 1,000–1,500 birds, of which about 200 Pintail are the most noteworthy. There are 2,000–3,000 waders as well. The area has been very little watched.

Access

Roads lead down to several points on each side of the estuary. On the south-east side, the road south-west of Labasheeda which runs to Kilkerin Point, has two right turns off it, both of which lead down to the estuary. The road from Labasheeda to Kilrush runs around the northern side of the bay. To see the north-west side, take the road for Killimer and follow either of the two left turns down to the estuary (1 km apart), about 3 km after you cross the bridge over the Clon river at the head of the bay.

41 POULNASHERRY BAY

OSI ½" map: sheet 17
Q95

Habitat and Species

This is a relatively isolated bay on the north-west side of the Shannon estuary and it has been very little watched. It is much more sheltered than Clonderalaw and holds a flock of 200 or so Brent Geese, about 1,000 Wigeon and smaller numbers of Shelduck, Mallard, Teal and Scaup. There are 2,000–3,500 waders in winter.

Access

Several roads run to the shore of this estuary. Driving from Kilrush for Moyasta, take the second left turn (about 3 km from Kilrush). Beyond Moyasta, several left turns lead to different sections of the estuary.

42 MUTTON ISLAND AND LURGA POINT

OSI ½" map: sheet 17
Q97

Habitat and Species

Mutton Island is a 75-hectare island lying off the west coast. The island is windswept and rocky with a cover of maritime grass. It has one of the largest wintering flocks of Barnacle Geese in the country, the total sometimes reaching over 400, though more usually being about 200–250.

Opposite the island on the mainland, at Seafields, Lurga Point, large counts of Purple Sandpipers have been recorded, some of the largest ever in Ireland. Up to 230 have been counted in March. Turnstones and Sanderlings also winter in the area.

Access

Lurga Point is reached from Quilty, which is south of Spanish Point. Take the road along the coast south-west from Quilty. Mutton Island can be viewed from the mainland by telescope.

43 BALLYVAGHAN

Habitat and Species

Ballyvaghan Bay is on the southern side of Galway Bay. Its shoreline is stony as befits the northern rim of the Burren. Off the beaches there are concentrations of divers in winter. Great Northern Divers are particularly numerous but Red-throated also occur. More importantly, this is the best place in Ireland for seeing Black-throated Divers. There are usually a few throughout the winter and up to 38 have been seen. Up to 150 Brent Geese are sometimes found on the shore. Snow Buntings have been seen in winter at Rue Point.

Access

Ballyvaghan is well signposted from Kinvarra to the east or Lisdoonvarna to the south-west. If travelling in the area in spring or summer, extend your trip to see Black Head to the west and do some 'botanising'.

44 LOUGH ATEDAUN

Habitat and Species

Lough Atedaun is a small, shallow lake east of Corrofin which holds large numbers of wildfowl when it is not being shot over. It is a good site for both Whooper and Bewick's Swans. Up to 200 Whooper and smaller numbers of Bewick's can be found here in winter. Large numbers of Wigeon and Teal also winter here and smaller numbers of Tufted Ducks. Pintail, Shoveler and Pochard can also be seen. Significant numbers of Dunlins and Black-tailed Godwits have also been recorded.

Access

From Corrofin the lake can be viewed at several points. Drive on the Gort road and turn right at the fork after 1.5 km. This road gives views of the northern side. The western side can be easily viewed by taking the first right turn off the Gort road for Corrofin, following the signpost for Lough Atedaun. The road leads to a slipway at the edge of the lake. The south-western side can be seen from the road south for Ennis. Take the first left turn (after about 1.5 km) to get access to the southern side.

TIPPERARY

Introduction

Tipperary is a large county bordered on the north-west side by Lough Derg and the River Shannon, on the north by the Little Brosna and on the south by the Galtee Mountains. To the east stretch fertile agricultural lands.

Because the county has no large centres of population and no coastline it was underwatched until the mid-1980s. Since about 1983 a Tipperary Ringing Group has been very active; this formed the nucleus of a branch of the IWC which has discovered a number of useful bird sites in the county, two of which are described below.

Sites

Minor sites:

45	Gortdrum Mines	*Gulls, migrant waders.*
46	Lough Avan	*Wild swans and Greenland White-fronted Geese.*

One of the best sites in the county is the Little Brosna, but this site is more easily approached from the Offaly side so it is dealt with under that county.

References

Tipperary Birds 1986–1987.
Tipperary Birds 1988–1990.
Both are reports published by the Tipperary branch of the IWC.

MINOR SITES

45 GORTDRUM MINE

OSI ½″ map: sheet 18
R84

Habitat and Species

Gortdrum is the site of a large and heavily worked but now abandoned mine in the valley between the Galtee Mountains to the south and the Slievefelim Mountains to the north. It has an 8-hectare lake and a 30-hectare mud plain to the south of it. Slag heaps surround the entire area.

The mine has one of the largest Irish roosts of Lesser Black-backed Gulls. Up to 2,000 occur in autumn and smaller numbers in winter. This is a site where unexpected birds can occur. In recent years Dotterel, American Golden Plover, Avocet and Wood Warbler have been recorded.

Access

Gortdrum Mine is difficult to find as it is not shown on the half inch map. Drive north from Tipperary on the road for Nenagh. After 1 km turn left and, after another 1.5 km bear right at a fork. Drive straight through the Boheratreene Crossroads (after about 3 km), cross over the railway line (after another 1 km) and you will see the spoil heaps which surround the mine on your left just after the left turning immediately beyond the railway. The mine is privately owned and permission to enter should be sought at the house at the main gate.

46 LOUGH AVAN

Habitat and Species

Lough Avan is a small lake close to Lough Derg and is a feeding site for wild swans and geese. Up to 40 Whooper Swans and 50 Greenland White-fronted Geese use it in winter.

Access

The lake is west of Borrisokane. Take the road for Ballinderry from Borrisokane and turn left after 6 km. The road goes over the river immediately after the turn. Drive straight along this road for 3 km until you see Lough Avan to your left.

CONNACHT

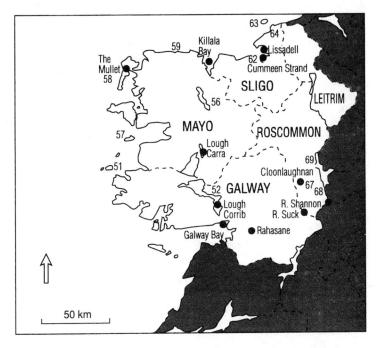

Connacht: counties, major sites (named) and other sites (numbered)

Galway
47. GALWAY BAY
48. LOUGH CORRIB
49. RAHASANE TURLOUGH
50. RIVER SUCK
51. Inishbofin and Inishshark
52. Rostaff Lake

Mayo
53. THE MULLET
54. LOUGH CARRA
55. KILLALA BAY
56. Lough Cullin
57. Clare Island
58. Inishkea Islands
59. Illanmastir

Sligo
60. CUMMEEM STRAND
61. LISSADELL
62. Ballysadare
63. Inishmurray
64. Bunduff Lake

Leitrim

Roscommon
65. RIVER SHANNON, ATHLONE
   TO SHANNONBRIDGE
66. CLOONLAUGHNAN
67. Lough Croan
68. Lough Funshinagh
69. Lough Ree

GALWAY

Introduction

Galway is a large county with an extremely indented coastline to the west and south-west, the rolling Slieve Aughty mountains to the south, the Rivers Shannon and Suck to the east and a mixture of lowland and hilly blanket bog to the north. Lough Corrib separates the western mountains and blanket bogs from the eastern lowlands.

Apart from Galway Bay itself, which is an important site, there is relatively little mudflat or saltmarsh to provide wildfowl or wader feeding on the coast, and there are few mainland cliffs to provide breeding sites for seabirds. Some of the offshore islands have breeding seabird colonies but they have been little studied.

The western blanket bog is difficult to traverse, as there are few roads crossing it, but it holds small populations of Merlins, Golden Plovers and Red Grouse in summer, scattered flocks of Greenland White-fronted Geese in winter and a large population of Grey Herons which nest on lake islands and feed on the coast. The mountains are little known and would repay visiting at any time of year.

Inland the most obvious physical features of the county are Ireland's second largest lake, Lough Corrib, and to the west the peaks of the Twelve Bens.

The most significant wetlands for birds are Lough Corrib, Rahasane turlough and the Shannon and Suck system which border the eastern side of the county.

Sites

47 GALWAY BAY   *Brent Geese, scarce gulls.*
48 LOUGH CORRIB   *Large lake, diving ducks, Coots.*
49 RAHASANE TURLOUGH
                      Whooper and Bewick's Swans, Greenland White-fronted Geese, ducks.
50 RIVER SUCK   *Callows, Whooper and Bewick's Swans, Greenland White-fronted Geese, ducks.*

Other sites:
51 Inishbofin and Inishshark
                      Corncrakes, Corn Buntings.
52 Rostaff Lake   *Whooper Swans, Greenland White-fronted Geese, ducks.*

References

Fitzpatrick, Trish and Whilde,Tony. *Insider's Guide to Connemara, Galway and the Burren* (Gill and Macmillan, Dublin, 1992).
Ruttledge, R.F. *Birds in Counties Galway and Mayo* (IWC, Dublin, 1989).
Whilde, Tony. *Birds of Galway and Mayo* (IWC, Galway, 1977).
Whilde, Tony. *Birds of Galway, a Review of Recent Records and Field Studies* (IWC, Galway, 1990).

47 GALWAY BAY

Habitat

Galway Bay is a broad bay, about 10 km wide, bordered on the southern side by the limestone hills of the Burren in Clare, on the northern side by the west Galway hills and at its eastern end by lowlying agricultural land.

There is a boulder shore on the southern side from Black Head (in Clare) to Kinvarra and on the northern side from Barna westwards, neither of which is particularly productive for birds. The best bird sites are all in the inner bay, which is divided into two sections by Tawin Island. The south-eastern part from Kinvarra to Clarinbridge has rather little inter-tidal sand or mud, but the section from Clarinbridge to Oranmore, and including Tawin Island, has a number of areas of mud and sand, several areas of saltmarsh and some shallow inlets and lagoons.

From Oranmore to Barna are stretches of mud at Oranmore Bay, stretches of sand and mud close to Galway city, a brackish inlet at Lough Atalia and a sandy bay at Loc Ruisin near Barna.

Galway refuse dump, to the north of the city, provides a source of food for several species of gull.

The birds of the inner bay have been counted regularly by the local IWC branch since 1976 so they are well known.

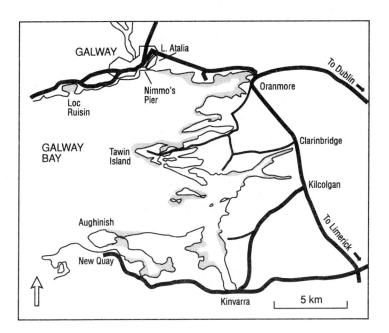

Galway Bay, Cos Galway and Clare

91

Species

The outer reaches of the bay hold wintering populations of divers. Great Northern are the most frequent, with many counts of over 20 in the bay, but Red-throated and Black-throated also occur, mainly south and west of Tawin. Great Crested Grebes in contrast tend to winter to the north of Tawin, though numbers are variable with up to 70 having been counted in the bay in the recent past. These are probably birds which breed on the nearby Lough Corrib. At the Claddagh, right in Galway city, over 300 Mute Swans assemble in spring and early summer and up to 600 moult on Lough Corrib in August.

Brent Geese arrive in the bay in late October and build up to reach a peak in the period from January to March. As elsewhere in the country, numbers have been increasing and now reach almost 600 in the bay. The bays on the south side of Tawin hold the largest numbers but, as the population has increased, so they have spread around the northern side of Galway Bay as well. Up to 1,500 Wigeon have been counted in the bay in winter, widely dispersed around the shoreline, but numbers of Shelduck, Mallard, Teal and Shoveler are much lower.

Some diving duck winter. A small flock of Scaup usually spends the early winter on Lough Atalia and some also occur on the south side of Tawin. Very small parties of Long-tailed Duck (up to 14) occur in late winter or early spring in the southern part of the bay. Common Scoter sometimes occur on open water in the bay but do not winter regularly. Red-breasted Mergansers are widely distributed, with large numbers on Lough Atalia at times.

Galway Bay has the typical wintering waders of much of the Irish coastline. Oystercatchers winter in numbers up to 600; Ringed Plovers are numerous, probably reflecting the extent of sand in the bay, and have exceeded 900. Golden Plovers and Lapwings can be found in winter on many parts of the bay. Grey Plover are most easily met with near Tawin. Dunlins, Bar-tailed Godwits, Curlews, Redshanks and Turnstones are all quite numerous. Small numbers of Greenshanks winter, and slightly more occur in autumn and spring; Loc Ruisin is usually the best place for them. Knots are scarce and Black-tailed Godwits curiously rare.

The bay is an excellent place for gull watching. Nimmo's Pier provides a vantage point for seeing large gulls which feed on the shore and smaller gulls which may be farther out in the bay. Great Black-backed, Herring and Common Gulls are common; Black-headed Gulls are numerous. Glaucous and Iceland Gulls should be sought for at Nimmo's Pier, although you should not expect a repeat sight of the 80 Glaucous Gulls seen here in February 1981 at the time of an exceptional sprat fishery. Galway dump is an alternative place to seek out gulls. The dump has produced several records of Kumlien's Gull and one of a bird believed to be the first European record of Thayer's Gull. Little Gulls should be looked for at Nimmo's Pier, especially between January and March, when quite large influxes can occur (once over 150 birds). Ring-billed and Mediterranean Gulls are both near annual and Ross's Gull has been seen here twice.

Timing

The Bay is at its best from October to the end of March. Goose and most duck numbers are highest after December. Scarcer gulls are most frequently recorded from January to March, though Glaucous and Iceland can be found in early winter as well.

Birdwatching is much easier at low tide at all locations mentioned above.

Access

All the sites referred to are easily accessible by road. On the southern side there are a number of turns to the left off the main road from Kinvarra to Clarinbridge which lead down to the edge of the bay. To the west of Kinvarra, driving west towards Black Head, there is a right turn, about 2 km from Kinvarra, which leads to Aughinish causeway and provides a number of viewing points for the outer reaches of the bay.

Tawin Island, in reality a peninsula, is an essential area to visit. Turn left at Clarinbridge off the main Limerick–Galway road. After 4 km take the right hand turn at a T-junction and turn left after a further 1.5 km. Follow the road out to Tawin and stop wherever birds are seen. Excellent views can be had of geese here.

Drive back to the main Limerick–Galway road and follow the signposts for Galway. Lough Atalia comes into view on the left hand side of the main road.

In Galway City follow the coast road beside Lough Atalia and around the docks to the Claddagh. The River Corrib flows south into Galway Bay at this point and Nimmo's Pier is on the western side of the little harbour. Cars can be parked and the area explored on foot. The entire Galway docks area should be checked for gulls.

Drive west through Galway, pass Salthill and 5 km later Loc Ruisin can be seen on your left. Take the left turn just after the bay, follow the signposts for Silver Strand and park your car at the beach.

Calendar

All year: Cormorant, Shag, Mallard, Great Black-backed Gull, Herring Gull.

Autumn: Early wildfowl and waders. Black-headed and Common Gull.

Black-throated Diver

Winter: Divers, Great Crested Grebe, Brent Goose, Shelduck, Wigeon, Teal, Mallard, Shoveler, Scaup, Long-tailed Duck, Red-breasted Merganser, Oystercatcher, Ringed Plover, Golden Plover, Grey Plover, Lapwing, Dunlin, Snipe, Bar-tailed Godwit, Curlew, Redshank, Greenshank, Turnstone, Black-headed Gull, Common Gull, Glaucous Gull, Iceland Gull, possible Little Gull and Ring-billed Gull.

Spring: Late wildfowl and waders. Possible influxes of Little Gulls. Glaucous and Iceland Gull, probable Ring-billed Gull.

48 LOUGH CORRIB

**OSI ½″ map: sheets 11, 14/
1:50,000 map: sheet 38
M22 M23 M33 M24 M34**

Habitat

Lough Corrib, with an area of 17,000 hectares, is the second largest lake in Ireland. It can be divided conveniently into two sections. The narrow, south-eastern arm is very shallow, with a maximum depth of about 6 m, and lies on limestone. The much larger and broader northern part is considerably deeper and lies mainly on granite, schist, shales and sandstones. A depth of up to 45 m has been recorded in this part.

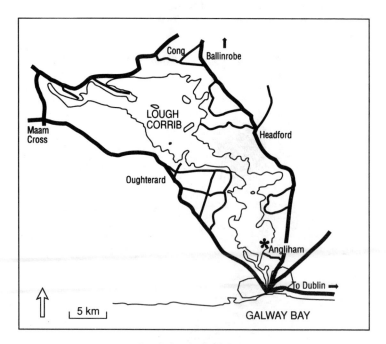

Lough Corrib, Co Galway

Much of the lake is surrounded by bare limestone or a thin covering of bog over the limestone. At the southern end is an extensive area of fen. The lake is one of Ireland's finest brown trout fisheries.

The shallower southern end, Lower Lough Corrib, is far and away the best for winter wildfowl.

Species

This is an excellent wildfowl lake in winter with large flocks of Pochard and Coots the highlight, although numbers have declined since the mid-1970s when over 20,000 Pochard and 16,000 Coots were counted. Nowadays, the peak counts are in the region of 4,000 Pochard and 6,000 Coots. Smaller numbers of Tufted Duck occur among the Pochard, together with some Goldeneyes, and, on the shoreline, there are small parties of Wigeon, Teal, Mallard and Shoveler.

Pochard probably breed in small numbers, but the large numbers result from immigration commencing in late July and building to a peak in October or November, before declining again. Presumably these are birds moulting on Lough Corrib.

Coot numbers appear to be very volatile. Large numbers have been seen in September, October and December, but in some years there are very few in mid-winter. There is a substantial breeding population.

In summer Great Crested and Little Grebes nest and as one would expect there is a good scattering of breeding Mute Swans and Mallard. Gadwall and Shoveler probably nest at the Mount Ross inlet and Tufted Ducks and Red-breasted Mergansers breed on many of the islands. In recent years a small breeding population of Common Scoters has become established as well.

The islands on the lake hold sizeable colonies of breeding Black-headed and Common Gulls. There are about 2,600 pairs of Black-headed and nearly 350 pairs of Common. A few pairs of Lesser Black-backed Gulls also nest, but Herring Gulls, which once bred in numbers up to 300 pairs, are reduced to a handful of pairs (three in 1992). The decrease, which mirrors similar declines all over Ireland, has been attributed to death of adult birds from botulism. A few Great Black-backed Gulls also nest. Terns can be found on the small islands as well: Common and Arctic Terns both breed in small numbers. The colonies are scattered on islands around the lake.

There were records in February and March 1990 of several thousand Common and Black-headed Gulls in the upper lough, presumably on passage to breeding grounds in Scotland. This was not repeated in 1991, 1992 or 1993 so appears not be a regular phenomenon.

Timing

Winter wildfowl are best seen from August to February. As the lake is large, and flocks of diving ducks can be well offshore, a calm and bright day is recommended. Gulls and terns, as well as nesting ducks, should be watched for from April to July.

Access

This is an enormous lake and, unfortunately, the road does not always run around the water's edge providing vantage points for viewing. At the southern end, the best place for getting good views is Angliham Marble Quarries where diving duck, often including Goldeneye, can be seen and, in the narrows, the Mount Ross inlet holds wintering Gadwall and breeding Shoveler and Gadwall.

Angliham is reached by taking the road for Headford out of Galway. After about 5 km, at the village of Ballindooly, take the left turn and follow it down to the lake shore.

Mount Ross is reached by taking the same road from Galway, but driving almost as far as Headford. Turn left at Clooneen about 3 km before Headford and follow the road to the lake shore.

Pochard

Calendar

All year: Cormorant, Little Grebe, Mallard, Tufted Duck, occasional Red-breasted Merganser, Coot, Black-headed Gull, Herring Gull, Great Black-backed Gull.

Autumn: Great Crested Grebe, Gadwall, a few Shoveler at the southern margin, Pochard, large numbers of Coots, other wildfowl.

Winter: Great Crested Grebe, Wigeon, Teal, Shoveler, Pochard, Lapwing, Snipe, Curlew.

Spring: Whimbrel, early terns, return of breeding gulls, passage of migrant gulls.

Summer: Breeding wildfowl, gulls and terns. Breeding Common Scoter, Ringed Plover, Redshank and Curlew, migrant Whimbrel.

49 RAHASANE TURLOUGH

Habitat

Rahasane is one of the few remaining turloughs in Ireland and is certainly the best for wildfowl of those which survive. There are a number of different kinds of turlough, and some have argued that Rahasane is not really one (turloughs are lakes which fill with water at times and then drain off through underground channels). Two aquatic mosses are found at most turloughs: *Cinclidotus fontinaloides*, a blackish moss, and *Fontinalis antipyretica*, a dark green one. Both can be seen at Rahasane.

The doubt about Rahasane's authenticity as a turlough arises because of arguments whether the water fills the lake through swallow-holes or rises purely due to the flooding of the Dunkellin river.

Whatever the case, this is an area of rich, green, alluvial pasture in summer with a narrow river running through it. When the winter rain comes, the water level rises and a shallow lake about 3 km long and 1 km wide appears within hours. The blackthorn around the lake is the habitat of one of Ireland's scarcest butterflies, the brown hairstreak.

In late autumn 1992, drainage works lowered the water level significantly. The long term effect of this change remains to be seen.

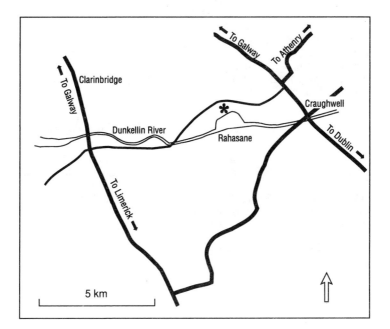

Rahasane, Co Galway

Species

This is a wonderful wildfowl haunt in winter and, at times, a good place for wader watching.

Up to 5,000 Wigeon occur in winter, together with smaller numbers of Mallard, Teal, Pintail, Shoveler, Tufted Duck and Pochard. Both Whooper and Bewick's Swan can be seen throughout the winter and a flock of about 100 Greenland White-fronted Geese is frequently present. Pintail are now a scarce duck in Galway and numbers at Rahasane are generally low.

Flocks of up to several thousand Lapwing and Golden Plover, and small numbers of Curlews, Black-tailed Godwits, Redshanks and Dunlins are regular. Larger flocks of godwits occur in spring on passage north to Iceland.

In winter the fields and hedgerows hold large numbers of Redwings and Fieldfares.

Water levels fluctuate and there can be a lot of disturbance at times, so bird numbers are unpredictable. Galway Bay is not far and birds move in and out of Rahasane frequently.

Timing

The best time to visit Rahasane is when the turlough is flooded to a level where there are grassy islets still visible. When the water level is very high some ducks find difficulty in grazing and leave the area.

It could repay autumn visits as the habitat looks ideal for migrant waders and Ruffs have been recorded, perhaps an indicator that more intensive watching could produce American vagrants.

Access

Rahasane is approached by turning right off the main Limerick-Galway road at Kilcolgan, where the signpost indicates Craughwell. Follow the narrow road for about 5 km until you see the turlough to the south on your right hand side. Park the car and scan the water from the roadside or, if the water level permits, walk across the pasture to the edge of the water and watch from there.

Calendar

All year: Grey Heron, Mallard, Meadow Pipit, Skylark, Reed Bunting.

Autumn: Teal, Shoveler, Wigeon, Pintail, Pochard, Tufted Duck, Golden Plover, Lapwing, Dunlin, Ruff, Curlew, Black-tailed Godwit, Redshank.

Winter: Whooper Swan, Bewick's Swan, Greenland White-fronted Goose, Teal, Shoveler, Wigeon, Pintail, Pochard, Tufted Duck, Golden Plover, Lapwing, Dunlin, Black-tailed Godwit, Curlew, Redshank.

Spring: Late wildfowl and waders.

50 RIVER SUCK

Habitat

The River Suck rises north of Lough O'Flyn in Roscommon and meanders in a generally south-south-east direction to join the Shannon at Shannonbridge. From close to Athleague it forms the border between the counties of Galway and Roscommon until it reaches the Shannon.

It is a narrow, slow-flowing river surrounded by extensive bogs and poorly drained agricultural land. The flood plain is lowlying and floods frequently in late autumn and winter. The flooded callows, or water meadows, which occur at Muckanagh to the south of Ballygar, between Ballyforan and Ballinasloe, and between Ballinasloe and the Shannon, provide feeding for large numbers of wildfowl.

In patches there are areas fringed with reeds and behind them rushy pastures where Lapwings and Golden Plovers feed.

Species

The species found are those typical of the Shannon system. Whooper and Bewick's Swans are widespread; there is a flock of several hundred White-fronted Geese at Muckanagh; thousands of Wigeon and Teal can be seen and smaller numbers of Mallard and Shoveler. Some Tufted Ducks and Pochard and good numbers of Coots occur.

The callows and the rough pasture are frequented by thousands of Lapwings and Golden Plovers and smaller numbers of Curlews and

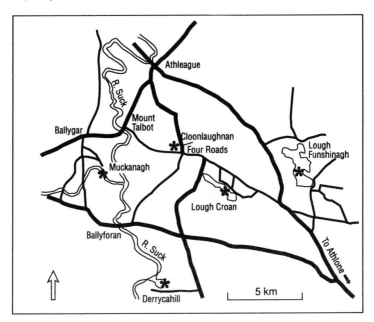

*River Suck, Cloonlaughnan, Lough Croan and Lough Funshinagh,
Co Roscommon*

Snipe. Some Redshanks occur and Black-tailed Godwits can sometimes be found.

Timing
This is very much a winter wetland. Visits are best when the river has flooded.

Access
Because this is a meandering river with no road running along its bank, access is often difficult. However, there are two particularly good spots.

Muckanagh, to the south of Ballygar, is a marvellously wild place for watching geese and swans in winter. Drive from Mount Talbot to Ballygar and turn left in the village on the Ballyforan road. After just over a kilometre turn left down a narrow road and follow the lane for 2 km to a fork; take the right turn and follow the road to the callows where you should have excellent views of wildfowl.

Derrycahill, to the south of Ballyforan, gives access to the next stretch of the river to the south. Take the road from Ballyforan for Athlone and, after about 1 km turn right and follow the road for about 5 km to a right turning. Take this turn to Derrycahill and access to the river.

Access to the stretch between Ballinasloe and Shannonbridge is difficult but several narrow roads lead close to the river and may produce views of wildfowl.

Calendar
All year: Grey Heron, Mallard, Meadow Pipit, Skylark, Reed Bunting.

Autumn: Wigeon, Teal, Pintail, Pochard, Tufted Duck, Golden Plover, Lapwing, Curlew, Redshank.

Winter: Whooper Swan, Bewick's Swan, Greenland White-fronted Goose, Teal, Shoveler, Wigeon, Pintail, Pochard, Tufted Duck, Golden Plover, Lapwing, Dunlin, Black-tailed Godwit, Curlew, Redshank.

Spring: Late wildfowl and waders.

OTHER GALWAY SITES

51 INISHBOFIN AND INISHSHARK

OSI ½" map: sheet 10/
1:50,000 map: sheet 37
L46 L56

Habitat and Species
These two islands lie off the Connemara coast. Inishbofin, much the larger at 936 hectares, is inhabited by about 250 people but Inishshark which comprises only 235 hectares is long deserted. The southern part of Inishbofin is cultivated and the remainder is rough moorland and bog. There are some hedges and shrubs, and a garden near the harbour,

which provide cover for passerines. Inishshark is much bleaker and has no cover at all.

Inishbofin is notable for its surviving populations of Corncrakes and Corn Buntings. Both are now very scarce in Ireland and, while they have declined on Inishbofin, they can be easily found in the cultivated quarter. Corncrakes were once so numerous that they were quite impossible to count at night. Nowadays there are a few pairs left, mostly at the east end of the island.

Inishshark has good numbers of nesting Fulmars and small numbers of other breeding seabirds. Peregrines nest on the island.

Access
The ferry for Inishbofin leaves from Cleggan near Clifden. There are two small hotels on the island and some self-catering accommodation. Inishshark can only be reached by making special arrangements with local boatmen.

52 ROSTAFF LAKE

Habitat and Species
Rostaff is a shallow lake close to Lough Corrib overlooked by a hide built by the local branch of the Irish Wildbird Conservancy in conjunction with the Black River Gun Club and the National Parks and Wildlife Service.

A flock of between 100 and 200 Greenland White-fronted Geese, small parties of Whooper Swans, occasional Bewick's Swans, several hundred Wigeon, up to 150 Teal and up to 70 Shoveler are regularly present in winter. Peregrines are frequent visitors.

Access
The lake is close to the road from Headford to Ballinrobe. It is on the left hand side of the road, about 3 km from Headford. The hide is reached about 4.5 km from Headford. This area holds most birds in autumn and winter when the lake floods.

MAYO

Introduction
Mayo is another large county, but the landscape is very different from that of Galway, with much more extensive areas of blanket bog and, particularly in the north-east, large tracts where there are no roads. The human population density is low, and birdwatchers are very few. The visitor, therefore, has a good chance of finding something new, especially on the coast or one of the lakes.

The western coastline has a variety of habitats. From Killary Harbour north to Roonah Quay the shoreline is lowlying, despite Mweelrea Mountain dominating the skyline. The shore is sandy, with Sanderling and Ringed Plover the principal wader species, but there are a number of small lakes behind the sand dunes which attract a number of other species and look as though they should attract migrant waders. Clew Bay has numerous islands and is difficult to watch because of the relative inaccessibility of so much of the habitat.

The Mullet peninsula forms the north-western corner of the county and has a number of good bird sites. Off the Mullet are the Inishkea Islands, long deserted by humans, but now providing a refuge for wintering Barnacle Geese and breeding terns and waders. Several smaller islands have large seabird colonies: Inishglora, in particular, has a large Storm Petrel colony and Illaunmaistir off the north Mayo coast has substantial numbers of Puffins.

The north coast has steep cliffs with breeding Fulmars, Kittiwakes and auks as well as good numbers of Choughs and Peregrines. However, access is chiefly on foot as there are few roads.

Killala Bay, the estuary of the river Moy, forms the eastern boundary of the county on the northern coast and has a history as a good bird site. Richard Warren, one of the authors of *Birds of Ireland*, published in 1900, spent much of his life here and made many interesting observations of seabirds, wildfowl and waders.

There are several large lakes in the centre of the county. Lough Mask is famous for fishing but is generally too deep for birds. Lough Carra, to its north, is shallower and well worth a visit. Farther north, Loughs Conn and Cullin have not been very well watched, but appear to have potential, especially Lough Cullin.

Sites

53	THE MULLET	*Breeding waders, Corncrakes, Corn Buntings, seawatching, winter wildfowl, possible American vagrants.*
54	LOUGH CARRA	*Breeding and winter wildfowl, breeding gulls and terns.*
55	KILLALA BAY	*Estuary and open bay, skuas.*

Other sites:

56	Lough Cullin	*Moulting and wintering wildfowl.*
57	Clare Island	*Breeding seabirds.*
58	Inishkea Islands	*Breeding seabirds, wintering Barnacle Geese.*
59	Illanmastir	*Breeding Puffins and other seabirds.*

References

Chapman, Bob. Site guide: Moy valley, Co. Mayo (*Irish Birding News* 1: 47–53, 1990).

Lloyd, C.S. The Birds of Clare Island, Co. Mayo in June 1982 (*Irish Naturalists' Journal* 21: 212–216, 1984).

Ruttledge, R.F. *Birds in Counties Galway and Mayo* (IWC, Dublin, 1989).

Whilde, Tony. *Birds of Galway and Mayo* (IWC, Galway, 1977).

53 THE MULLET

Habitat

The Mullet is a long peninsula, really almost an island as the inlets of Broadhaven to the north and Blacksod Bay to the south virtually meet at the town of Belmullet. The western side of the peninsula mainly comprises sandy beaches with dune systems behind them and areas of wet machair. To the west are the long and low Inishkea Islands and several smaller islands including Inishglora, famous for the Storm Petrels which nest in its boulder beach. The entire area is wild and windswept.

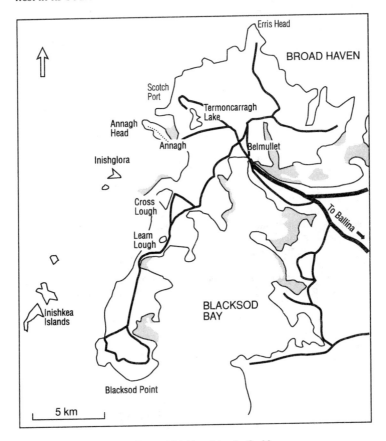

The Mullet and Inishkea Islands, Co Mayo

There are several headlands on The Mullet and both Erris Head to the north, and Annagh Head to the west, are good seawatching promontories. These promontories have very little cover but look attractive for buntings and pipits. Along the main road, which runs along the Mullet, are some small gardens which should hold migrant passerines.

Three lakes on The Mullet are well worth visiting: Termoncarragh Lake to the north, Cross Lough in the centre and Leam Lough towards the south all have the potential to attract interesting wildfowl and waders. The eastern end of Termoncarragh Lake is owned by the Irish Wildbird Conservancy.

Termoncarragh is a relatively shallow lake surrounded by stands of clubrush. A number of streams flow into the lake and, where they enter the lake, there are marshy areas. There is damp grassland surrounding the lake, classic damp machair, providing habitat for nesting waders.

Annagh Marsh, to the west of Termoncarragh Lake, is a marshy area which provides excellent breeding wader habitat. This marsh was purchased in the 1950s by the Irish Society for the Protection of Birds as a sanctuary for the long established colony of Red-necked Phalaropes there. When the ISPB merged with other organisations in 1968 to form the Irish Wildbird Conservancy, ownership passed into the hands of the new body.

The town of Belmullet has a small winter flock of gulls, which is principally famous because it was here that Ireland's first Ring-billed Gulls were seen. Glaucous and Iceland Gulls are regular.

Species

Termoncarragh has a flock of up to 40 White-fronted Geese in October and wintering Whooper Swans and duck. Barnacle Geese formerly visited the lake but fencing has apparently made the area less attractive for them. The principal duck species are Mallard, Teal, Wigeon and Tufted Duck. Large numbers of Lapwing, Golden Plover and Curlew pass through in autumn and many also winter. Ruffs occur on passage and rarities such as Green-winged Teal and American Golden Plover have been seen.

This is one of the few remaining places where Corncrakes and Corn Buntings can be found, though there may be as few as ten pairs of the latter remaining. The margins of Termoncarragh are a good place to search for them. Water Rails also nest here as well as Lapwing, Snipe and Dunlin.

Annagh is famous for its breeding Red-necked Phalaropes, but it also has nesting Lapwing, Snipe and Dunlin. Scarcer waders can also occur, and Wilson's Phalarope and Buff-breasted Sandpiper have both been seen in the area. One or two pairs of phalaropes arrive in most years and usually a pair breeds, but the birds should not be disturbed under any circumstances.

Seabird passage has been shown to be excellent at times. Great and Sooty Shearwaters and Great, Pomarine and Arctic Skuas are all regular and the site is so far west that Long-tailed Skuas, which are known to migrate well off the west coast of Ireland, could be expected in strong westerlies. They have been seen in spring in the past from the Inishkeas so some should be seen from Annagh or Erris Head in May or in autumn. Erris Head is probably the best site in autumn when birds moving south across Donegal Bay pass very close, while Annagh Head is better in spring.

Timing

The Mullet is a place which can be visited at almost any time. In summer the nesting waders, Corncrakes and Corn Buntings are an attraction. In spring and autumn, there is the possibility of good seawatching.

The area is so far west that it must get American waders and passerines most years. Red-eyed Vireo has been seen and some waders but the Mullet has been seriously underwatched in autumn. When a Bird Observatory functioned here for a couple of seasons Lapland Buntings and Snow Buntings were seen frequently.

In winter there can be a good variety of wildfowl and again the chance of some exotic vagrant. In the nineteenth century, this was the best place in Ireland for seeing Snowy Owls. So who knows what might be found here?

Access

The Mullet is a long drive from Dublin, Belfast or Cork. It is hardly a place for a day trip, but an excellent place for a full weekend or a few days.

Termoncarragh Lake can be viewed from the public road which runs north-west from Belmullet to Scotch Port.

Cross Lough and Leam Lough are both accessible from the road south along the peninsula.

Annagh marsh is at the southern end of Termoncarragh and can be visited by turning left off the road for Scotch Port, about 3 km beyond Belmullet and following the narrow road down to the inlet. The marsh is a bird reserve, with a local warden, and visitors should not walk in places where waders may be breeding.

Lapwing chick

Calendar

Autumn: Divers, Fulmar, Manx Shearwater, Sooty Shearwater, Gannet, Oystercatcher, Ringed Plover, Golden Plover, Lapwing, Dunlin, Sanderling, Ruff, Curlew, Redshank, Greenshank, skuas. Migrant passerines, particularly Snow and Lapland Buntings. Possibility of American waders and passerines.

Winter: Divers, White-fronted Goose, Wigeon, Teal, Mallard, Tufted Duck, Long-tailed Duck, Red-breasted Merganser, Oystercatcher, Ringed Plover, Golden Plover, Lapwing, Dunlin, Bar-tailed Godwit, Curlew, Redshank, Greenshank, Turnstone, Glaucous Gull, Iceland Gull, possible Ring-billed Gull.

Spring: Late wildfowl and waders. Sea passage, including Pomarine Skua and possibility of Long-tailed Skua.

Summer: Breeding seabirds, Lapwing, Snipe, Dunlin, Red-necked Phalarope, Corncrake, Water Rail, Corn Bunting.

54 LOUGH CARRA

OSI ½" map: sheet 11/
1:50,000 map: sheet 38
M16 M17

Habitat

Carra is a 1,500-hectare very shallow lake lying to the north-east of Lough Mask. It is situated on limestone at the western edge of what geologists term the central lowlands. The lake is narrow in the middle and has a number of small wooded islands. The maximum depth is about nine metres.

The shoreline is a mixture of woodland, grassland, limestone pavement and fen. The limestone pavement, which is very important botanically, is located at the southern tip where Lough Carra drains into Lough Mask.

Species

The lake is a very important breeding area for Mallard and Tufted Duck and a wintering area for a number of species of duck. In autumn, when numbers are at their highest, Mallard peak at up to 1,500 birds. Winter numbers are usually lower. A long-term ringing programme at the lake in the late 1960s and early 1970s showed that the Mallard population was virtually sedentary and that seasonal fluctuations in numbers were due to the production of young in summer and to local movements.

Other duck species wintering in reasonable numbers include Wigeon (up to 900), Teal (up to 900), Shoveler (up to 500), Gadwall (up to 50), Tufted Duck (up to 500), Pochard (up to 800) and Goldeneye (up to 75). Numbers vary enormously, both from week to week and from year to year and the figures quoted are maxima.

Over 1,000 pairs of Black-headed Gulls, several hundred pairs of Common Gulls and one or two pairs of Lesser Black-backed Gulls nest on islands on Carra.

The lake was very well watched in the early 1970s but in recent years there have been far fewer observations.

Some rarer ducks have been seen, including Long-tailed Duck and Green-winged Teal.

Timing

In summer the duck are nesting and not so visible as from autumn to spring, but the gulls on the various islands are very obvious. Lough Carra has more potential in winter, however, when duck are at their most numerous.

Shooting is prohibited, so disturbance is not a major problem.

Access

The southern and western sides of Lough Carra can be seen from the main road between Ballinrobe and Castlebar. The lake comes into view on the right hand side about 5 km from Ballinrobe and is accessible again by taking the right turn off the main road after another 4 km. The lake is again visible from the main road about 3 km further on.

The northern and eastern sides are less easy to get close to, but several minor roads run close to the shore.

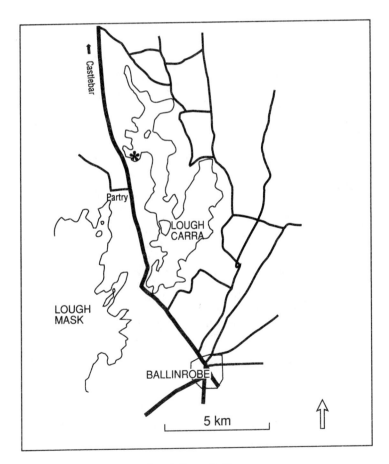

Lough Carra, Co Mayo

Calendar

All year: Mallard, Tufted Duck.

Autumn, winter, spring: Wigeon, Gadwall, Teal, Shoveler, Pochard, Goldeneye.

Summer: Black-headed Gull, Common Gull, Lesser Black-backed Gull.

55 KILLALA BAY

OSI ½" map: sheet 6
G23 G22

Habitat

Killala Bay comprises the estuary of the Moy river, from Ballina north-wards to the sand dunes of Bartragh Island, and the outer bay which is reasonably sheltered from westerly winds. The inner estuary is muddy but the strata are sandier close to Bartragh Island.

Any visitor seeking a historical account of this estuary should dip into Ussher & Warren's great *Birds in Ireland*, published in 1900. Richard Warren, one of the authors, lived in this area for much of his life and the book contains many observations of birds around Bartragh Island and in the bay generally.

Species

In winter, there is a flock of up to 300 Brent Geese, several hundred Wigeon and smaller numbers of Teal and Mallard in the estuary. This section of the bay is one of the better places to see waders on the west coast and Curlews, Oystercatchers, Golden Plovers, Lapwing, Red-shanks, Dunlin and a few Knot and Grey Plovers can all be seen. In autumn Black-tailed Godwits, Spotted Redshanks, Curlew Sandpipers and Little Stints have been seen but not every year.

The outer bay holds Great Northern and Red-throated Divers, Red-breasted Mergansers, a small number of Common Scoters and a hand-ful of Long-tailed Ducks in winter.

In autumn seawatching can be excellent if north-westerlies funnel birds into the bay. Large numbers of skuas of each of the three common species have been seen in these conditions.

The sand dunes have Snow Buntings in late autumn and winter.

Timing

The estuary is at its best between August and May.

Access

The inner bay is difficult to cover adequately, but it can be reached by walking west along the sand dunes from Inishcrone.

The western side of the bay, and in particular the outer bay, is easier

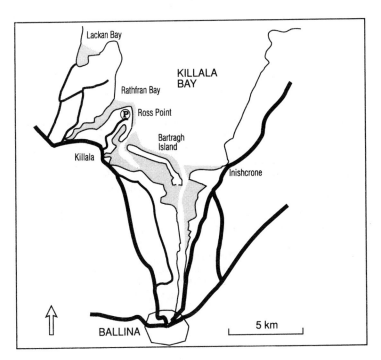

Killala Bay, Co Mayo

to see. Drive from Ballina towards Killala and, just before the town, park your car and walk east along the edge of the bay.

Killala Pier and the carpark at Ross beach, just before Ross Point, are both excellent vantage points.

Calendar

All year: Shelduck, Mallard, Oystercatcher, Curlew, gulls.

Autumn: Seabirds including Gannet, Fulmar, Manx Shearwater, Arctic Skua, Pomarine Skua, Great Skua, terns. First wildfowl and waders. Migrant waders including Curlew Sandpiper and Little Stint in most years.

Winter: Red-throated Diver, Great Northern Diver, Brent Goose, Wigeon, Teal, Red-breasted Merganser, Common Scoter, Long-tailed Duck, wintering waders including Golden Plover, Grey Plover, Lapwing, Knot, Dunlin, Redshank, Greenshank.

Spring: Late wildfowl and waders.

Summer: A few terns.

OTHER MAYO SITES

56 LOUGH CULLIN

OSI ½" map sheet 6
G20

Habitat and Species

Lough Cullin is a moderate-sized lake, about 1,100 hectares in extent, which lies to the south of the much larger Lough Conn. The village of Pontoon divides the two lakes. Conn is much deeper than Cullin, so its wildfowl populations are much smaller. Most of Lough Cullin is no more than four metres deep, though there are substantial fluctuations in water level between summer and winter, and the shallow waters provide feeding for large numbers of diving ducks.

A small population of Common Scoters breed on Loughs Conn and Cullin, but the best time for birdwatching is from July onwards. A moulting flock of Tufted Ducks, which is present from July, is joined by up to 2,000 Pochard and 1,500 Coots in October. Rarer species are sometimes among them and, in recent years, Scaup, Goosander, Smew, Ring-necked Duck and Ferruginous Duck have all been recorded.

The lake was well watched in the later 1980s, and the value of regular observations was shown by the list of rare ducks and, in addition, the recording of Mediterranean and Bonaparte's Gulls among the Black-headed Gulls.

Access

Cullin is best viewed from the peninsula which projects south into the lake about 1 km west of Pontoon Bridge and from the bridge itself. There are also several places where a car can be parked on the north-east shore on the road from Pontoon to Foxford.

57 CLARE ISLAND

OSI ½" map: sheet 10/
1:50,000 map: sheet 30
L68 L78

Habitat and Species

Clare Island lies off the west Mayo coast, just outside the mouth of Clew Bay. It is a particularly hilly island with a summit of approximately 400 m. The island is famous in the scientific literature because of the study of its natural history carried out in 1909–1911 under the auspices of the Royal Irish Academy. In the past few years research into the island's natural history has recommenced with the objective of updating the original Clare Island Survey. As the island has a hotel and guest houses, birdwatching can be carried out in some comfort.

The island has spectacular cliffs on the north side which hold breeding Fulmars, Kittiwakes, Razorbills and Guillemots. A small number of Puffins and Black Guillemots also nest, and Lesser Black-backed, Herring, Great Black-backed and Common Gulls all breed in scattered little colonies. In 1978, Gannets were first found breeding on the island, the single pair choosing a low stack north-east of the old tower. Breeding continues.

Choughs are numerous, up to 25 pairs nesting, and Peregrines and Sparrowhawks are present in summer, perhaps breeding. Skylarks,

Swallows, Wrens, Blackbirds, Wheatears, Meadow Pipits, Rock Pipits and Linnets are among the commoner land birds.

Access

The ferry for Clare Island leaves from Roonah Quay. From Westport, drive west to Louisburgh. In Louisburgh, follow the signposts for Roonah Quay.

58 INISHKEA ISLANDS

OSI ½" map: sheet 6
F52 F51

Habitat and Species

The Inishkeas are two low windswept islands, each measuring about 2.5 km long and 1 km wide. They are separated by a channel about 30 m wide. The vegetation is a sward of red fescue *Festuca rubra*, ribwort plantain *Plantago lanceolata* and creeping bent *Agrostis stolonifera*. There is a small lake on the northern island.

Grey seals are abundant: the islands have the largest breeding colony in Ireland.

The Inishkeas hold the largest wintering concentration of Barnacle Geese in the country. The flock has been studied for many years and over 2,000 birds winter.

In summer a small number of Common, Arctic and Little Terns nest on the islands. The islands are also well situated for watching sea passage and small numbers of Long-tailed Skuas have been seen moving north offshore in May. Judging by the numbers of both Pomarine and Long-tailed Skuas recorded off the west coast of Scotland in spring in recent years, there seems little doubt that this site in good conditions would provide views of flocks of these species.

Access

Access is only possible by negotiating passage with boatmen on the adjoining Mullet peninsula.

59 ILLANMASTIR

OSI ½" map: sheet 6
F94

Habitat and Species

The island is small but rather steep and is one of the finest Puffin colonies in the country. At least 2,000 pairs nest here.

Peregrines, Choughs and Ravens are usually to be seen on the cliffs opposite the island and a small number of Twites breed.

Access

Illanmastir is much the most remote site mentioned in this book. Access to the island itself is prohibited by the Irish Wildbird Conservancy, which owns the site, but it can be scanned well with binoculars and telescope from the mainland cliffs. To get to the cliff requires a walk across country of about 5 km from Porturlin to the west or a more difficult walk of about 6 km over hillier countryside from Belderg Harbour to the east. The walk, however, provides spectacular views of cliff scenery and open bog.

Belderg Harbour is north of Belderg, a village west of Ballycastle on the road from Killala to Belmullet. Porturlin is reached by turning right at Glenamoy on the road from Belderg to Belmullet. Follow the road for 8 km to a fork. At the junction turn right (follow the signposts) for Porturlin.

SLIGO

Introduction

Sligo has a varied coastline backed by impressive mountains. From Killala Bay in the west, the coast is rocky to Ballysadare Bay, but then the inner reaches of the shallow, sandy and muddy Sligo Bay are met. There are three separate bays here — Ballysadare Bay, Cummeen Strand and Drumcliff Bay — before the coast swings around north-eastwards from Raghly to Mullaghmore.

Inland, the Ox Mountains dominate the south-west of the county and the Curlew Mountains the south-east. There are several fine lakes, including Lough Gill, made famous by the poet William Butler Yeats. The scenery is very different from any other part of Ireland, and the spectacular Ben Bulbin dominates the view from Sligo town northwards.

Sites

60	CUMMEEN STRAND	*Brent Geese, Wigeon.*
61	LISSADELL	*Barnacle Geese.*

Other sites:

62	Ballysadare	*Estuary.*
63	Inishmurray	*Breeding seabirds, Eiders.*
64	Bunduff Lake	*Whooper Swans, Greenland White-fronted Geese.*

60 CUMMEEN STRAND

OSI ½" map: sheet 7/
OSNI ½" map: sheet 3/
1:50,000 map: sheets 16, 25
G63

Habitat

The large, shallow bay between Sligo town and the sea is shaped rather like a bottle with Coney Island, at the mouth, forming a loosely fitting cork. The sea has a narrow exit to both north and south of Coney Island and most of the bay drains dry at low tide, giving access to Coney Island by a narrow road. The sand flats are most extensive at the southern side of the bay, known as Cummeen Strand.

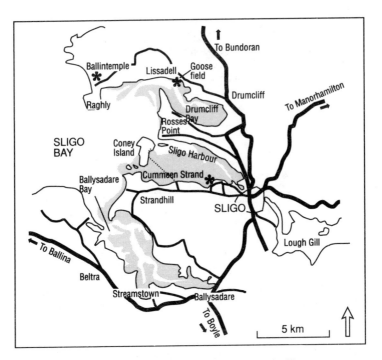

Cummeen Strand, Lissadell and Ballysadare, Co Sligo

Species

Cummeen Strand is a place of arrival in autumn for large numbers of Brent Geese and Wigeon. In October and November there are brief periods when over 800 Brent Geese and about the same number of Wigeon occur; numbers decline later. Shelduck and Mallard also winter.

Some hundreds of waders spend the autumn and winter. Oyster-catchers, Ringed Plovers, Lapwing, Dunlin and Curlew all occur, and the location of the bay, at the western side of the country, is such that occasional American vagrants should occur.

Over 2,000 gulls frequent the town dump and inner estuary. Glaucous and Iceland Gulls are seen every winter and rarer species have also been recorded.

Timing

Late autumn is much the best for this site, as wildfowl peak at this time. Since the tide runs out for 3 km, the best time for a visit is within two hours of high tide.

Access

The upper part of the strand can be watched from the Rosses Point road north-west of the town and along the edge of the inner bay. The strand itself is best watched from the end of the narrow road which turns right off the Sligo-Strandhill road and crosses the strand to Coney Island. Take the road west for Strand Hill out of Sligo and turn right after 4 km. The narrow road reaches Cummeen Strand after about a kilometre.

Calendar

Autumn-winter-spring: Brent Goose, Shelduck, Wigeon, Teal, Mallard, Red-breasted Merganser, Oystercatcher, Ringed Plover, Lapwing, Dunlin, Curlew, Redshank, Greenshank, gulls including Glaucous and Iceland, and possibility of Ring-billed and Mediterranean.

61 LISSADELL

OSI ½″ map: sheet 7/
OSNI ½″ map: sheet 3/
1:50,000 map: sheet 16
G64

Habitat

A large field between Lissadell and the north shore of Drumcliff Bay is the finest site on the Irish mainland for Barnacle Geese. The site is managed by the National Parks and Wildlife Service for the geese and the field has been fertilised specifically to improve the grass for them. A hide provides excellent viewing.

Species

This site is one where Barnacle Geese are the highlight. Some ducks and waders do winter on the mudflats of Drumcliff Bay, but the numbers are lower than at Cummeen Strand or Ballysadare. Lissadell has over 1,000 Barnacle Geese at times nowadays, having increased from only 300 or so in the mid-1970s. This increase has been due to good management, as it far exceeds the rate of increase in the wintering population generally, but the birds move about the general area on the north side of Drumcliff Bay and spend much of their time at Ballintemple.

Timing

The geese are present from October to April.

Access

Take the road from Sligo to Drumcliff. Just beyond Drumcliff, turn left for Lissadell and drive for about 5 km, forking left at Carney village. The geese can be seen easily from the road to Lissadell. To see them from the hide which overlooks the field traditionally used by the birds, enter the driveway to Lissadell House and walk back in an easterly direction through the trees along the shoreline, taking care not to disturb the geese.

Ballintemple is farther out along the road towards Raghly and should also be explored.

Calendar

Autumn-winter-spring: Barnacle Goose.

OTHER SLIGO SITES

OSI ½″ map: sheet 7/
OSNI ½″ map: sheet 3/
1:50,000 map: sheet 25
G53 G63 G62

62 BALLYSADARE

Habitat and Species

Ballysadare is the most southerly of the three inlets of Sligo Bay. It is the estuary of the Ballysadare river and is a long inlet. The upper reaches of the estuary are muddy and hold wintering Shelduck, Mallard, Teal, Wigeon, Red-breasted Mergansers and Goldeneye. Oystercatcher, Curlews, Bar-tailed Godwits, Redshanks, Greenshanks and Dunlin are also found here. Some Brent Geese also winter: they can be found in most parts of the bay, but tend to prefer the Streamstown inlet.

In autumn, the sand bank at the mouth of the bay attracts feeding terns. It should be a good place for interesting gulls.

Access

The head of the bay is best viewed from the shoreline by Ballysadare Quarry. The inlet by Streamstown, to the west of Ballysadare and accessible by taking the first right turn about 1.5 km outside Ballysadare on the Ballina road, is good for seeing Brent Geese. The mouth of the estuary can be reached most easily by taking the road from Ballysadare to Strandhill and stopping on the road as it passes alongside the bay.

OSI ½″ map: sheet 7/
OSNI ½″ map: sheet 3/
1:50,000 map: sheet 16
G55

63 INISHMURRAY

Habitat and Species

Inishmurray is a small and lovely island comprising less than 600 hectares, situated about 7 km off the north Sligo coast. It was inhabited until 1948, and has remarkable monastic ruins. Nowadays, the absence of humans has kept the island free from disturbance in winter, when Barnacle Geese graze, and in summer there are breeding Storm Petrels, Eiders, Common and Arctic Terns and gulls.

Access

A visit to Inishmurray requires negotiation with a boatman as the island is uninhabited. Rosses Point or Mullaghmore are the best places to make enquiries.

OSI ½″ map: sheet 7/
OSNI ½″ map: sheet 3/
1:50,000 map: sheet 16
G75

64 BUNDUFF LAKE

Habitat and Species

North of Sligo, close to Mullaghmore, lies Bunduff Lake, a small lake surrounded by marshy fields, which holds up to 180 Whooper Swans in October and about 50 in winter. Small numbers of Teal, Mallard, Tufted Duck and Pochard also winter here, together with occasional Scaup.

It looks an ideal site for a Nearctic duck.

Access

Take the road from Sligo to Bundoran and take the left turn for Mullaghmore, just after passing through the village of Cliffony. Bunduff Lake is on the right hand side of the road, about a kilometre after the junction. Bunduff Lake can be well viewed from the road which leads to the right immediately after passing the south-west end of the lake.

LEITRIM

General

Leitrim is undoubtedly the least birdwatched county in Ireland. It suffers from having only a very short coastline, but has numerous small lakes. There are no sites known to be of especial importance for birdwatching but Fermanagh, which adjoins this county, has been better watched and found to have a very rich mix of breeding birds.

Lough Allen, the large lake in the centre of the county, is deep and holds relatively few birds. Loughs Boderg and Bofin on the Shannon, at the south-eastern end of the county, hold Whooper Swans and good numbers of duck. These lakes are difficult to access, other than from a boat on the river.

In summer, Great Crested Grebes nest on many of the Leitrim lakes and Garden Warblers nest on the shorelines of some.

Overall, this is a county about which little is known of its birds but which might well repay more intensive study.

ROSCOMMON

Introduction

Roscommon is a large county bordered to the east by the River Shannon, to the south-west by the Suck, a tributary of the Shannon, to the north-west by the Curlew Mountains and stretching out in the west to the landscape of small fields mixed with areas of bogland which dominates east Galway and Mayo.

The Suck and the Shannon are surrounded by bogs and, to the west of these rivers, there are a number of shallow lakes and turloughs which hold quite large numbers of passage and wintering wildfowl and waders.

The Suck, which divides Roscommon from Galway, is dealt with under that county.

65 RIVER SHANNON, ATHLONE TO SHANNONBRIDGE
Wildfowl, Corncrakes.
66 CLOONLAUGHNAN   *Wintering wildfowl.*

Other sites:
67 Lough Croan   *Breeding and wintering duck.*
68 Lough Funshinagh   *Breeding and wintering duck.*
69 Lough Ree   *Wintering duck; breeding Common Scoter.*

65 RIVER SHANNON, ATHLONE TO SHANNONBRIDGE

OSI ½″ map: sheets 12, 13
N03 M93 M92

Habitat

The River Shannon between Athlone and Shannonbridge is surrounded by extensive bogs and poorly drained agricultural land. In winter it floods and the surrounding callows hold large numbers of birds. The river is difficult to access because the only road crossings between Lough Ree and Lough Derg are at Athlone, Shannonbridge and Banagher where eskers, which formed under the glacial ice sheet, provide firm ground on both banks. The roads run along the eskers at right angles to the river, rather than following the line of the Shannon.

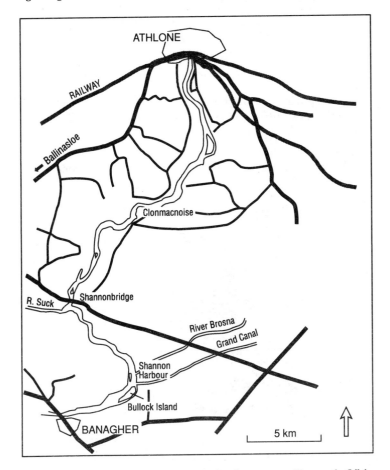

River Shannon, Athlone to Shannonbridge, Cos Roscommon, Westmeath, Offaly and Galway

The pasture land on either side of the river provides excellent feeding for wildfowl when the river floods.

Species

The principal species to be seen in winter are those typical of the Shannon system generally: parties of Whooper and Bewick's Swans, Greenland White-fronted Geese, huge flocks of Wigeon and smaller flocks of Teal and Mallard. Mute Swans are common. In winter the fields hold great clouds of Lapwing and Golden Plovers, and smaller numbers of Curlews. The drains are full of Snipe and small flocks of Black-tailed Godwits can often be found.

In summer the wildfowl mostly return to the north to breed and only some Little Grebes, Moorhens, Mute Swans and Mallard nest. However, this is one of the last refuges of the Corncrake. As the water drains from the fields which have flooded in winter, a glorious growth of meadow emerges and this provides cover for Corncrakes. They can be heard at night, and sometimes by day, along much of this stretch of river.

Some wader species also nest here. Snipe, Redshanks, Curlews and Lapwing all breed in small numbers, especially in the vicinity of Clonmacnoise, and Black-tailed Godwits have nested in the past.

Timing

To see the breeding birds and hear the Corncrake, the best time to come is in June or early July.

For wildfowl the best time is from October to the end of March. Weekends should be avoided if possible as the river is very heavily shot over.

Access

Much the best way to see birds on the Shannon is from a boat. Cruisers can be hired at Portumna, Banagher and Athlone and provide a great

Snipe

summer holiday. In winter they are not available, so the wildfowl enthusiast must take the various roads which cross the river or, alternatively, come close to the Shannon. There are a number of points where access has been provided to the river for coarse fishing.

The road crosses the river at Shannonbridge and at Athlone and comes close to the river at Clonmacnoise and a number of points on both banks south of Athlone.

Calendar

All year: Little Grebe, Heron, Cormorant, Moorhen, Mute Swan, Mallard, Curlew, Snipe, Kingfisher, Reed Bunting.

Autumn-winter-spring: Whooper Swan, Bewick's Swan, Greenland White-fronted Goose, Wigeon, Teal, Golden Plover, Lapwing, Black-tailed Godwit.

Summer: Redshank, Corncrake, Swallow, Sand Martin, Sedge Warbler.

66 CLOONLAUGHNAN

OSI ½″ map: sheet 12
M85

Habitat

Cloonlaughnan is a turlough close to Mount Talbot which has the great advantage of being much easier to watch than the rather inaccessible callows on the Shannon and the Suck. This shallow lake lies in a large field partially hidden from the road by high hedgerows. The area is very open so geese and duck can see danger from a considerable distance, yet the hedges provide cover for the birdwatcher.

Species

When Cloonlaughnan is flooded a flock of up to 100 Greenland White-fronted Geese, parties of Whooper and Bewick's Swans, hundreds of Wigeon, Teal and Mallard and smaller numbers of Shoveler and Pintail can be seen well. At times, indeed, there are well over 1,000 Wigeon here.

Large numbers of Lapwing and Golden Plover occur, as is usual on wet land in the Shannon valley, and Curlews and Black-tailed Godwits as well. Less common in the Shannon are the wintering Dunlin which can also be found.

Timing

This is a site to be visited only in winter. It is best between October and March.

Access

Cloonlaughnan is not marked on the half inch Ordnance Survey map. It is best located by taking the road from Athlone for Mount Talbot. Turn right at Four Roads, a junction about 5 km before Mount Talbot. Cloon-laughnan is on the left hand side of the road just after the crossroads.

Calendar

Autumn-winter-spring: Whooper Swan, Bewick's Swan, Mute Swan, Greenland White-fronted Goose, Wigeon, Teal, Mallard, Shoveler, Pintail, Golden Plover, Lapwing, Dunlin, Black-tailed Godwit, Curlew.

OTHER ROSCOMMON SITES

67 LOUGH CROAN

OSI ½" map: sheet 12
M84 M85

Habitat and Species

Croan is a small permanent lake which holds a reasonable wildfowl population in winter and is an excellent breeding site for duck in summer. The lake has up to 900 Wigeon and smaller numbers of Teal, Mallard, Shoveler and Pintail in winter. Lapwing, Golden Plovers and Curlews utilise the surrounding pastures.

In summer Great Crested and Little Grebes nest and Black-necked Grebe has been proved to breed in the past. A number of duck species breed including Mallard, Teal and Shoveler.

The lake dries out considerably in summer and the breeding duck are vulnerable to disturbance so the area should not be walked over.

Access

Lough Croan is close to the road from Athlone to Mount Talbot. Take the left turn about 2 km before Four Roads and then take the narrow road to the left which is found after about 2 km. This road runs along the edge of the lake and provides good views.

68 LOUGH FUNSHINAGH

OSI ½" sheet 12
M95 M94

Habitat and Species

Funshinagh, like Croan, is a famous wildfowl breeding lake. It may not be quite as productive as Croan nowadays, but in the past this lake was the stronghold of the Irish Black-necked Grebe breeding colony which was plundered by egg-collectors year after year. As well as the rare Black-necked, both Great Crested and Little Grebe bred. Mallard, Teal, Gadwall, Pintail, Shoveler, Tufted Duck, Pochard, Red-breasted Merganser, Mute Swan, Coot, Moorhen, Lapwing, Ringed Plover, Snipe, Common Sandpiper, Redshank and Dunlin have all been known to nest.

The lake has a naturally fluctuating water level and extensive stands of clubrush and reeds, which make observation of both wintering and breeding birds very difficult. Undoubtedly, the area would repay further investigation as it is very much underwatched since egg-collecting has fallen out of favour (as well as being illegal).

Access

The best way to approach Funshinagh is by turning right off the road from Athlone to Mount Talbot. Take the first right turn after passing through Milltown Pass, about 2 km after the village. Follow the road straight through the crossroads which is reached after 1.5 km. The road shortly runs past south-east corner of the lake. A narrow road runs along the southern side.

69 LOUGH REE

OSI ½″ map: sheet 12
M96 M95 M94 N06
N05 N04

Habitat and Species

Lough Ree is the second largest lake on the Shannon system but has rather low numbers of wintering duck when compared with the great flocks which occur on the callows. At times in winter, when the water level is low, the east side in particular can hold good numbers of duck. The north-east holds over 1,000 Tufted Duck and the south-east several hundred Wigeon, Mallard and Teal.

There are a number of islands and these provide nest sites for Tufted Duck, Red-breasted Mergansers, Mallard and, in recent years, a small but growing population of Common Scoters.

Some Common Terns and Black-headed Gulls also nest on the lough.

Access

In summer, access is best by boat, but the lake is very broad and can be dangerous when winds get up.

In winter, the wildfowl can be best seen by driving down to the shore-line at the many points where access is available. The coast is very indented and there are quite extensive reedbeds in parts so bird-watching is frequently rather unsatisfactory. One gets the feeling that only a small proportion of the birds are being seen.

LEINSTER

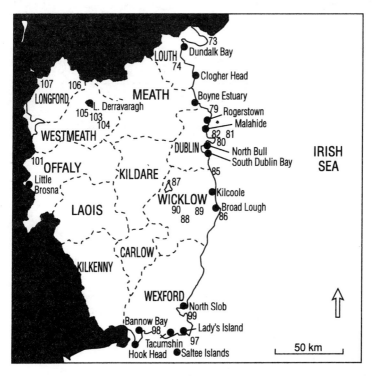

Leinster: counties, major sites (named) and other sites (numbered)

Louth
70. DUNDALK BAY
71. CLOGHER HEAD
72. BOYNE ESTUARY
73. Carlingford Lough
74. Braganstown
Meath
Dublin
75. ROGERSTOWN ESTUARY
76. MALAHIDE ESTUARY
77. NORTH BULL
78. SOUTH DUBLIN BAY
79. Skerries
80. Howth Head
81. Ireland's Eye
82. Baldoyle Estuary

Wicklow
83. KILCOOLE
84. BROAD LOUGH
85. Bray Head
86. Wicklow Head
87. Blessington Reservoir
88. Glendalough
89. Devil's Glen
90. Glenmalure
Wexford
91. NORTH SLOB
92. LADY'S ISLAND LAKE
93. TACUMSHIN LAKE
94. SALTEE ISLANDS
95. HOOK HEAD
96. BANNOW BAY

LOUTH

Introduction

Louth is the most northerly county in Leinster, pressing up against the mountainous south-east corner of Down. The coastline is largely low-lying and there are extensive mudflats on the shore of Carlingford Lough and, especially, around the sweep of Dundalk Bay which resembles an enormous bite taken out of the county. South of Dundalk Bay the headlands of Dunany Point and Clogher Head project out into the Irish Sea. Sandy beaches run from Dunany Point southwards to Baltray and the Boyne Estuary where the county boundary with Meath follows the line of the river to the sea.

Inland, the Cooley peninsula, dividing Carlingford Lough from Dundalk Bay, incorporates a wild stretch of hill country with few roads. Most of the remainder of the county is lowlying, flat agricultural land.

A number of rivers flow from west to east, entering the sea in Dundalk Bay or farther south. The Fane, for example, runs into Dundalk Bay at Lurgangreen, and the Dee at Annagassan. The Boyne, which enters the Irish Sea at Baltray, runs through Meath for much of its length rather than Louth.

Sites

70	DUNDALK BAY	*Estuary.*
71	CLOGHER HEAD	*Migration watchpoint.*
72	BOYNE ESTUARY	*Estuary.*

Other sites:

73	Carlingford Lough	*Estuary, divers, sea-duck.*
74	Braganstown	*Geese.*

References

Irish East Coast Bird Reports.

Lenehan, L. J. The Birds of the Meath and South Louth coasts (*Irish East Coast Bird Report 1990*: 50–59, 1991).

Lenehan, L. J. Wintering Wildfowl at Stabannon-Braganstown, Co. Louth (*Irish East Coast Bird Report 1991*: 77–81, 1992).

70 DUNDALK BAY

OSI ½" map: sheets 9, 13
J10 J00 O09 O19

Habitat

Dundalk Bay is an enormous sandy bay with extensive inter-tidal flats where wildfowl and waders feed securely at low tide. Behind these flats are a number of areas of saltmarsh where large roosts form.

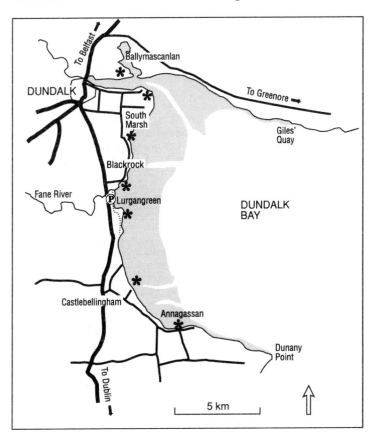

Dundalk Bay, Co Louth

Ballymascanlan in the north is a small muddy inlet which has rich feeding for Redshanks and Black-tailed Godwits. To the immediate south, Dundalk Harbour at low tide is also quite muddy. However, these two inlets represent only a tiny part of the wader feeding area. The tide exposes an area of sand and mud which stretches for up to 3 km between the high tide mark and the water's edge. This expanse stretches from Giles' Quay on the Cooley peninsula in the north to Annagassan in the south and covers 4,500 hectares.

The land behind the bay is all very lowlying but at the South Marsh and Lurgangreen there are extensive saltmarshes. The South Marsh lies to the east of the town of Dundalk and is a large area of mixed pasture and saltmarsh, divided in places by muddy channels, many of which are impassable, especially at high tide. Lurgangreen lies to the south of Blackrock, just south of where the Fane river meets the bay. It too is an area of saltmarsh, divided by channels, and behind it are fields protected from the sea by embankments.

Farther south again, near Annagassan are shingle banks where waders frequently roost at high tide.

Species

The outer bay holds small numbers of divers and grebes. Both Red-throated and Great Northern Divers can be seen from Giles' Quay and some Great Crested Grebes also occur. Slavonian Grebe has been recorded and might well be found more frequently if the area was more thoroughly covered by birdwatchers. Common Scoters and Red-breasted Mergansers also winter off Giles' Quay.

Wildfowl numbers are not particularly high when one considers how large the area is, but there is great diversity. Mute Swans congregate at Dundalk docks; Whooper Swans are occasional visitors to Lurgan-green; Greylag and White-fronted Geese come and go at both Dundalk Bay and Lurgangreen; Brent Geese are regular in autumn and spring; Shelduck, Wigeon, Teal, Mallard, Pintail, Shoveler and Goldeneye all winter in varying numbers. Wigeon and Teal gather principally at the South Marsh and Lurgangreen, Mallard at Ballymascanlan and off Annagassan. Shoveler are probably the scarcest of the regularly occurring ducks.

The bay is best known among birdwatchers, however, for its enormous wader numbers. In Ireland as a whole, only the Shannon estuary and Strangford Lough have had more waders recorded. On the Atlantic coast of Europe and north Africa it ranks among the top twenty estuaries.

About 10,000 Oystercatchers winter, and many more occur in autumn. Winter numbers of Lapwing and Golden Plover are among the highest on the east coast, with flocks of several thousand of each. Bar-tailed Godwits, Curlews, Redshanks, Dunlin and Knot all winter in numbers over 1,000. Winter flocks of Black-tailed Godwits at both Ballymascanlan and Dundalk Harbour have been building steadily over many years and now number several hundred at each site.

Many other wader species also occur, but in small numbers. Grey Plover, Ringed Plover and Greenshanks all winter in small numbers. Ruffs and Spotted Redshanks occur in autumn and sometimes in winter. Curlew Sandpipers are seen in autumn most years and Little Stints occasionally. Common Sandpipers teeter about the estuary at Bally-mascanlan and Dundalk Harbour in late July.

Gulls roost in the bay and terns feed in late summer.

Overall, this bay has potential which has hardly been touched. Regular watching should turn up many more species, but, even for a brief day visit, the sight of huge wader flocks swirling over the saltmarsh at the South Marsh or Lurgangreen is well worth a detour.

The South Marsh is probably the best site on the Leinster coast for wintering Twites. Over 50 have been seen in the area from Soldier's Point southwards.

Curlew

Access

Begin a visit from the north at Giles' Quay. Take the Belfast road north from Dundalk and turn right after 3 km on the road to Carlingford. Follow the road past Ballymascanlan and on for 7 km to a right turn for Giles' Quay. Turn down the narrow road to the quay. The open bay can be scanned from here and from several points on the road back towards Ballymascanlan.

The top of Ballymascanlan Bay can be seen from the road west of Ballymascanlan village. The outer part of the bay is accessible on the west side from a narrow road which runs to the east from the main Belfast road about 600 m north of Dundalk.

Dundalk Harbour is readily worked by following the road to the east along the edge of the harbour out to Soldier's Point. Park the car here and explore the north part of the South Marsh. Much of the marsh is not directly accessible because of the drains which cross it, but most of the birds can be seen with the use of a telescope. The south part of the marsh can be seen from the road from Dundalk to Blackrock, just where it joins the coast.

At low tide, or on a dropping tide, the estuary can be seen well from the road to Blackrock. Just west of Blackrock, the road joins the main Dundalk-Dublin road. A couple of hundred metres to the south, the road south crosses a bridge over the River Fane. Park on the south side of the bridge and follow the lane down to the edge of the saltmarsh. There is a path south to the sea-wall and, from there on to the south, the embankment provides cover for viewing the roosting flocks of birds.

The south part of Dundalk Bay can be seen by driving south to Castle-bellingham and then turning left for Annagassan. The road runs along the side of the bay for a couple of kilometres and good views are available at the old mill at Annagassan.

Timing

The bay is best from August to March, but passage waders in April and May could be interesting. Observations are much easier if the tide is within two hours of high water. At low tide most of the birds are too far distant, even with a good telescope, but they can be well seen as they are pushed up by a rising tide to the roosts. At full tide, many of the waders are hidden among the long grass on the saltmarsh but they become visible again as the tide ebbs. The best conditions of all are about one hour after high tide in the afternoon, with the sun behind the observer.

Calendar
Autumn, winter, spring: Red-throated Diver, Great Northern Diver, Great Crested Grebe, Mute Swan, Whooper Swan, Greylag Goose, White-fronted Goose, Brent Goose, Shelduck, Wigeon, Teal, Mallard, Pintail, Shoveler, Goldeneye, possibility of Long-tailed Duck, Oystercatcher, Ringed Plover, Golden Plover, Grey Plover, Lapwing, Knot, Dunlin, Black-tailed Godwit, Bar-tailed Godwit, Curlew, Redshank, Greenshank, Turnstone.

Autumn: Curlew Sandpiper, possibility of Little Stint, Ruff, Spotted Redshank, Common Sandpiper.

71 CLOGHER HEAD
OSI ½" map: sheet 13
O18

Habitat
Clogher Head protrudes well out into the Irish Sea and is well situated for seawatching and searching for passerine migrants. Its potential was first thoroughly explored by a small group of Dublin birdwatchers in the early 1970s. They were anxious to see if the variety of migrants which could be seen at Saltee in Wexford and Cape Clear in Cork might be found on the east coast, and they visited Clogher Head regularly at weekends throughout the year for a period, but eventually the lure of rarities in Wexford and Cork drew them away. Clogher Head is now very much underwatched.

The head itself has a scattering of cover in gardens above the harbour of Port Oriel. The harbour is busy and attracts gulls, especially where the water outflows from the fish processing plant to the west of the harbour. There is rocky shore each side of the harbour, and a sandy beach from a few hundred metres west of Port Oriel which stretches north to Dunany Point.

Species
Systematic seawatching in spring and autumn showed that quite substantial passage could be seen from the head. In the autumn of 1974 all four species of skua were recorded as were Cory's Shearwater, Sooty Shearwaters, Sabine's Gull, Little Gulls and Black Terns. Subsequent observations have been far less regular but have shown that Arctic and Great Skua are both regular and Pomarine Skua occasional. The Irish

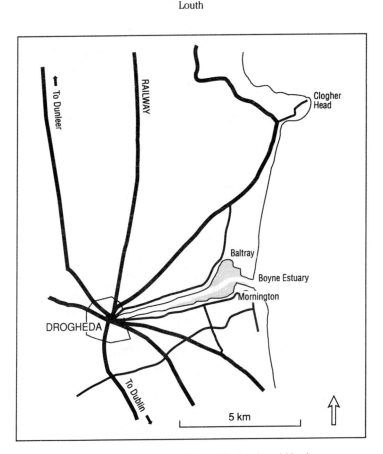

Clogher Head and Boyne Estuary, Cos Louth and Meath

Sea, in the right conditions, obviously has considerable numbers and diversity of seabirds and Clogher Head is an ideal headland for sea-watching.

Large numbers of gulls appear off the harbour, especially in winter, and Glaucous and Iceland are regular. Up to 13 Glaucous and 12 Iceland Gulls have been present at the one time. Mediterranean Gulls often occur among the Black-headed Gulls which roost on the beach to the north of the head. In December 1988, a Laughing Gull was found at the harbour and seen later at the beach.

Passerine migration is good in both spring and autumn. Clogher Head's rarest bird, Ireland's only Rock Thrush, was found in May 1974. Willow Warblers, Chiffchaffs, Wheatears, Whinchats, Whitethroats, Grasshopper Warblers, Sedge Warblers and Spotted Flycatchers all pass through in April and May. Other species recorded in spring include Turtle Dove, Serin and Red-breasted Flycatcher.

In autumn, Blackcaps and Garden Warblers are probably annual. Rarities seen in autumn have included Barred Warbler, Yellow-browed Warbler and Lesser Whitethroat.

Late in autumn Clogher Head has good numbers of finches, including occasional Twites.

Timing

Visits are worthwhile in spring from March to early June and in autumn from August to the end of October if seawatching or passerine watching is planned. The best conditions for skuas are after periods of strong westerly and south-westerly gales accompanying the passage of areas of low pressure.

Passerines are best in both spring and autumn in quite different conditions, when the winds are south-easterly or during periods of calm weather accompanying high pressure systems.

Access

Clogher Head is easily found. Drive from Drogheda for Termonfeckin and follow on through the village to Clogher Head. Park the car at the harbour and explore on foot.

Male Wheatear

Calendar

All year: Fulmar, Red-breasted Merganser, Oystercatcher, Curlew, Turnstone, Black-headed Gull, Herring Gull, Lesser Black-backed Gull, Great Black-backed Gull, Kittiwake, Guillemot, Razorbill, Linnet, Tree Sparrow.

Autumn: Red-throated Diver, Great Northern Diver, Manx Shearwater, Gannet, Arctic Skua, Pomarine Skua, Great Skua, passerine migrants.

Winter: Divers, Common Scoter, Golden Plover, Lapwing, Purple Sandpiper, Iceland Gull, Glaucous Gull, finch and thrush flocks.

Spring: Divers, seabird passage with likelihood of Arctic Skua, passerine migrants including Grasshopper Warbler, Sedge Warbler, Whinchat.

72 BOYNE ESTUARY

Habitat

The Boyne estuary divides the eastern margin of the counties of Louth and Meath. The land is lowlying on both sides and the estuary is muddy with some saltmarsh. Various efforts have been made over the years to reclaim parts of the estuary and there are a number of sea walls.

The estuary is narrow from the town of Drogheda downstream as far as Mornington where it broadens out to about 1.5 km in width. This is the widest part of the estuary; shortly afterwards the estuary narrows again to reach the sea through an exit between the sand dunes of Baltray to the north and Queensborough to the south.

Species

This is a rather good site for seeing wildfowl and waders, but it has been overshadowed by the impressive sites of Dundalk Bay to the north and the North Bull to the south. The site has been surveyed regularly and duck numbers appear to have been reasonably stable over the past 20 years. Up to 120 Shelduck, 800 Wigeon, 300 Teal and 250 Mallard can be expected and, in recent years, as their Irish wintering population has exploded, a small flock of Brent Geese occurs. The geese are most regular in spring.

The wader species are typical of those of the east coast, but the Boyne has the largest numbers of Black-tailed Godwits (up to 450) of any estuary north of Wexford. Passage waders also occur and Spotted Red-shank, Little Stint and Ruff are annual. Rarities recorded include Little Egret, Avocet and Pectoral Sandpiper.

The dunes at Baltray hold a small colony of Little Terns in summer and a handful of Ringed Plovers. Carrion Crows are more often reported from the Baltray area than any other part of Leinster.

Timing

The best time for visiting the estuary is within two hours of high tide. However, timing is not so critical as at Dundalk Bay as the estuary is relatively narrow and easily watched.

Access

Both sides of the Boyne can be watched by driving east from Drogheda. To see the northern side take the road for Baltray and stop where birds are seen. The southern side, which is not usually so good, can be watched by taking the road for Mornington. To cover the area thorough-ly, both sides must be watched.

Calendar

Autumn-winter-spring: Brent Goose, Shelduck, Wigeon, Teal, Mallard, Oystercatcher, Golden Plover, Grey Plover, Lapwing, Knot, Dunlin, Black-tailed Godwit, Curlew, Redshank, Greenshank.

Autumn: Spotted Redshank, Ruff, Curlew Sandpiper, Little Stint, Whim-brel.

Summer: Terns, especially Little Tern.

OTHER LOUTH SITES

73 CARLINGFORD LOUGH

OSI ½" map: sheet 9/
OSNI ½" map: sheet 4
J11 J21

Habitat and Species

Carlingford Lough is divided in two by the border between Northern Ireland and the Republic. This section, therefore, deals only with the south-west shore. The north-east side is dealt with under the accounts for County Down.

The lough is a deep fjord-like sea lough surrounded by mountains. The Mourne Mountains loom over the Down side and the Carlingford Mountains dominate the Cooley peninsula on the Louth side. The mouth of the lough is shallower than much of the lough itself, a characteristic of fjords, and the bay is surrounded by moraines.

The lough holds an impressive population of sea-duck. Over 500 Scaup and up to 100 Goldeneye, 50 Red-breasted Mergansers and in some years over 50 Long-tailed Ducks winter here. Great Crested Grebes are common, but divers are very thinly distributed. Some Brent Geese, Shelduck, Teal, Mallard and Wigeon and small numbers of Grey Plovers, Golden Plovers, Lapwing, Oystercatchers, Dunlin, Bar-tailed Godwits, Redshanks and Greenshanks winter here. The muddy area between Greenore and Carlingford is the best part of the bay for waders.

Access

Access could hardly be easier. From Dundalk, take the main road for Greenore. Park at Greenore and scan the bay. Work back along the road to Carlingford and then back to Omeath. The border crossing is just beyond Omeath.

74 BRAGANSTOWN

OSI ½" map: sheet 13
O09

Habitat and Species

Braganstown, just to the north of Stabannon, has become an important swan and goose wintering site since the early 1980s. In the maps of Louth, which form part of the centrepiece of the *Irish East Coast Bird Report*, it did not appear until 1984. The site is an area of farmland on the southern edge of the River Glyde between Ardee and Castle-bellingham, which attracts large numbers of Greylag Geese and smaller numbers of wild swans and other geese. The farm was formerly marsh-land but was drained and is now farmed intensively for grass, cereals and root crops.

Up to 1,000 Greylag Geese are regular, though numbers do fluctuate considerably. Some few Pink-footed and White-fronted Geese are usually among the Greylags and Barnacle Goose has been recorded. Whooper and Bewick's Swans are both regular, with Whooper the commoner. Up to 50 Whoopers could be expected, whereas Bewick's are often absent. As well as wildfowl, there are flocks of Golden Plovers, Lapwings and Curlews, as well as good numbers of wintering thrushes and finches. This is a good spot for seeing Bramblings.

The best time for a visit is between late October and March.

Access

The birds can be watched by taking the road north from Ardee towards
Dundalk and turning right for Castlebellingham about 1 km beyond
Ardee. The road runs along the north side of the River Dee. Drive for
about 5 km to Stabannon. At Stabannon, turn left at the junction and
Braganstown is reached on the left side of the road after about 1.5 km.
The estate is strictly private, but most of the birds can be viewed from
the road.

MEATH

General

Meath is a large county with rich agricultural land. The coastline is small
and limited to a stretch of shelving beach between the Boyne estuary
(see under Louth above) and the Dublin border. Inland the county is
relatively flat and has very few areas of standing water.

For a county so close to Dublin, there have been surprisingly few
unusual species found.

Bird records are included in the annual *Irish East Coast Bird Report*.

Coastal birdwatching at Laytown and Gormanston is good in winter.
Red-throated and Great Northern Divers occur in small numbers. Large
flocks of Common Scoters winter in some years, though numbers
fluctuate from year to year, and small numbers of Velvet Scoters and an
occasional Surf Scoter can be found among them. A small flock of
Scaup sometimes winters on this coast as well.

Waders, some Wigeon and Teal and a small flock of about 50 Brent
Geese winter on the estuary just to the south of Laytown. A few Purple
Sandpipers can be seen on the rocky coast north of Laytown.

The lakes in the west and north of the county have breeding Great
Crested Grebes and Blackcaps.

DUBLIN

Introduction

Dublin is dominated by the city which sprawls both inland and along
the coast to north and south from Dublin Bay. About a million people
live in the capital and its suburbs, and inevitably they put pressure on
the best places for birds. Yet the county has a magnificent series of
estuaries, large seabird colonies on sea cliffs and fine mountains.

The coast from the Meath border south to Rogerstown estuary is
lowlying with a shelving beach off which scoters and Red-breasted
Mergansers feed. Then there is a series of estuaries: Rogerstown,
Malahide, Baldoyle and Dublin Bay. On the north side of Dublin Bay the
promontory of Howth Head projects far enough out to be a useful seawatching site and its cliffs support large numbers of seabirds. South of
Dublin Bay, the coast swings around the arc of Killiney Bay and then,
just across the border with Wicklow, the shallow coast terminates at
Bray Head.

Offshore, there are several islands. Rockabill, a tiny rock marked with a lighthouse, lies off Skerries, but visiting is prohibited. The island has the largest colony of Roseate Terns in north-west Europe and a team of wardens protect them from disturbance. The birds can be seen in summer from the adjacent coast. Farther south, Lambay Island has wintering geese and large numbers of breeding seabirds but is privately owned so not accessible. Ireland's Eye, a smaller island off Howth, can be reached by boat from Howth Harbour and also holds a seabird colony.

Inland, there are attractive habitats for riverine birds along the River Liffey and the banks of the Royal and Grand Canals. The Phoenix Park, on the western side of Dublin city and within easy reach of the centre city by public transport, has a long list of the commoner breeding and wintering land birds.

The birds of the county are probably the best watched in the country as there is a greater concentration of birdwatchers here than anywhere else. The IWC has three branches and its headquarters are at Ruttledge House, 8 Longford Place, Monkstown in south Dublin, close to Dun Laoghaire.

There are plans in progress for a new book on the birds of the east coast which will, of course, include those of Dublin.

Perhaps the finest aspect of birdwatching in Dublin is that most of the sites can be reached easily by public transport.

Sites

75	ROGERSTOWN ESTUARY	*Estuary; Brent Geese.*
76	MALAHIDE ESTUARY	*Estuary; Brent Geese.*
77	NORTH BULL	*Estuary; close views of large numbers of birds.*
78	SOUTH DUBLIN BAY	*Divers and grebes, sea-duck, gulls, terns.*

Other sites:

79	Skerries	*Islands; rocky shore; gulls, seabirds.*
80	Howth Head	*Breeding seabirds, seabird and passerine migrants.*
81	Ireland's Eye	*Breeding seabirds.*
82	Baldoyle Estuary	*Estuary, grebes.*

References

Hutchinson, C. *The Birds of Dublin and Wicklow* (IWC, Dublin, 1975).
Jeffrey, D.W. *et al.* (ed) *North Bull Island, Dublin Bay – a Modern Coastal Natural History* (Royal Dublin Society, Dublin, 1977).
Jeffrey, D.W. and Walsh, Edward. *A Student's Guide to North Bull Island* (Royal Dublin Society, Dublin, 1983).
Irish East Coast Bird Report.
McManus, F., McNally, J. and Cooney, T. The Wildfowl and Waders of Rogerstown Estuary (*Irish East Coast Bird Report 1991*: 54–72, 1992).

75 ROGERSTOWN ESTUARY

OSI ½″ map: sheet 13
O25

Habitat

Rogerstown is the most northerly of the Dublin estuaries and is situated in the heart of the rich vegetable-growing belt of north County Dublin. The estuary is broad and muddy, but is divided in two by the causeway which was built in 1844 to carry the railway line between Dublin and Belfast.

Above the causeway, the estuary is very muddy and is edged with salt-marsh at the inner end. The mud is quite treacherous and slopes down

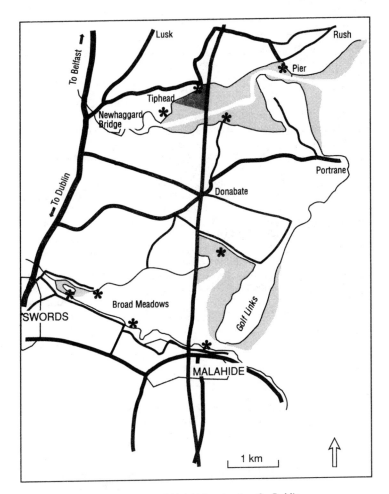

Rogerstown and Malahide estuaries, Co Dublin

135

to the meandering river channel at low tide. There are clumps of *Spartina anglica* and a large expanse of *Salicornia europaea*. On the northern side is a large and expanding tiphead, operated by Dublin County Council since the early 1970s. The tip has reduced the area of mud by about 50 hectares and has covered what used to be one of the main wildfowl feeding areas.

The outer section of the estuary has coarser sediments and is scarred with mussel beds. There are extensive beds of green algae *Enteromorpha* and *Ulva lactuca* which provide feeding for Brent Geese. Large areas of *Ruppia maritima* are grazed by Wigeon. The estuary is partly impounded by terminal sand dune systems to both north and south and narrows sharply before meeting the sea.

The outer portion of the estuary is a National Nature Reserve and a Ramsar site. Although shooting is prohibited at the inner section, this part of the estuary, which includes the tiphead, does not have nature reserve status.

Species

Rogerstown is very much an estuarine site with its best birdwatching between late August and March. The principal wildfowl species here are Brent Geese (up to 800), Shelduck (up to 700), Wigeon (fluctuating from 300–1,100), Teal (up to 900), Mallard (peaking at about 700 in August when local breeding birds assemble), Pintail (20–30) and Shoveler (20–60). In addition, occasional Gadwall are seen and, in among the Brent Geese, one or two Black Brant and one or two Dark-bellied Brent have been seen in most recent years among the Pale-bellied birds.

Numbers of duck have decreased somewhat in the past 20 years.

Wader numbers are quite high with the principal species being Oystercatcher (up to 900), Ringed Plover (up to 180 in autumn), Golden Plover and Lapwing (occasional large flocks in winter, especially after cold weather), Grey Plover (up to 130), Knot (fluctuating between 100 and 1,700), Dunlin (2,000–2,500), Black-tailed Godwit and Bar-tailed Godwit (a hundred or two of each), Curlew (up to 1,000), Redshank (up to 900 in autumn), Greenshank, Spotted Redshank and Green Sandpiper (a few of each).

The estuary is far and away the best place on the east coast to see Green Sandpipers and is also the most likely place to come upon an American vagrant in autumn. Seven species of American wader have been recorded here, with Pectoral Sandpiper the most frequent.

Green Sandpipers can be found in late summer and autumn along the river between Newhaggard Bridge and the saltmarsh, but the land here is privately owned and warning notices have been erected.

Other scarce migrant waders, such as Curlew Sandpipers, Little Stints and Ruffs, have also been seen here in autumn with some regularity.

This is an excellent site for birds of prey in winter. Peregrines and Merlins are regular; Hen Harriers are seen each winter and Buzzard and Marsh Harrier have been seen in recent years. The rough pastures provide suitable habitat for Short-eared Owls which can sometimes be seen in winter.

The fields around the estuary hold large flocks of thrushes and finches in winter and are among the best sites in the country for flocks of Tree Sparrows.

Timing

The estuary is best visited between August and March. Green Sandpipers can be found from July, sometimes June, so an earlier visit could be worthwhile.

Most of the Brent Geese arrive at this site in November.

Access

Take the bus or drive along the main Dublin-Belfast road to a point 5 km north of Swords where the North Dublin Growers Co-Op warehouse can be seen on the right hand side. Turn right here if you have a car and turn right again at the fork about 1 km on, following the signs to Balleally tiphead. If you have travelled by bus, you will have to leave it at the main road and continue on foot.

The tiphead provides the best accesspoint for the western end of the estuary. A track continues to the eastern end as well, but the visitor with a car will prefer to take the road on to the little pier at the mouth of the estuary.

On the south side, the best access route is by the road which runs directly north from Donabate village to the edge of the estuary.

Calendar

All year: Grey Heron, Mute Swan, Shelduck, Mallard, Sparrowhawk, Kestrel, Oystercatcher, Curlew, Herring Gull, Great Black-backed Gull, Stonechat.

Autumn: Passage waders and arriving wintering wildfowl. Green Sandpiper, Common Sandpiper, Ruff, Curlew Sandpiper, possibility of American waders, terns at the mouth of the estuary.

Winter: Brent Goose, duck and wader species, Tree Sparrow.

Spring: Late wildfowl and waders, Whimbrel, Common Sandpiper, terns.

76 MALAHIDE ESTUARY OSI ½″ map: sheet 13
O14 O24

Habitat

This estuary, the next one south after Rogerstown (see map on page 135), is similar in that it is also divided in two by a causeway built to carry the railway northwards from Dublin. The habitat, however, is rather different because the area impounded behind the causeway is here an expanse of open water with only a slight tidal rhythm.

This estuary can be considered to have three principal habitats for birds. East of the railway causeway is open mudflat exposed at low tide and with some mussel beds and extensive swards of *Zostera angustifolia* and the scarcer *Z. noltii.*

Immediately west of the causeway is an area of water known as Broad Meadows (after the River Broad Meadow which empties into it) which is deep and only drops a few centimetres on the ebb tide. This is a popular sailing and windsurfing area.

At the head of this part of the estuary, just below Lissenhall Bridge, is a small area of grassy islands and muddy creeks.

The whole area has changed dramatically in the past 20 years as housing estates have extended around both Malahide and Swords, and as boating has become more popular on the open water.

Arctic Tern

Species

On the open mudflat, a large flock of Brent Geese and smaller numbers of duck winter. Numbers have decreased in recent years. Up to 330 Shelduck, 30 Wigeon, 80 Teal, 50 Mallard and a handful of Pintail occur. Among them are 700 or more Oystercatchers, occasional large flocks of Golden Plover and Lapwing, up to 1,000 Dunlin and smaller numbers of Bar-tailed Godwits, Black-tailed Godwits, Curlews and Redshanks.

The deeper waters at Broad Meadows hold up to 25 Great Crested Grebes, 100 Pochard (as many as 400 have been seen), 100 Goldeneyes, a handful of Scaup, one or two Long-tailed Duck and the possibility of something unusual such as a Smew or a Ring-necked Duck, both of which have been recorded here.

The head of the estuary, traditionally known as Swords estuary, holds a large flock of Mute Swans which have been studied for many years as part of a research programme on the swans of County Dublin. Many of them have white numbered rings on their legs. Indeed, Mute Swans ringed in Dublin as part of this programme have been seen as far east as Wales, as far south as Wexford and as far west as Cork.

The muddy creeks among the small islands at the head of the estuary are perfect habitat for migrant waders in autumn. They have held as many as five species of American wader and hold Spotted Redshank, Curlew Sandpiper, Little Stint and Ruff almost every autumn. Gulls roost here and Mediterranean Gull should be looked for at any time of the year.

In summer and early autumn terns feed in the estuary. Common, Arctic, Sandwich and Little all occur regularly and Roseates from the Rockabill breeding colony occasionally.

Timing

The estuary is best from August through the winter to April. Wildfowl and wader numbers are highest and there is always the possibility of a rarity in autumn. Coverage is best within two hours either side of high tide.

Access

The main wader roost on the outer estuary can be viewed well from the southern shore, about 200 m east of Malahide village. The road along the southern shore of Broad Meadows has several points where a car can be parked and the area scanned in comfort.

A road runs around the entire head of the estuary, providing excellent viewing at a number of points.

Calendar

All year: Grey Heron, Mute Swan, Shelduck, Mallard, Oystercatcher, Curlew, Herring Gull, Great Black-backed Gull.

Autumn: Passage waders and terns; early wildfowl; Ruff, Curlew Sandpiper, possibility of American waders.

Winter: Brent Goose, duck and wader species.

Spring: Late wildfowl and waders, terns.

77 NORTH BULL

Habitat

The North Bull is a dune-covered sandy spit which runs parallel to the coast between Clontarf and Sutton on the northern side of Dublin Bay for a distance of 4.85 km. The island is bordered to the south by the Bull Wall which was completed in 1825 with the objective of improving the approaches to Dublin Harbour. The word 'bull' may derive from 'ball', which means a sand bank. Certainly, there was a sand bank here in the late eighteenth century, which emerged following extensive dredging activities and the construction of new walls on the south side of the port. A map drawn by Captain Bligh (of Bounty fame) in 1800 shows a tiny area of permanent dry sand.

After the Bull Wall was built, the island extended rapidly. Sand was deposited on the seaward side of the bank and what was described by the Directors-General of Inland Navigation in Ireland as soft ooze from the sewers of the city was swept down from the river and deposited on the strand opposite the growing island.

In 1964, a causeway was completed to carry traffic across the middle of the muddy lagoon to the centre of the island.

There are two golf courses on the Bull and the beach on the seaward side is a very popular recreational area.

There are several habitats of special interest to the birdwatcher, and the inter-tidal flats and saltmarsh are the principal ones. The inner side of the Bull, from Clontarf out to Sutton, is an extensive inter-tidal zone where thousands of wildfowl and waders feed at low tide. The area of

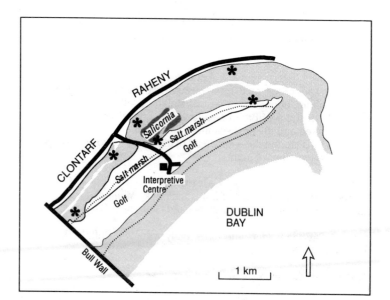

North Bull Island, Co Dublin

140

flats to the north of the causeway comprises a mixture of bare mud and *Salicornia*-covered mudflat. Farther to the north, and to the south of the causeway, most of the remaining inter-tidal flats are comprised of sandier sediments.

Above the intertidal zone, an extensive saltmarsh runs almost the entire length of the island between the dune complex and the high water mark of neap tides. When there are high spring tides, the entire saltmarsh is inundated at high water. The saltmarsh has numerous drainage channels and shallow, muddy pans.

Towards the tip of the island, about 1 km from the end, is the Alder Marsh, an area of lowlying ground with a stand of alder trees and a terrestrial marsh vegetation. This habitat, quite different from others on the Bull, attracts occasional passerine migrants.

The Bull has been much studied and written about. A very attractive little book, *An Irish Sanctuary – Birds of the North Bull*, was published in 1953 by Rev P.G. Kennedy S.J. but is long out of print. More recently, the Royal Dublin Society sponsored the publication of a major volume on the natural history of the island (see references) and a slim paperback, entitled *A Students' Guide to North Bull Island*, subsequently appeared which distilled the main points.

Dublin Corporation, which manages the island, has an Interpretative Centre at the island end of the causeway.

Species

The great attraction of the North Bull is that so many species can be seen so closely within the confines of a capital city. At the end of 1992, a total of 198 species had been recorded. The variety of habitats provides opportunity for seeing virtually anything, even the strange discovery on the beach of the remains of both Bridled and Royal Tern.

Off the point and out to sea, divers, grebes, Common Scoters and seabirds which have come into Dublin Bay can be seen. On the sandy beach few birds occur apart from a flock of Ringed Plovers and Sanderling at the Point, though White Wagtails sometimes pass through in autumn and Snow Buntings occasionally feed by the high water mark.

The inter-tidal zone between the island and the shore is where the most spectacular sights are to be seen. Up to 1,500 Brent Geese, 1,300 Shelduck, 2,000 Wigeon, 1,500 Teal, 100 Mallard, 400 Pintail, 330 Shoveler and small numbers of Red-breasted Mergansers are the main wildfowl species.

The geese feed in different areas depending on the time of year. In early November they feed on what remains of the *Zostera* beds at Sutton strand and on mats of *Enteromorpha* near Kilbarrack. From early December many move onto grassland around Dublin Bay. They feed on the football pitches in St Anne's Park, across the road from the Bull causeway, on the golf courses and on mown grass close to the road at Clontarf.

The Shelduck congregate at both sides of the causeway where they feed on the small snail *Hydrobia*. Wigeon, which graze exclusively, concentrate off Raheny but can be found all along the inter-tidal flats. Teal, which have a more catholic diet, also gather at Raheny, but the largest numbers are found on the *Salicornia* flats. Pintail are found mainly between Raheny and the causeway, and Mallard and Shoveler both favour the outlets of the streams to the south of the causeway. All the common duck species can usually be seen at low tide from the causeway as they feed or roost on the mud on both sides. Depending on the light, they can be seen well from the road on the mainland or from the causeway.

Many rarer ducks have been seen including American Wigeon, Black Duck, Blue-winged Teal and Green-winged Teal. Gadwall occur occasionally.

Even larger numbers of waders winter, but they use the North Bull as a roosting area and spread out over much of Dublin Bay to feed. Only when the tide is flooding in do large numbers feed in the Bull channel. The roosts, however, are spectacular and include at peak 2,200 Oystercatchers (autumn), 300 Ringed Plovers (autumn), 350 Grey Plovers, 2,000 Knots, 6,000 Dunlins, 250 Black-tailed Godwits, 1,800 Bar-tailed Godwits, 1,000 Curlews, 1,600 Redshanks (autumn) and 250 Turnstones. Peak numbers of most species occur in winter, but some, as indicated, pass through in larger numbers. All these birds roost on the saltmarsh but many of them feed on the south side of Dublin Bay (see the account which follows) or off Clontarf.

Scarcer species such as Spotted Redshank, Ruff, Curlew Sandpiper and Little Stint are annual. Rarities include Buff-breasted Sandpiper, Pectoral Sandpiper and Wilson's Phalarope, the last of which has been recorded three times. Avocets have been seen at the North Bull on a number of occasions and at one stage in the early 1970s seemed likely to winter every year. The appearance of six in November 1992 marked a welcome return.

The Bull has a large wintering gull population, but tends not to be the best place for rarer species. In summer a small colony of Little Terns struggles against all the odds to produce young on a popular beach and, in some years, succeeds. A handful of pairs of Ringed Plovers nest among the terns.

In autumn and winter the Alder Marsh and dunes are worth scouring.

Several Short-eared Owls usually winter on the saltmarsh and in the vicinity of the golf courses. The southern end of the saltmarsh is usually the best place to look for them. Peregrines and Merlins are frequent in winter. Passerine migrants such as Wheatears, infrequent Whinchats, and just occasionally something more exotic such as a Lapland Bunting or Shore Lark have been seen.

Close to the Bull Wall a small party of Snow Buntings can usually be found on the beach in mid-winter.

The Bull Wall itself prvides good views of divers and Red-breasted Mergansers in winter and has a small number of Purple Sandpipers among the Turnstones at the tip. In summer it is a good place for watching terns.

Timing

The Bull is worth a visit at any time of the year. The best time for wildfowl and waders is from August to March, but interesting birds can turn up at any season and, in summer, there are usually breeding Little Terns.

Covering the entire North Bull takes most of a day, but to see the wildfowl and waders best try to ensure that part of your visit covers the period within three hours of high tide. The duck are best watched from the road rather than the island as walking on the saltmarsh causes disturbance.

Access

To see most of the species in a short time, make your way to the causeway opposite St Anne's and walk along the path beside the road to both south and north. Having seen the duck on either side of the causeway, walk across the causeway and scan the flats on either side. Many of the common wader species should be seen.

A thorough visit requires much more time. Ideally, the visit should start at Clontarf and combine a walk along the shoreline opposite the North Bull as far as Kilbarrack with a complete traverse of the saltmarsh and a visit to the Alder Marsh.

Calendar

All year: Cormorant, Shelduck, Mallard, Oystercatcher, Curlew.

Autumn: Returning wildfowl and waders, including first Brent Geese. Migrant waders including Curlew Sandpiper and Little Stint. Possibility of migrant passerines.

Winter: Red-throated Diver, Great Northern Diver, Brent Geese, Wigeon, Teal, Pintail, Shoveler, large numbers of waders, especially Dunlin, Knots and Bar-tailed Godwits, small numbers of Purple Sandpipers on the Bull Wall. One or two Black Brant and possibly a Dark-bellied Brent Goose. Short-eared Owls, Snow Buntings.

Spring: Late wildfowl and waders. Brent Geese remain into early May. In May there is movement of Whimbrels, Ringed Plovers and Sanderling.

78 SOUTH DUBLIN BAY
OSI ½″ map: sheet 16
O13 O23 O24

Habitat

South Dublin Bay is a broad arc, which swings from the Poolbeg Lighthouse at the mouth of Dublin port around Sandymount and Merrion strands and out to Dun Laoghaire. The habitat includes the shallow water of Dublin Bay, the extensive sand flats of the inter-tidal zone, the weedy edges of the piers and the small marsh at Booterstown.

The bay is very shallow; the 5-fathom line stretches north from Dun Laoghaire more or less directly to Howth Head. This depth provides feeding for divers, grebes and sea-duck in winter and for terns in summer and autumn. The low tide mark runs from close to Blackrock north to the South Wall. A number of shallow pools mark the strand, the largest of which is known as the cockle lake. Cockles are in profusion across the sand. There is a large bed of *Zostera* which provides feeding for Brent Geese.

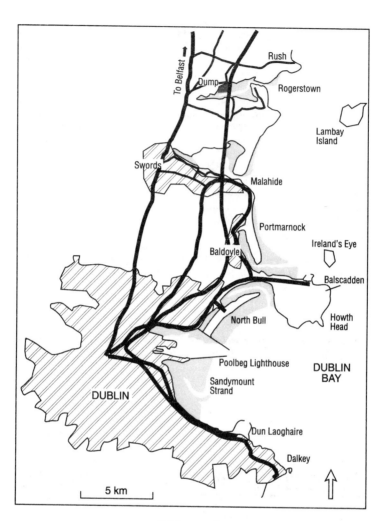

Dublin estuaries

Both the South Wall and the West Pier, Dun Laoghaire project well out into Dublin Bay and provide vantage points for scanning the water for duck.

Species

The shallow waters attract divers, grebes and duck in winter. Great Northern and Red-throated are regular. Black-throated occurs in most but not in all winters. Great Crested Grebes are regular off both the South Wall and the West Pier. Slavonian has been seen and Red-necked has also been recorded, but very rarely. The commonest sea-duck are Common Scoter and there are usually 25–50 between the South Wall and Dun Laoghaire. A few Red-breasted Mergansers and Goldeneyes and one or two Long-tailed Ducks are also usual.

Flocks of gulls feed around the piers and roost on the water. Among the commoner species are the occasional Iceland or Glaucous in winter and at almost any season there is the possibility of Mediterranean, Little or Ring-billed. All of these species are annual in Dublin Bay. The piers at Poolbeg or Dun Laoghaire and the sand at Merrion Gates, when the tide is rising, are among the best places to search.

On the strand there are 250–350 Brent Geese in late winter and a few Wigeon, but the most numerous birds are waders. Flocks of Oyster-catchers (up to 800), Bar-tailed Godwits (up to 100), Sanderling (up to 220), Ringed Plovers (up to 130), Redshanks (up to 200), Knots (up to 200) and Curlews (up to 50) feed on the beach, with smaller numbers of other species. At one time it was thought that these were all birds from the North Bull which move over here to feed, but it is now known that many of the waders feeding on the south side of Dublin Bay roost here as well.

The strand in late July and August is a quite spectacular place with large numbers of roosting terns. Towards dusk, thousands of terns, which have been feeding on the sand banks several kilometres east of Dublin Bay, fly in to settle on the beach. Most of them are Common and Arctic Terns but Roseate Terns, presumably from Rockabill, can usually be distinguished by call and, in calm weather when the birds are approachable, by plumage tone as well. An occasional Black Tern turns up at this time of year in most years. The calls of the terns as they rise before a flooding tide are a wonderful sound on a clear night.

Behind the railway line at Booterstown is a small marsh which holds Teal and Snipe and, at high tide, small numbers of roosting waders.

The piers at both the South Wall and Dun Laoghaire have small populations of Purple Sandpipers as well as the ubiquitous Turnstones. The West Pier sometimes has Snow Buntings in late winter and occasional winter and late autumn Black Redstarts.

Access

The entire south side of the bay is ringed by roads and can be viewed at many points. The DART rapid transit railway line stops at stations at Booterstown, Blackrock, Seapoint and Dun Laoghaire which provide immediate access to the shore and good points for placing a telescope.

A thorough search of the area would start with a drive out towards the South Wall, parking the car at Poolbeg and walking out to the lighthouse. Return, stopping the car at various points where birds are congregating, finally parking near Seapoint and walk out along the West Pier. On a Sunday afternoon, the Pier is thronged with people taking the air or walking their dogs, but there are usually a number of birdwatchers among them.

Timing

South Dublin Bay is interesting at any season, but is best from late July through to May. The South Wall and the West Pier are best at high tide, when the feeding divers, grebes and ducks come closest. The sandy beach is best a couple of hours before high tide, when the feeding waders and gulls are pushed close to the road.

Calendar

Autumn: Common Scoter, possibility of Little Gull, terns including Roseate Tern and occasional Black Tern, waders.

Winter: Red-throated Diver, Great Northern Diver, Great Crested Grebe,

Brent Goose, Wigeon, Common Scoter, Goldeneye, Long-tailed Duck, Red-breasted Merganser, Sanderling, Purple Sandpiper, gulls including likelihood of Mediterranean, Ring-billed, Iceland and Glaucous Gulls, Black Redstart, Snow Bunting.

Spring: Late divers, grebes, duck, waders, Whimbrel, arriving terns.

OTHER DUBLIN SITES

79 SKERRIES

OSI ½″ map: sheet 13
O25 O26

Habitat and Species

Skerries is a small coastal village with a largely stony shoreline and several small flat-topped islands offshore. The shoreline holds wintering Brent Geese (up to 200 in late winter), Wigeon (up to 150), Oyster-catchers, Ringed Plovers, Grey Plovers, Dunlin, Sanderling, Redshanks and Curlews. On the islands a few Greylag Geese winter each year.

Large numbers of gulls winter on the shoreline. Up to 2,000 Great Black-backed Gulls congregate in September, but numbers are reduced in winter to 500–700. Both Iceland and Glaucous Gulls are regular.

This is a good seawatching spot. Good passage of Manx Shearwaters and Fulmars is recorded and small numbers of Storm Petrels pass between July and October. Arctic, Great and Pomarine Skuas are seen each autumn and Long-tailed Skuas were recorded in 1991.

In summer there are breeding Shags, Cormorants, Great Black-backed Gulls, Lesser Black-backed Gulls and Herring Gulls on the islands. Roseate Terns breed on Rockabill island about 6 km off the coast and can be seen from Skerries in summer when they fish along the coastline.

Access

Skerries is easily visited by car, train or bus. The harbour lies north of Rush and is reached by turning right off the main Dublin-Belfast road about 5 km north of Swords. Follow the signposts through Lusk to Skerries.

80 HOWTH HEAD

OSI ½″ map: sheet 13
O23 O33

Habitat and Species

At the northern extremity of Dublin Bay the hilly promontory of Howth Head drops sharply to the sea at its north-east and eastern sides, the resulting cliffs providing nest sites for a growing seabird nesting colony. There are a number of gardens, many of which are not accessible, but some between Howth Harbour and Balscadden can be viewed.

There were only a few gulls, some Black Guillemots and a handful of pairs of Manx Shearwaters breeding here in the late 1940s. The shear-waters may still nest, though nobody knows for certain, but there are now over 100 Fulmar nest sites, 1,700 Kittiwake nests, several hundred pairs of breeding Guillemots and Razorbills, a few pairs of Cormorants and Shags, several Black Guillemot nest sites and small numbers of gulls. Up to about ten years ago, there were about 1,000 pairs of Herring Gulls nesting here, but numbers have declined drastically. The breeding colony is easily seen. A small roof-nesting population in the village has not declined with the coastal population.

Seabird passage can be worthwhile. Manx Shearwaters often occur in good numbers and Arctic and Great Skuas are fairly frequent. Storm Petrels are regular from July to October. Rarer species seen off Howth Head include Sooty Shearwater, Pomarine and Long-tailed Skua.

Passerine migrants certainly appear on the Head, but many of the best looking sites are in very private gardens. However, an area of hillside near Balscadden on the north-east side of the Head produced Radde's Warbler, Pallas's Warbler, Firecrest and a number of other migrants in October 1988, and local birdwatchers usually find migrant Ring Ouzels and Grasshopper Warblers here in early May without too much difficulty. Blackcaps, Garden Warblers, Whinchats and the occasional Redstart are regular in autumn.

Access

Howth Harbour is readily accessible by bus. The Harbour itself should be looked at for interesting gulls. Then walk east along Balscadden Road and follow the track which leads along the top of the cliff. From this path, many of the nesting seabirds can be seen.

Seabird watching can be carried out from the Nose of Howth, but the cliffs are dangerous and great care should be taken if visiting them. Passerine migrants should be searched for in the trees and on the hill-side around the north-east side of the head, in the gardens between the harbour and the carpark at Balscadden, and in the gardens near the Baily lighthouse. Remember that all these gardens are private property and should not be entered without permission.

81 IRELAND'S EYE

OSI ½″ map: sheet 16
O24

Habitat and Species

Just to the north of Howth Head lies the small island of Ireland's Eye. The island has grassy slopes with steep cliffs on the north-east corner and a sheer stack offshore. There is a martello tower at the north-west corner.

The island has an important seabird breeding colony. Its small Gannet colony is the most recent in Ireland. Breeding commenced in 1989, and by 1992 there were 47 nests. The most numerous nesting birds are the Kittiwakes (950 nests), Guillemots (over 700 pairs) and Razor-bills (over 150 pairs). Fulmars, Cormorants, Shags and Black Guillemots also breed and there is a small colony of Great Black-backed, Lesser Black-backed and Herring Gulls. As elsewhere along the coast, the Herring Gull population has collapsed in recent years. There were over 1,000 nests in the early 1970s, but now there are only a handful.

A very few Puffins nest here. Nine pairs were estimated in 1987.

Shelduck, Oystercatcher, Ringed Plover and Whitethroat also breed on the island.

Manx Shearwaters were believed to be nesting and were proved to do so in the early 1950s.

In winter both Brent and Greylag Geese frequently graze the grassy slopes. They can be seen from the mainland without much difficulty.

Access

The only way to visit Ireland's Eye is to hire a boat. During the summer, trips are easily arranged at Howth Harbour.

To see the seabirds and particularly the Gannets well, the boat should be taken around the entire island.

82 BALDOYLE ESTUARY

OSI ½″ map: sheets 13, 16
O24 O23

Habitat and Species

Baldoyle is the smallest of the impressive chain of estuaries which stretches along the Dublin coast from Rogerstown to Dun Laoghaire, and it is also the one most damaged by the growth of *Spartina anglica*. The estuary is a narrow finger-like bay, sheltered from the sea by sand dunes which provide, as at Malahide and the North Bull, an excellent surface for golf links. The head of the estuary, near the village of Portmarnock, is like a field of *Spartina* and rather few birds are found.

In winter, surface-feeding duck congregate around the freshwater stream which enters the estuary at Mayne Bridge. Small numbers of Shelduck, Wigeon, Teal and Pintail are found. Further south in the estuary, Brent Geese and waders feed at low tide. The species are similar to those found at the nearby North Bull: Oystercatcher and Dunlin are the most numerous.

The beach on the seaward side of Portmarnock sand dunes holds good numbers of Sanderling and large numbers of gulls. Offshore there are usually Red-throated Divers, Great Northern Divers, Great Crested Grebes, Common Scoters and Red-breasted Mergansers. One or two Slavonian Grebes are usually here in winter. The inlet to the estuary at high tide is probably the best place on the Dublin coast for seeing this species.

A few pairs of Ringed Plovers nest at Portmarnock Point and Little Terns attempt to breed each year.

Access

The estuary can be watched easily from the road between Sutton and Portmarnock which runs along the west side of Baldoyle Bay. The strand can be walked from Portmarnock.

WICKLOW

Introduction

The landscape of Wicklow is dominated by the granite and slate of its mountains, contrasting sharply with the limestone lowlands of Dublin.

West and central Wicklow is mountainous and still has a considerable area of blanket bog. The highest mountain in Ireland outside Kerry is Lugnaquillia, but there are a number of other peaks jutting up from the spine of land over 300 m which runs down the centre of the county.

Some of the bog on these mountains has been drained and coniferous forests planted on it and the rough pasture and heathland farther down the hillsides. Below the rough pasture is permanent pasture with numerous hedges and small deciduous plantations. The whole area provides habitat for Hen Harriers, a few pairs of which nest in young plantations, Ravens, Peregrines, Stonechats, Chaffinches, Siskins, Linnets, Reed Buntings and, in summer, Whinchats and Grasshopper Warblers. The coniferous plantations at Cruagh Wood, Coronation Plantation and Lough Tay provide habitat for Crossbills which should be looked for between July and September.

There are a number of fine stands of deciduous woodland which provide breeding habitat for Goldcrests, Chiffchaffs, Blackcaps and a small number of Wood Warblers and Redstarts. Pied Flycatchers have bred on occasions in the past and should be looked for. The oakwoods at the Vale of Clara and the Glen of the Downs, the mixed woods at the Devil's Glen, Shillelagh and Glendalough and the hazel woods at Glenasmole are examples of a relatively scarce Irish habitat.

The coast is mainly lowlying, but is broken by the promontories of Bray Head and Wicklow Head where seabirds nest. Behind the sandy and shingle beach, which runs from Greystones to Wicklow, is lowlying poorly drained pasture and reedbeds with several small pools at Kilcoole and Newcastle and a lagoon at Broad Lough. There is another small pond at Arklow, used in summer for boating, but interesting in winter for birds. The sandy beach from Wicklow town south extends on eventually to Wexford Harbour.

Wicklow has a large body of standing water at Blessington Reservoir in the north-west corner of the county near the Dublin border. Several other lakes in the mountains such as Lough Tay, Lough Dan, the Glendalough lakes and the Vartry Reservoir are deep and only occasionally good for wild swans or a few duck.

Sites

| 83 | KILCOOLE | *Coastal lagoon; breeding terns.* |
| 84 | BROAD LOUGH | *Coastal lagoon; breeding Reed Warblers.* |

Other sites:

85	Bray Head	*Breeding seabirds.*
86	Wicklow Head	*Breeding and passage seabirds. Passerine migrants.*
87	Blessington Reservoir	*Greylag Geese, wildfowl.*
88	Glendalough	*Woodland.*
89	Devil's Glen	*Woodland.*
90	Glenmalure	*Mountains; Ring Ouzel.*

References

Hutchinson, C. *The Birds of Dublin and Wicklow* (IWC, Dublin, 1975).
Irish East Coast Bird Report.

83 KILCOOLE

OSI ½″ map: sheet 16/
1:50,000 map: sheet 56
O30

Habitat

Kilcoole marsh lies south of Greystones on the flat stretch of lowland lying behind the shingle bank stretching south to Wicklow Head. The railway line from Dublin to Wexford runs along the bank. It consists of a series of channels where small streams meander about the fields before converging and cutting through the shingle bank to the sea. The cut, known as the 'breeches', carries the tide in as well as providing an exit for the river. Hence the channels are muddy and estuarine in appearance. Scattered about the area are a number of small, brackish pools. In recent years embankments have been built to restrict the effect of flooding and sheep have grazed the grassland.

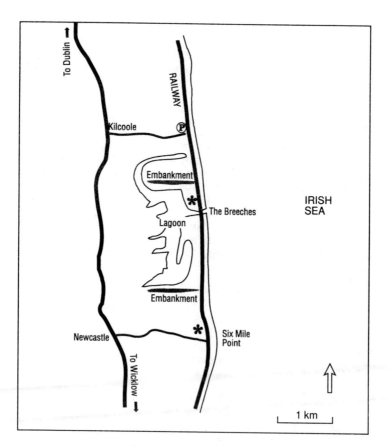

Kilcoole, Co Wicklow

Species

In winter quite large numbers of wildfowl use this area. Up to 400 Grey-lag Geese, 500 Brent Geese and small numbers of both Bewick's and Whooper Swans are perhaps the most spectacular. The largest numbers of Brent Geese are seen in March when they move onto grassland, having exhausted the easier pickings on the north Dublin estuaries, though they return to Dublin Bay each evening to roost. Some hundreds of Wigeon, Teal and Mallard also winter. A few Pintail, Shoveler, Gadwall and Shelduck also occur in most winters.

Wader numbers are lower than on the nearby north Dublin estuaries as would be expected. Curlews and Redshanks are much the most numerous species, but there is diversity. Ruffs, Little Stints, Spotted Redshanks and Green Sandpipers are probably annual. Rarities seen in recent years include Baird's Sandpiper and Lesser Yellowlegs. Ringed Plovers and Oystercatchers both breed.

Off the beach Red-throated Divers are scattered along the shore in winter. Little Gulls appear with more frequency and in greater numbers than anywhere else in Ireland. The largest numbers are usually in February and up to 400 have been seen at Greystones, with smaller numbers farther south at Kilcoole.

In summer Little Terns and Ringed Plovers nest on the beach. The Little Tern colony has been very successful in most recent years, partly because of regular wardening and the construction of enclosures around the nests to protect them. Unfortunately, these enclosures proved counter-productive in 1990 when a Kestrel found that they provided ideal perches for convenient dining on the chicks.

In autumn sea passage can be sizeable. Large numbers of Manx Shearwaters pass and occasional Great and Arctic Skuas are among them.

Migrant passerines are often present on this coast in spring and autumn, especially Whinchats in autumn, and several species of bird of prey are regular. Kestrel and Merlin are the most regular in winter but Hen Harrier, Peregrine and Sparrowhawk are occasional, and Marsh Harrier sometimes appears in May.

Access

Much the best way to see the birds of this coast is to walk south along the side of the railway track from Greystones. This gives opportunities to see birds at sea, on the beach and on the fields to the north of Kilcoole. Walk at least as far as the breaches before turning back and walking to Kilcoole railway station where a road leads up to Kilcoole village and a bus stop. Alternatively, the visitor can walk as far as Newcastle railway station where a similar road leads to a bus stop in Newcastle village.

For a quick inspection of the marsh, travel to Kilcoole village and turn left there for the strand. Park the car at the car park by the railway station and walk south along the side of the railway track. The marsh is private property and should not be entered upon.

Timing

Kilcoole is best in autumn and winter for wildfowl and waders. Early spring is the best time for Little Gulls and summer is obviously the time for nesting Little Terns.

A calm day makes birdwatching easiest at Kilcoole. The state of tide makes very little difference.

Calendar

Autumn: Early ducks and waders including Curlew, Redshank, Greenshank, Dunlin, possibility of Little Stint, Ruff, Green Sandpiper. Seawatching from the old station.

Winter: Whooper Swan, Bewick's Swan, Greylag Goose, some Brent Geese, Wigeon, Teal, possibility of Pintail, Shoveler and Gadwall, Dunlin, Curlew, Redshank, Little Gull.

Spring: Late ducks and waders, large numbers of Little Gulls at times.

Summer: Breeding Ringed Plover and Little Tern; early seabird passage.

84   BROAD LOUGH

OSI ½″ map: sheet 16/
1:50,000 map: sheet 56
T39

Habitat

Broad Lough lies about 10 km south of Kilcoole and is in a similar situation behind the shingle bank. However, it is a much broader expanse of water, though the edge is muddy and estuarine in appearance because of the tidal inflow at the southern end. The Vartry river reaches the sea through Broad Lough after flowing east from Ashford and the Devil's Glen. The lough is long, narrow and very shallow at the southern end; at its northern extremity it broadens out into a reed-fringed lake. Shooting is prohibited and the area is an Irish Wildbird Conservancy reserve by arrangement with certain of the local landowners. The site is not wardened.

Species

This is an excellent site for wintering swans, geese and ducks. Mute Swans are the commonest swan species, but Whooper Swans occur most winters and Bewick's Swans are seen in hard weather. A flock of 100–250 Greylag Geese moves between this lough and Kilcoole to the north and appears to be expanding in size. Small numbers of Shelduck and larger numbers of Teal, Wigeon and Mallard winter. Occasional parties of White-fronted Geese spend a few days but this is not a regular site.

The most common waders are Curlews and Redshanks, but most of the common species occur in small numbers in autumn and winter.

There is a fine roost of gulls and terns in autumn, and both Little Gull and Mediterranean Gull are regular.

This site would repay much more frequent observation in autumn as it seems ideal for passage migrants.

In summer Reed and Grasshopper Warblers breed. Bearded Tits have bred here in the past. This is an ideal site for seeing Water Rails with their chicks in late June or July. Normally very elusive, the birds show well on calm mornings and evenings.

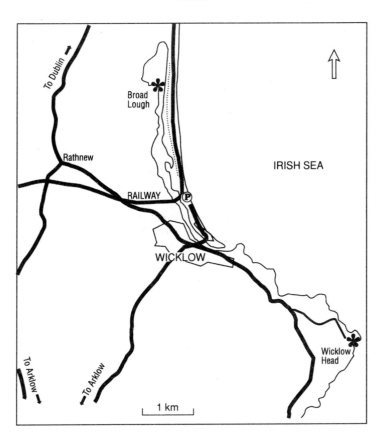

Broad Lough and Wicklow Head, Co Wicklow

Access
Broad Lough is approached most readily from Wicklow town. Travel north along the seafront and out onto the grassy path which runs north along the edge of the sea. At the end of the path there is a turnstile on the left where the railway track can be crossed. The lough can be approached from here.

Timing
This is best from autumn through winter to spring. As with Kilcoole, the state of tide does not matter greatly.

Calendar
Autumn: Early ducks and waders including Dunlin, possibility of Little Stint, Ruff, Curlew, Redshank, Greenshank, Green Sandpiper.

Winter: Occasional Whooper Swan, regular Greylag Goose, Wigeon, Teal, possibility of Shoveler, Dunlin, Curlew, Redshank, Little Gull.

Spring: Late ducks and waders, Little Gulls.

OTHER WICKLOW SITES

85 BRAY HEAD

Habitat and Species

Bray Head has the only cliffs between Dublin Bay and Wicklow Head. A granite cliff rises from the sea for about 25 m to the Dublin to Wexford railway track which runs round the headland. Above the railway line, the cliff rises another 50–70 m to a public footpath. Above the path there are further cliffs.

The cliffs below the railway hold a colony of nesting seabirds of which the Black Guillemots are the most striking, being easily visible from the train as it passes the cliffs. About 60 pairs of Fulmar, a few Cormorants, Shags and Herring Gulls, over 750 pairs of Kittiwake and 50–100 pairs each of Razorbill, Guillemot and Black Guillemot breed. Manx Shearwaters have been heard calling over the head in summer but birds have not been seen on the ground since the late 1960s. An interesting investigation would be a search for birds outside nesting burrows in summer.

A Puffin was seen here in 1987, but breeding has not been proved. Ravens also nest on these cliffs.

Access

The cliffs are best viewed from the public footpath which runs around the headland, above the line of the railway. Direct access to the seabird cliffs is difficult and not advisable, both because it is dangerous and likely to cause unnecessary disturbance. Most of the birds can be seen quite well from the footpath.

86 WICKLOW HEAD

Habitat and Species

This is the most easterly projecting headland south of Co Down and, while it has cliffs with nesting seabirds, it is at least as important as a birdwatching site for its potential for seawatching and passerine migrants.

The nesting seabirds are rather similar to those at Bray Head to the north and include Fulmars, Shags, Herring Gulls, Great Black-backed Gulls, Kittiwakes, Guillemots, Razorbills and Black Guillemots. The colony is doing well, with most species increasing. Peregrines and Ravens also nest here.

On the head itself a few native Grey Partridges may still be found, and one or two introduced Red-legged Partridges may also survive. For many years, this has been one of the most reliable sites in Ireland for the rapidly disappearing Grey Partridge, but numbers have reduced and the birds may even have become extinct here.

The headland is an excellent seawatching site and the trees and hedges on the way out to the head provide cover which looks ideal for land migrants. There is more cover to the south of the head which could be good for holding birds after a fall. In recent years, Pied Flycatcher, Black Redstart and Yellow-browed Warbler have been seen in autumn and Wood Warbler and good numbers of Grasshopper Warblers in spring.

Access

The head is reached by driving south from Wicklow town on the main road for Wexford. Turn left down a narrow road about a kilometre after leaving the town. This road leads to the lighthouse at the tip of the head.

87 BLESSINGTON RESERVOIR

OSI ½″ map: sheet 16
N91 N90 O01 O00

Habitat and Species

The large reservoir at Blessington, which supplies much of the water for Dublin city, is an excellent site for Greylag Geese and ducks.

Between 200 and 400 Greylag Geese occur in winter, but numbers vary throughout the season, probably because there is movement to and from the nearby coast. Small numbers of Whooper and, less often, Bewick's Swans occur as well. Wigeon, Teal, Mallard, Pochard, Tufted Ducks and Goldeneyes winter. Mallard and Tufted Duck nest, as do Common Sandpipers.

This lake holds a large winter flock of Lesser Black-backed Gulls.

While the ducks are scattered around the lake, the geese tend to prefer the south-western end near Valleymount.

Access

The road provides access to most of the reservoir. Drive south-west from Dublin through Tallaght and on to Blessington. Follow the road around the reservoir, stopping when birds are seen.

88 GLENDALOUGH

OSI ½″ map: sheet 16
T19 T09

Habitat and Species

Glendalough, with its monastic settlement and spectacular views of two lakes and high cliffs, is a famous Wicklow beauty spot and is much visited by tourists in summer. The birdwatcher will be attracted more by the deciduous woodlands which provide nest sites for a wider diversity of species than can be found in most Irish counties. As well as Chaffinches, Chiffchaffs, Robins and Wrens, these woods hold Sparrowhawks, Blackcaps and a small scattering of Wood Warblers and occasional Redstarts. Above the woods, on the rocky slopes, one or two Ring Ouzels breed, but they are extremely difficult to find. A visit in May or early June is essential for seeking these passerines, as they are best picked up on song. Early morning is best and Wood Warblers can usually be found in the pines beside the car park.

Grasshopper Warblers breed by the lower lake and Dippers can be seen throughout the year on the stream between the two lakes.

In winter there are sometimes Whooper Swans on the lakes.

Wren

Access

Take the road to Laragh, and follow the signposts to Glendalough, about 3 km west of the village. There is a large public car park and a number of walks through the woodland on the southern side of the lakes.

89   DEVIL'S GLEN

OSI ½″ map: sheet 16
T29

Habitat and Species

This is another deciduous wood with similar species to those in the woodland at Glendalough. It consists of an area of deciduous woodland in the valley of the Vartry river above the town of Ashford. There are no lakes and no habitat suitable for Ring Ouzels, but it is a beautiful place for a walk on an early morning in late May or June. Wood Warblers nest here in some years and Blackcaps are quite common.

Access

From Ashford, take the road west for Annamoe. After about 1.5 km the road crosses the river. A car park is on the right a few hundred metres later. There are paths here leading along the edge of the river.

90   GLENMALURE

OSI ½″ map: sheet 16
T09

Habitat and Species

Much wilder than the Devil's Glen and Glendalough, this Wicklow valley is long, rugged and glaciated. There is a rocky hillside on the north-east side of the road which holds Ring Ouzels. They are difficult to find, but can sometimes be picked up by listening for their distinctive call. The Glenmalur river tumbles down the valley and there are several patches of deciduous wood which hold Blackcaps and, at times, Wood Warbler and Redstart as well as the commoner breeding birds.

Peregrines nest in this area and there is also the possibility of Merlin and Hen Harrier. Kestrels are common. Red Grouse nest on the open moor, though they are nowhere numerous.

Access

Drive south from Laragh on the road for Rathdrum. After 2 km take the turn to the right which rises through Derrybawn wood (another good site for Wood Warbler) onto open mountain. This is an old military road built to provide access for the British army to rebel retreats. Follow the road until you reach the cross roads at Drumgoff Bridge in Glenmalure. Turn right here and follow the road up to the carpark at Baravore. This is a good stopping place and one of the best sites for finding Ring Ouzels. Peregrine, Raven, Siskin and Redpoll can usually be seen (or heard) from the carpark and Crossbills can be found in the plantation opposite it.

WEXFORD

Introduction

Wexford is one of the best birdwatching counties in Ireland, with a list of species recorded second only to that of Cork. Its location in the south-east of the country marks the first landfall for many spring migrants returning from Africa; its estuaries and lagoons are habitat for a diversity of wildfowl and wader species; the great reclaimed sloblands in Wexford Harbour are the best goose wintering area in the country; and the relatively short distance from Dublin means that it is well watched.

The eastern coastline is lowlying, with long sandy beaches backed by fine dune systems. The shallow waters here provide feeding for sea-ducks, divers and grebes. Wexford Harbour is the only estuary facing east, but the extensive mudflats, with the reclaimed land on either side, make it one of the most important wetland habitats in Ireland. Carnsore Point, at the south-east corner of Ireland, is a good seawatching point.

The south facing coastline has a spectacular choice of bird habitats. The brackish lagoons of Lady's Island Lake and Tacumshin hold a rich diversity of wildfowl and waders. Farther west the muddy estuaries at The Cull and Bannow Bay are typical of the series of estuaries which stretch right along the south coast of Ireland to west Cork. Offshore, the Saltee Islands have over 50,000 breeding seabirds on the cliffs and Great Saltee is also one of the best migration watchpoints in the country. Hook Head, on the western edge of the county, does not have large seabird breeding colonies but rivals Saltee in the number of scarce passerine migrant species seen. It is also a good seawatching point.

Inland, the Blackstairs Mountains in the north-west of the county hold nesting Red Grouse and Hen Harriers. Farming is varied and the county has a great deal of tillage. Many wooded areas remain, however, and these are the habitat for the common woodland songbirds.

The slow-moving River Slaney flows through the middle of the county. In its lower reaches, extensive reedbeds hold nesting Sedge

Warblers and, increasingly, Reed Warblers as well as Reed Buntings, Moorhens and Water Rails.

So, while Wexford is a very rich county ornithologically, the accounts which follow will concentrate on the major sites. This should not deter the visitor from exploring the many other parts of this wonderful county.

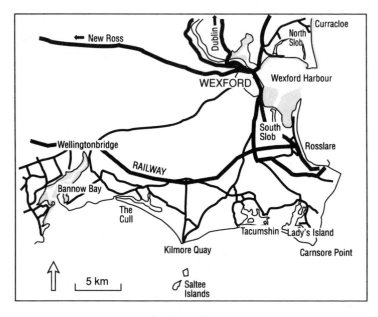

South-east Wexford

Sites

91	NORTH SLOB	*Geese; ducks; estuary.*
92	LADY'S ISLAND LAKE	*Shallow lake; ducks.*
93	TACUMSHIN LAKE	*Brackish lagoon; rare waders.*
94	SALTEE ISLANDS	*Seabird breeding colony; passerine migrants.*
95	HOOK HEAD	*Seawatching; passerine migrants.*
96	BANNOW BAY	*Estuary.*

Other sites:

97	Carnsore Point	*Seawatching; passerine migrants.*
98	The Cull	*Estuary.*
99	Rosslare Back Strand	*Estuary.*

References

Lovatt, J, K. *Birds of Hook Head 1883–1983* (IWC, 1984).

Merne, Oscar J. *The Birds of Wexford, Ireland* (South East Tourism and Bord Failte, 1974).

Perry, Kenneth W. and Warburton, Stephen W. *The Birds and Flowers of the Saltee Islands* (Privately published, Belfast, 1977).

Roche, R. and Merne, O. *Saltees: Islands of Birds and Legends* (O'Brien Press, Dublin, 1977).

91 NORTH SLOB

Habitat

The North Slob, on the north side of Wexford Harbour, consists of 1,000 hectares of lowlying land reclaimed from the sea in the 1840s. A dyke constructed from just north of Raven Point at the entrance to Wexford Harbour to the shore near Wexford town enclosed a large area of inter-tidal mud and several islands. These islands remain as low undulations on the otherwise flat expanse of farmland. A wide channel runs through the west, north and east of the Slob and this collects much of the rainwater which drains off the land. Drainage ditches separate many of the fields and empty into larger channels. A pump station at the southern edge of the channel is operated by the North Slob Commissioners to ensure that surplus water is pumped into Wexford Harbour.

The land has been farmed since it was reclaimed and there are four groups of farm buildings, a dwelling house on Begerin Island, and a complex of buildings surrounding a reception area for the Wexford Wildfowl Reserve. Begerin Island has a cluster of deciduous trees and there are stands of conifers nearby. Otherwise, a small number of rows of hedges provide what cover there is on this flat landscape. A network of untarred roads provides access for farm vehicles and reserve workers to all the fields.

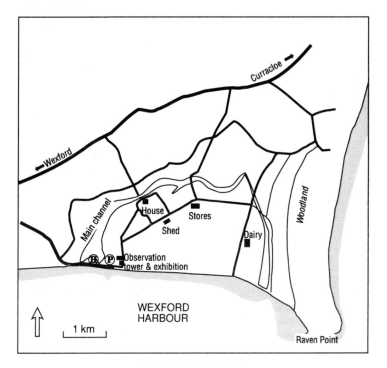

North Slob, Co Wexford

Up to the late 1940s, the land was largely pasture with a relatively small amount of tillage. In the early 1960s most of the North Slob was acquired by one landowner who drained the fields very effectively, making it possible to grow larger areas of cereal and tillage. In 1968, the Irish government and the Irish Wildbird Conservancy jointly purchased 100 hectares and obtained a long lease of another 50 hectares, and these lands were kept under pasture. A resident warden has been present since 1968 and the observation tower, hide and reception area were opened to the public in 1974. In 1990 a further 90 hectares were purchased, again jointly by the government and the IWC, thus enlarging the reserve substantially.

An extensive area of sand dunes borders the eastern edge of the North Slob, stretching from the Raven Point north to Curracloe and Ballinesker. These have been planted with conifers. Offshore the shallow seas provide rich feeding for divers, grebes and sea-ducks.

Species

The North Slob is famous for its geese. From October to April thousands of Greenland White-fronted Geese feed on the Slobs. In recent years the total on both North and South Slob has reached 10,000 birds, the largest number recorded since these geese first started to come to the Slobs in the 1920s. The geese are being studied by workers at the reserve, so you may notice some birds with red neckbands. Most of these have been caught and marked in Ireland, many of them on the North Slob, though a few were marked in Greenland.

Among the White-fronted Geese each winter are a small number of Pink-footed Geese and, in most winters, a blue phase Snow Goose or a white Snow Goose and a few Canada Geese. Sometimes the Canada Geese are of one of the very small subspecies, indicative of a trans-atlantic origin rather than an escape from a collection in Ireland or a wanderer from the feral population in Britain. Brent Geese feed in the harbour and increasingly also use the fields on the southern side of the North Slob close to the sea wall. Other geese recorded include Greylag Geese and Barnacle Geese (both regular in the past but now very rare), Russian White-fronted Geese (a few in most winters), Bean Geese (very rare) and Lesser White-fronted Goose (once).

Bewick's Swans have built up to good numbers in recent years on the North Slob and, occasionally, a North American Whistling Swan has been seen with them. Whooper Swans are rather scarce. Mute Swans are present throughout the year.

Most of the common duck species winter on the North Slob. Shelduck, Mallard, Teal, Gadwall, Wigeon, Pintail, Shoveler, Scaup, Tufted Duck, Pochard, Goldeneye and Red-breasted Merganser all occur on the North Slob, though Scaup and Red-breasted Merganser are best seen from the sea wall, looking south into Wexford Harbour. Over the years the North Slob has added three species to the Irish list: Lesser White-fronted Goose, Western Sandpiper and Paddyfield Warbler. Other rarities have included Black Duck, Blue-winged Teal and Green-winged Teal from North America.

Off Curracloe and Ballinesker there are large rafts of wintering Common Scoter. Velvet and Surf Scoters sometimes accompany them and a scattering of divers and grebes are usually interspersed among the ducks. Great Northern and Red-throated Divers and Great Crested and Slavonian Grebes occur each winter and there is always the possibility of one of the rarer grebes.

The North Slob has large wintering numbers of Lapwings, Golden Plovers and Curlews, and smaller numbers of Black-tailed Godwits, Redshanks and Dunlins. The harbour area has Oystercatchers, Ringed Plovers, Grey Plovers, Turnstones, Bar-tailed Godwits, Redshanks, Spotted Redshanks, Greenshanks and Dunlins. Rare waders recorded on the North Slob include Upland Sandpiper and Pectoral Sandpiper as well as the first Irish Western Sandpiper, on the small pool in front of the reception area, in autumn 1992.

Birds of prey quarter the slob regularly. Kestrels and Sparrowhawks occur throughout the year. Hen Harriers, Merlins and Peregrines are regular in winter. Marsh Harriers, Ospreys, Short-eared Owls and occasional Buzzards have been recorded.

The farm buildings are excellent sites for watching finches. Greenfinches and Chaffinches are common and there are usually some Tree Sparrows and a few Bramblings among them.

Timing

The best time to visit the North Slob is from October to April when geese are present. A visit in August or September can sometimes coincide with migrant waders. The state of the tide does not make much difference, but it is important to avoid visiting the Slob on the morning of a shoot. There are organised shoots on the area of the North Slob outside the reserve at weekends: the entire Slob appears relatively birdless after the disturbance so check with the Warden in advance.

Access

The North Slob is approached from the road north from Wexford to Gorey. After crossing the bridge in Wexford town, drive for about 3 km to the first right turn. This is signposted for the Wexford Wildfowl Reserve and the turn is situated just before a garage on the right hand side. Follow the narrow road for 1.5 km to the carpark and reception area. There is an observation tower at the reception area from which much of the North Slob can be scanned. The Pat Walsh hide provides viewing of the main channel; the harbour can be examined from the sea wall.

Access to the rest of the North Slob is restricted but, if the Warden gives permission, the road across the North Slob can be travelled by car. Under no circumstances should the visitor get out of the vehicle, as this disturbs the geese. A car in fact operates as a very effective hide.

To view the Curracloe area, return to the reception area and leave the Slob. Take the first turn to the right and follow the road around to Curracloe. The scoter flocks can be seen from the sand dunes by taking one of the right turns off the road which runs north along the edge of the dunes.

The Warden is Chris Wilson, Wexford Wildfowl Reserve, North Slob, Wexford (telephone 053–23129).

Calendar

All year: Great Crested Grebe, Mute Swan, Mallard, wildfowl collection (for those who must see geese out of season !), Kestrel, Sparrowhawk, Tree Sparrow.

Autumn: Early geese, ducks, waders, possibility of Marsh Harrier, terns and possible Black Terns, some passerine migrants.

White-fronted Geese (Wexford Wildfowl Reserve)

Winter: Bewick's Swan, Greenland White-fronted Goose, Pink-footed Goose, Brent Goose, possible Snow Goose and Canada Goose, Spotted Redshank, Ruff, finches. Divers, grebes, Common Scoter, Velvet Scoter at Curracloe. Peregrine, Merlin, Short-eared Owl.

Spring: Bewick's Swan, Greenland White-fronted Goose, Pink-footed Goose, Brent Goose, terns in Wexford Harbour. Divers, grebes and scoters at Curracloe.

Summer: Black-tailed Godwits summering; terns in Wexford Harbour.

Note: The map of the North Slob is redrawn from the Wexford Wildfowl Reserve map.

92 LADY'S ISLAND LAKE

OSI ½″ map: sheet 23
T00 T10

Habitat

Lady's Island Lake lies south of Rosslare, on the south coast of the county, just around the corner from Carnsore Point. The lake is about 4 km long and 2 km wide at its broadest. It is fed by a number of small streams and is impounded from the sea by a broad shingle bank. From time to time an exit channel is dug through this bank and the water level falls rapidly. Southerly gales quickly close the exit, but while it is open there can be a considerable expanse of sand and mud at the northern end of the lake providing good feeding for waders.

The lake is named after Lady's Island, a small island joined to the mainland by a broad causeway, which has the ruins of a Norman castle on it. The island is a place of pilgrimage in August and prevention of flooding of the pilgrims' route around the island is the reason for cutting through the shingle bank at the southern end of the lake.

Off the west side of Lady's Island is a small, very low island named Scarageen, which is completely covered by water when the level is at its highest. To the south is a larger island named Inish which is farmed.

The shoreline is stony and backed by lowlying farmland. The little village of Lady's Island is at the north end of the lake. The southern side is a shingle bank with sand dunes. In the south-east corner is an area of enormous granite boulders, many of which have been removed in recent years for building work in Rosslare.

Ring Marsh, a small lagoon and marsh, lies to the east of the lake. This lagoon has more cover than Lady's Island Lake itself and the *Phragmites* beds provide nest sites for duck, Sedge and Reed Warblers.

At the south-west end of Lady's Island Lake there is a small isolated pool near the end of the road which has held Lesser Yellowlegs and Stone-curlew in the past. There is a farm nearby providing feeding for thrushes amd finches in winter.

Species

In summer there is an important tern colony on Inish island. Sandwich Terns are usually the most numerous but Common, Arctic and, in recent years, Roseate also breed. Roseate Terns are now very rare and, while Rockabill Island off the north Dublin coast has more birds, this is much the most accessible place to see the species in summer. Herring and Lesser Black-backed Gulls also nest on Inish and Black-headed Gulls nest at Ring Marsh. Ring has breeding Great Crested Grebes, Little Grebe, Mallard, Shoveler, Tufted Duck and Sedge and Reed Warbler. Little Grebes, Mallard, Coots, Moorhen and a colony of Mute Swans nest on Lady's Island Lake itself.

The lake is an important wildfowl and wader area in autumn and winter, though numbers are not so high as at Tacumshin. All the common dabbling and diving duck species can be seen. Numbers of waders are usually low, but most of the common species occur. Curlew Sandpipers, Ruffs and Little Stints are recorded in most years. A number of American species have been seen over the years.

On the sea, off the south-western corner of the lake, Black-throated Divers are regular in spring. This is probably the best place in Wexford to have a reasonable chance of seeing this species. Red-throated and Great Northern Divers also occur. This corner also has a small pool with potential for vagrant waders.

Timing

Lady's Island is worth a visit at any time of the year. In spring and summer there are migrant and breeding terns; in autumn there is always the possibility of scarce migrant waders; and in winter wildfowl numbers can be high. Ring Marsh has potential as a breeding site for most species of duck known to nest in Ireland and can also be

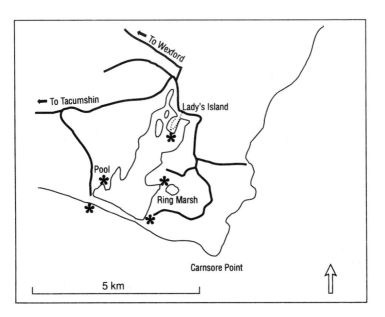

Lady's Island Lake, Co Wexford

interesting for wildfowl and waders throughout the remainder of the year.

The area is best visited in calm weather.

Access

Take the Rosslare road south from Wexford town and follow the signs for the ferry port at Rosslare Harbour. At Tagoat, about 4 km before Rosslare Harbour, take the second right turn, clearly marked for Lady's Island Lake, and drive the 4 km to the village which surrounds the large church at the north end of the lake. There is plenty of room to park a car at the causeway. A wide path runs around Lady's Island and this is well worth walking. The entire north shore can be well watched from this area.

To get to the south-east corner of the lake and to Ring Marsh take the road east from the village and follow the signs for Carne Beach. At the Lobster Pot bar, about 2 km from Lady's Island, take the right turn indicated for Carnsore Point. This road deteriorates after a few kilo-metres and eventually reaches the south-east corner of the lake.

Ring Marsh can be reached by turning right about 2 km after The Lobster Pot and following the narrow road down to the sand dunes.

The south-west end is reached by turning left off the road to Tacumshin, about 5 km from Lady's Island, and following the narrow road down to the sea.

Calendar

All year: Mute Swan, Mallard.

Autumn: Migrant waders including Greenshank, Curlew Sandpiper, Little Stint and possibility of American vagrants.

Winter: Wigeon, Teal, Gadwall, Shoveler, Pintail, Pochard, Tufted Duck, Scaup, Goldeneye, Red-breasted Merganser, Coot, Oystercatcher, Golden Plover, Lapwing, Curlew, Redshank, Greenshank. Occasional Black-throated Diver on the sea. Small grebes have been seen as well.

Spring: Late wildfowl and waders. Migrant terns including the possibility of Black Tern.

Summer: Breeding Great Crested Grebe, Shoveler, Sandwich Tern, Common Tern, Arctic Tern, Roseate Tern, Sedge Warbler, Reed Warbler.

93 TACUMSHIN LAKE

OSI ½″ map: sheet 23
T00

Habitat

Tacumshin is another lagoon only 2 km west of Lady's Island Lake. The water level is normally far lower than at Lady's Island, so this lagoon holds a much greater diversity of wildfowl and, in particular, waders throughout the autumn, winter and spring. The lake is separated from the sea by a shingle bank and dune system. The lagoon is not tidal, but the water fluctuates considerably. Rainwater drains off the surrounding fields into the lagoon and evaporates in dry sunny days in summer.

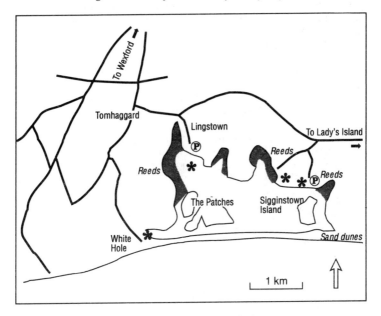

Tacumshin Lake, Co Wexford

Tacumshin is about 2 km from north to south and 5 km in length. There is one island at the eastern end, Sigginstown, and two at the western end, known as The Patches. The eastern island is farmed, but the two western islands are very lowlying and sandy, with *Salicornia* and other saltmarsh plants.

The south-eastern corner has a small area of saltmarsh and extensive reedbeds. The shoreline from Sigginstown around to the north-west corner has a number of reedbeds and stony beaches. The north-west corner at Lingstown has a large reedbed and a number of pools. The south-western corner has a subsidiary marsh known as The White Hole, which is separated from the main lake by a dyke and sluice.

The shingle bar at the southern edge of the lake has an extensive sand dune system, which has attracted its share of rare migrants.

Species

Tacumshin is a fine place for a visit at any time of the year. In summer there are Shelducks and Redshanks breeding on The Patches, Oyster-catchers and Ringed Plovers nesting on the shingle bar and always the possibility of a vagrant wader. Water Rails are a feature of Tacumshin, their squealing call being very striking to the visitor.

Autumn, however, is the peak time when birdwatchers can be found here daily. Duck numbers build up and Mallard, Teal, Shoveler, Gad-wall, Pintail, Pochard and Tufted Duck can all be seen. Garganey are almost annual in autumn. Wader diversity is remarkable, but the area is so extensive that a thorough investigation is very difficult. As a result, the visitor should not be despondent if there are a number of birdwatchers in the area. Rare birds can turn up at any time of the day and are not always found by the earliest arrival. All the common species occur, but the Dunlin flocks should be searched thoroughly. Pectoral, White-rumped and Baird's Sandpipers are near annual and most of the American species on the Irish list have been seen including the first Irish Short-billed Dowitcher, a number of Semi-palmated Sandpipers and up to nine Buff-breasted Sandpipers in a day.

European vagrants have also been seen, such as Broad-billed Sand-piper and Marsh Sandpiper. Marsh Harriers are regular in late summer and autumn.

In autumn large numbers of hirundines feed over the lake before migrating and White Wagtails and Wheatears feed on the saltmarsh and beach.

In winter there are large numbers of duck and regular winter flocks of Bewick's Swans and Brent Geese. The geese and Wigeon feed mainly on the saltmarsh on The Patches. Whooper Swans also occur in small numbers. At times, particularly when flooded, The White Hole attracts several hundred Bewick's Swans and Brent Geese.

Early spring is probably the quietest time but Little Gulls often occur in small parties from March onwards. Later on, there is the possibility of a Mediterranean Gull, or of Garganey, marsh terns or perhaps a Little Ringed Plover.

The reality of Tacumshin is that the unexpected turns up repeatedly and at all seasons. The area is worth a visit at any time of the year.

Timing

Tacumshin is good for birds all year round. Calm conditions are best, as the waders can be approached closely when there is little wind.

The lake is most frequented by birdwatchers on weekends in September and October.

Access

A visit could start at The White Hole, working back around the lake to Sigginstown. Take the road from Wexford for Kilmore Quay. After about 12 km turn left at a sign for Tomhaggard. Bear right through the village and then turn left, after about 1 km, following the narrow road until a small parking area is reached. The White Hole can be covered from here, and then Tacumshin itself can be seen by walking eastwards until a good view of The Patches can be had.

To get a better view of the birds in the north-west corner return to Tomhaggard, and take the right turn in the village, then, after almost 1 km, take the right turn marked cul de sac. This road leads down to the Lingstown corner. A car can be parked and this corner of Tacumshin explored on foot. The edge of the main lagoon should be scanned and all the bays checked carefully. There are a number of pools holding birds and these all deserve scrutiny. Make your way to The Patches and walk across much of the area. Not just waders but wagtails, pipits and buntings use this part.

The eastern end can be viewed from a couple of spots. Drive back from the Lingstown corner but, instead of turning left from Tomhaggard, turn right and drive for about 5 km until a right turn comes into view, with the ruins of an old castle beside it. Turn right here and then, at the fork, turn right, following the road down to the shore. The shore to the west should be walked as the area opposite here, known as The Forgotten Corner, has held interesting birds in the past. Returning to the fork, turn right, rather than returning to the main road, and follow the narrow road to a small car park overlooking Sigginstown island. The eastern corner of the lake can be explored from here.

Calendar

All year: Mute Swan, Shelduck, Mallard, Moorhen, Water Rail, Oyster-catcher, Ringed Plover.

Autumn: Waders including Curlew Sandpiper, Little Stint, Ruff, Black-tailed Godwit, Spotted Redshank, American vagrants. Early wildfowl, including Wigeon, Teal, Gadwall, Shoveler, Pintail.

Winter: Whooper Swan, Bewick's Swan, Brent Goose, ducks, Hen Harrier, waders.

Spring: Terns, migrant waders, Little Gulls, other migrants.

Summer: Breeding waders. Occasional breeding terns. Breeding Reed Warblers at Tomhaggard end.

94 SALTEE ISLANDS

Habitat

The two Saltee islands, Great Saltee and Little Saltee, lie between 4 and 6 km off the fishing village of Kilmore Quay. Little Saltee is about 1 km long and less than 0.5 km wide. It has no high cliffs and very little cover, and the island is no more than 30 m high. Great Saltee is a much larger island, being 2 km long and about 1 km wide at its broadest. The southern and western sides have steep cliffs, especially at the southern tip. The island slopes down to low boulder-clay cliffs overhanging the boulder beach which runs for much of the north-western shore. There are two houses on the island: an old stone farmhouse and a wooden bungalow. These are the property of the Neale family who own the island and made it a bird sanctuary. The family has erected a Throne near the mid-point of the island.

There are trees and the remnants of a garden around the old farmhouse and these provide cover for some passerine migrants. The island was farmed in the past but the fields are now overgrown with bracken and brambles.

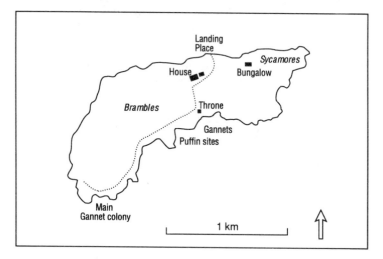

Great Saltee, Co Wexford

Species

The seabird colony on Great Saltee is much the most impressive sight for any visitor to the island in summer, and probably the main reason why so many people take a boat trip across from Kilmore Quay. Over 25,000 pairs of birds of twelve species nest on the two Saltees. Only Cormorants breed on Little Saltee, but Manx Shearwaters, Fulmars, Gannets, Shags, Guillemots, Razorbills, Puffins, Kittiwakes, Great Black-backed Gulls, Lesser Black-backed Gulls and Herring Gulls all nest on Great Saltee and all, except the Manx Shearwaters, which come to land only at night, can be seen with ease.

The Gannet colony, concentrated at the high cliffs at the southern tip of the island, is expanding rapidly, and has recently spread onto the Makestone Rock close to the Throne. Breeding was first proved in 1929; by 1960 there were 60 nests, by 1970 165, by 1980 350 and by 1990 1,050. This rate of increase shows no sign of slowing, and there is still plenty of room for more nest sites. There are thousands of Guillemots, Razorbills and Kittiwakes and hundreds of Puffins. The auks and Kittiwakes breed on the cliffs or, in the case of the Puffins, above the cliffs around the southern and western sides of the island. Gulls breed on the bracken-covered fields and on the shoreline.

As well as seabirds, Shelduck, Mallard, Oystercatchers, Ringed Plovers, Snipe, Ravens and Choughs also breed. Very few passerines nest.

In spring and autumn, however, Saltee is a great migration watch-point. There was a bird observatory here from 1950 to 1963, the first in Ireland, and pioneering studies were made. Nowadays, birdwatchers and bird ringers visit regularly in May and September, but there is not the intensive coverage there was in the past.

On a good day in spring hundreds of Willow Warblers feed in the bracken, Swallows and Cuckoos fly over, Redstarts and Whinchats show in ones and twos, and a rarity or two, such as a Hoopoe, Golden Oriole, Woodchat Shrike, or Tawny Pipit, appears for a few hours. Great Saltee experiences much larger falls of migrants than any other Irish site. In autumn these falls are not quite so spectacular, but there has been a long list of rarities including Greenish Warbler, Bonelli's Warbler, Olive-backed Pipit and Siberian Stonechat.

Seabird passage in autumn is not so good as off the headlands of Cork and Kerry but skuas and shearwaters can be seen when the wind is southerly or south-westerly.

Timing

The months of May to July are the best time to go to Great Saltee. In mid-May there is the chance of interesting migrant land birds and from then on the seabirds can be seen. A calm day with bright sunshine is best, and make sure to bring a picnic.

In autumn, the days are shorter and there are few seabirds remaining. At this time of year, a visit ideally should cover several days so that there is a good chance of hitting a period of south-easterly winds which may bring a fall of migrants. Permission from the owner is required to stay overnight.

Access

The islands are privately owned but visitors are welcome to come on day trips. Provided the weather is fine, particularly if the wind is not from the north, it is usually possible to find a fishing boat at Kilmore Quay to take one out to Great Saltee, especially in summer. Little Saltee is difficult to land on and has far less diversity of birds, so visits are rare.

Arrangements should be made well in advance with a boatman if a trip is being planned and the visitor is travelling a considerable distance to Kilmore Quay.

Calendar

All year: Cormorant, Shag, Great Black-backed Gull, Herring Gull, Pere-grine, Oystercatcher, Raven, Chough, Meadow Pipit, Rock Pipit.

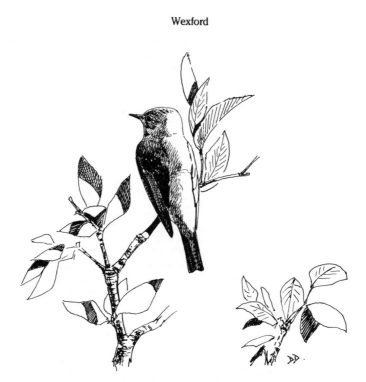

Spotted Flycatcher

Autumn: Warblers, Redstart, Pied Flycatcher, Spotted Flycatcher, scarce migrants.

Winter: The island has never been adequately watched in winter, but thrushes and finch flocks have been seen.

Spring: Willow Warbler, Chiffchaff, Wheatear, other spring passerine migrants, returning seabirds.

Summer: Nesting Fulmar, Gannet, Shag, Mallard, Lapwing, Snipe, Guillemot, Razorbill, Puffin, Herring Gull, Lesser Black-backed Gull, Great Black-backed Gull, Kittiwake.

95 HOOK HEAD

OSI ½″ map: sheet 23
S70 X79

Habitat

Hook Head is a promontory at the eastern side of Waterford Harbour projecting far to the south. The only part of Wexford county which

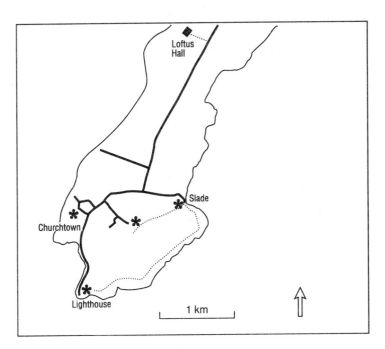

Hook Head, Co Wexford

extends farther south is the island of Great Saltee. This position means
that the headland is an excellent seawatching and passerine migration
watchpoint.

The head comprises lowlying limestone. The main cover on the head
is provided by dense hedgerows of blackthorn and bramble. There are
also a few gardens centred around the clusters of houses at Churchtown
and Slade. Otherwise, the overall impression is of a well farmed area
with a number of small fields. About half the area is tilled, most of the
remainder being grazed by cattle. Slade has a fishing harbour and is
dominated by the ruins of Slade Castle, the earliest part of which dates
from the late fifteenth or early sixteenth century. At the tip of the headland is Hook Head lighthouse, a striking and ancient tower. There has
been a tower here since the thirteenth century or earlier, and a lantern
on the tower since the late seventeenth century.

Species

This is a headland for watching spring and autumn migration. The
absence of high cliffs means that there are few suitable sites for breeding
seabirds, and the breeding land birds are those typical of south Wexford.

As a seawatching point, Hook has recorded large spring passages of
Pomarine Skuas in May, as many as 191 being seen in a day. Maximum
numbers of Manx Shearwaters and Gannets are also seen in spring. In
autumn, in optimal south-westerly winds with mist or rain, the passage
of Manx Shearwaters, Storm Petrels,

Gannets, auks and Kittiwakes can be joined by Great Skuas, Arctic
Skuas, Sooty Shearwaters and, occasionally, a Great Shearwater or
Sabine's Gull.

On the land, this is the second best spring migration site (after near-by Great Saltee). On a good day in early or mid-May the head can have large numbers of Swallows, Swifts, Wheatears and Willow Warblers and smaller numbers of Cuckoos, Turtle Doves, Redstarts, Blackcaps and Garden Warblers. Among the commoner birds are one or two rarities every year: Golden Oriole, Lesser Whitethroat, Subalpine Warbler and Woodchat Shrike are typical of the species which turn up.

In autumn, movement has been recorded from August to early November. Pied and Spotted Flycatchers, Whinchats and Blackcaps are all regular, and Icterine Warbler, Melodious Warbler, Lesser Whitethroat, Reed Warbler, Firecrest, Red-breasted Flycatcher and Red-backed Shrike have all appeared on several occasions. Major rarities recorded include Radde's Warbler from Siberia, Red-rumped Swallow and Lesser Grey Shrike from southern Europe and Upland Sandpiper, Bobolink and Red-eyed Vireo from North America.

Choughs do not breed on the Head but a few are regular in late autumn and winter.

Timing

Hook Head is best in spring and autumn. For passerine watching try to choose a day with light south-easterly winds. Seawatching is best, as elsewhere along the south coast, in south-westerlies with rain or mist. Birds are most active in the early morning.

Access

Hook Head is best approached from Wexford or New Ross by following the signposts for Fethard-on-Sea. In Fethard take the road south which is indicated for Churchtown and runs right to the lighthouse at the tip. The best area is from Slade south to the lighthouse and west to Church-town.

Calendar

All year: Cormorant, Shag, Herring Gull, Oystercatcher, Magpie, Hooded Crow, Jackdaw, Meadow Pipit, Rock Pipit, Pied Wagtail, Starling, House Sparrow, Tree Sparrow.

Autumn: Manx Shearwater, Sooty Shearwater, Storm Petrel, Gannet, Arctic Skua, Great Skua, Chough, scarce seabirds, warblers, Redstart, Pied Flycatcher, Spotted Flycatcher, scarce migrants.

Winter: Red-throated Diver, Great Northern Diver, wintering Golden Plover, Lapwing, Snipe, Curlew, Chough, thrushes and finches.

Spring: Seabird passage, especially Pomarine Skua. Willow Warbler, Chiffchaff, Wheatear, other spring passerine migrants.

96 BANNOW BAY

Habitat

This broad and long bay lies at the western end of the county, close to Hook Head. The bay is about 7 km from Wellingtonbridge, at the northern end, to the sea and about 3 km wide at its broadest. The intertidal zone comprises very extensive mudflats which hold large numbers of feeding wildfowl and waders. The estuary is fed by the Owenduff and Corock rivers which meet at Wellingtonbridge and by a number of smaller streams.

Species

Bannow Bay has rather small numbers of wildfowl. The main feature is its flock of several hundred Brent Geese, but it also holds some hundreds of Teal, up to 1,000 Wigeon and smaller numbers of Shelduck, Pintail, Mallard, Pochard, Tufted Duck, Scaup and Red-breasted Mergansers.

Wader numbers are quite high, with several thousand Lapwing and Golden Plover and over 1,000 Curlews, Redshanks and Dunlins recorded most years. There is a nice flock of 500–800 Black-tailed Godwits and small numbers of the scarcer species, such as Greenshank and Spotted Redshank, have been seen. Ruff, Sanderling and Curlew Sandpiper have been recorded.

Timing

This is of interest to the visitor principally from autumn through winter to the spring, the months August to March. Birdwatching is easiest two hours either side of high tide when the birds are forced close to the shore by the water level.

Access

Bannow Bay is a very difficult area to cover well as the mudflats are very extensive and the public road only runs along the edge of the bay at a handful of points. Try, therefore, to time a visit for high tide.

Most of the birds roost at three areas. The saltmarsh at Clonmines at the north end of the bay holds large numbers of waders and duck. It can be viewed from the road between Wellingtonbridge and Duncormick just south of Wellingtonbridge.

The saltmarsh east of Bannow Island, in the south-east corner, is another wader roost and frequently holds most of the Brent Geese. It can be viewed by taking the road south along the east side of the bay leading to the south-east corner.

The west side of the bay and the channel in the middle can be seen best by taking the road which runs along the shoreline between Wellingtonbridge and Saltmills. Just to the north-east of Saltmills the road provides excellent views.

Calendar

Autumn, winter, spring: Red-throated Diver, Great Northern Diver, Brent Goose, Shelduck, Wigeon, Mallard, Pintail, Teal, Pochard, Tufted Duck,

Scaup, Goldeneye, Red-breasted Merganser, Oystercatcher, Ringed Plover, Golden Plover, Grey Plover, Lapwing, Knot, Dunlin, Snipe, Curlew, Black-tailed Godwit, Bar-tailed Godwit, Spotted Redshank, Redshank, Greenshank, Turnstone.

OTHER WEXFORD SITES

97 CARNSORE POINT

Habitat and Species

Carnsore Point is at the south-east corner of Ireland and well situated for watching seabird passage and passerine migration. The promontory is of granite and is lowlying with little cover.

Many seabirds breeding in the Irish Sea pass Carnsore, going to and from their feeding areas in the Atlantic. Skuas, including large numbers of Pomarine Skuas at times, occur among the Manx Shearwaters, Gannets and auks which stream past. Because the point has such a wide field of view, ranging from north-east to south-west, the glare of the sun can usually be avoided.

Diurnal migration is frequently evident in both spring and autumn. Large numbers of hirundines, Swifts, Skylarks, Meadow Pipits and White Wagtails can often be seen coming in from the sea or heading out, depending on the season. Although there is very little cover, warblers and flycatchers can sometimes be found on the stone walls or boulders. In recent years rarities seen here have included Golden Oriole, Wryneck, Woodchat Shrike and Ireland's first Desert Wheatear.

Access

Carnsore Point is reached by following the road for the south-east corner of Lady's Island Lake (see above). Instead of turning right, take the lane to the south-east and drive through an area of bracken onto some low dunes and then east to the head. The car can be parked at the headland.

98 THE CULL

Habitat and Species

The Cull is a long, narrow estuary running from east to west parallel to the shore at Ballyteigue Bay.

The eastern part of the inlet has been reclaimed, but the western part, which extends for over 6 km and is less than 0.5 km wide, is a good wildfowl and wader site.

White-fronted Geese and Bewick's Swans are sometimes seen and small numbers of Mallard, Teal, Wigeon, Shelduck and Red-breasted

Mergansers winter. There are up to 1,000 waders in winter, but larger numbers in autumn. Passage species such as Common Sandpiper, Curlew Sandpiper, Little Stint and Ruff all occur occasionally. Rarities recorded here include Blue-winged Teal, Black-winged Stilt and Avocet.

Access

The best point for viewing The Cull is at Killag. From Kilmore Quay drive north for about 3 km to Killag. Turn left on the Duncormick road and drive for 2 km to Park. At Park, where the road turns sharp right, take the narrow lane to the left. This unsurfaced lane leads down to The Cull Bank where the pump-house can be seen. Most of the birds can be viewed from here.

99 ROSSLARE BACK STRAND

OSI ½" map: sheet 23
T01

Habitat and Species

The south-east corner of Wexford Harbour, between the South Slob and Rosslare Point, is known as the Back Strand. The northern part of this area is inter-tidal mudflat, grading to sandy beach close to Rosslare Point. The southern part, known as Hopeland, was once reclaimed land like the Slobs, but the seawall was breached in the 1930s and the area reverted to mudflat and saltmarsh. Much of this part of the Back Strand is infested with *Spartina*.

Many of the waders which feed in Wexford Harbour can be found here. Several hundred Oystercatchers, Ringed Plovers, Curlews, Black-tailed Godwits, Redshanks and Knot, and several thousand Dunlin, can be found here in autumn and winter. Scarcer species such as Curlew Sandpiper and Little Stint are seen in most autumns and some American species, such as White-rumped and Semipalmated Sandpipers, have been recorded.

Wildfowl numbers are varied, but Brent Geese, Shelduck and Wigeon usually feed here

In summer and autumn, terns are usually seen feeding in the area.

Access

Take the road north from Rosslare village past the golf links until Hopeland can be seen on the left. Walk on from here to Rosslare Point. Visits to Rosslare Point are best just after high tide when birds are starting to feed on the freshly exposed mud.

KILKENNY

General

The inland counties of south Leinster are very much understudied by birdwatchers, principally because few enthusiasts live in them and those that do find the lure of the nearby coast irresistible. Kilkenny is a large county with a variety of habitats but very few places where wildfowl congregate.

The best known wildfowl spot is Tibberoughney Bog in the south of the county on the edge of the River Suir. This is a large marsh with flooded areas of pasture. In winter the Greylag Geese, which feed at Coolfin in Waterford (see the separate account of that site), roost here. Whooper and Bewick's Swans and Wigeon, Teal, Mallard and Tufted Ducks also occur. The area is best approached from the village of Tibberoughney, about 2 km south-east of Piltown.

There are excellent woodland sites in a number of locations, but especially in the river valleys. Jays, Barn Owls, Kestrels and Sparrowhawks are all quite widespread.

In winter, flocks of Lapwings, Golden Plovers, Redwings and Fieldfares are widespread.

CARLOW

General

Carlow is a much smaller county than Kilkenny to its west, but the birds are very similar. The only medium-sized body of standing water is an artificial pond at Oak Park, owned by the Agricultural Institute, where Teal, Mallard, Tufted Duck and Pochard can be seen.

There are nesting Hen Harriers and Red Grouse on the tops of the Mount Leinster chain of mountains.

LAOIS

General

Laois is mainly a relatively lowlying agricultural county, but it does have the Slieve Bloom mountains on its northern border. This range holds Hen Harriers; the best place to visit is The Cut, where the road runs across the summit.

There are a few wetlands. The 'Curragh' between Rathdowney and Durrow, a stretch of rough meadow along the River Erkina south of Ballacolla in the south of the county, holds a small wintering population of Greenland White-fronted Geese. These birds move about a little, generally in response to disturbance, and sometimes can be found on the flats beside the River Nore near Borris-in-Ossory or at Lough Annaghmore.

KILDARE

General

Kildare is a flat, lowlying county with the River Liffey, the River Barrow and the Grand Canal providing varied bird habitat. There are few notable birdwatching sites, but the county as a whole has the typical birds of the Irish midlands. The Curragh is a large, flat area where Lapwings and Golden Plovers winter in large numbers. Whinchats nest on the fringes of young plantations. Jays and Blackcaps can be found in the deciduous woods.

Prosperous reservoir, the source of the Grand Canal, has a large colony of breeding Black-headed Gulls and smaller numbers of Little Grebes, Mallard, Snipe and Redshanks. A Savi's Warbler sang here for several days some years ago, and Marsh Harriers have been seen, so there is obviously sufficient potential to encourage a visit.

OFFALY

Introduction

Offaly resembles the other inland counties of Leinster in a number of respects: it is lowlying apart from the Slieve Bloom mountains on its southern fringe, it has few large woods, it has very few bodies of standing water. But, it has a huge advantage for the visiting birdwatcher in that its western edge is formed by the River Shannon and that several tributaries, including the Little Brosna, flow through the county.

The most northerly tributaries, the Rivers Brosna and Blackwater, which enter the Shannon at Shannon Harbour and a few kilometres to the north respectively, do not flood in winter and are not known to be of great importance for wildfowl. The Little Brosna, which looks on the map like a very similar river, has callows on either side which flood and provide wonderful habitat in winter and late spring.

The River Shannon between Athlone and Shannonbridge has been described under the sites of Roscommon, but between Shannonbridge and Meelick on the borders of Offaly and Galway, there are a number of other areas where large numbers of wildfowl occur in winter and where Corncrakes and waders breed in summer.

Sites

100   LITTLE BROSNA   *Greenland White-fronted Geese; wildfowl, waders.*

Other sites:

101   Bullock Island   *Breeding waders; Corncrakes.*

100   LITTLE BROSNA

OSI ½″ map: sheet 15
M91 M90 NOO

Habitat

The Little Brosna is a narrow, slow-flowing river which winds its way from the vicinity of Roscrea to Birr and then flows in a desultory fashion on to the Shannon just south of Meelick. The river in summer is popular among coarse fishermen and paths run alongside it. In autumn it floods and the surrounding meadows are inundated. Large areas of shallow water stretch for several kilometres on either side from above Newtown to the confluence with the Shannon.

The extent of flooding is variable, beginning in early autumn but with some areas remaining uncovered until late November. A system of surface drains prevents the callows, as they are known, from prolonged waterlogging.

Species

The Little Brosna is a spectacular place in late winter when thousands of Wigeon throng the shallow waters. Among them are hundreds of Mallard, Teal, Pintail and Shoveler, as well as 100 or more Whooper and Bewick's Swans. This area has one of the largest flocks of White-fronted Geese in the country away from the Wexford Slobs. Up to 500 geese feed on the callows and on the surrounding bogs.

The sight of geese here, on callows which have flooded for millenia, is far more stirring than seeing them on the reclaimed fields of the Wexford Slobs. The White-fronted Goose on the callows seems a much wilder bird in a much more fitting habitat.

It is not just a good place for wildfowl. Wader numbers are even larger. Some of the largest concentrations of Lapwing and Golden Plover in Ireland scatter over the callows and adjoining farmland. There are large numbers of Curlews and a flock of Black-tailed Godwits which peaks in late winter at up to 4,000 birds. Dunlin are also recorded in winter and over 1,000 can be seen at times. Redshanks, Greenshanks and, as would be expected, large numbers of Snipe are also to be found. Over 20,000 waders have been counted here.

The largest numbers of birds occur here in February and March, probably gathering to build up their fat reserves before returning to Iceland and other breeding grounds to the north.

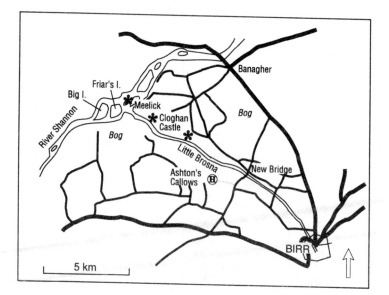

Little Brosna, Cos Offaly and Tipperary

Access

The entire length of the river from New Bridge, 6 km west of Birr, to Meelick on the Shannon and including Big Island and Friar's Island, is excellent for wildfowl and waders. Take the road from New Bridge along the north side of the Little Brosna and leave it where you can gain access to the callows at a sand and gravel quarry. Walk along the edge of the callows as far as Cloghan Castle, for here the largest number of birds normally occur and they usually include the geese. It will take most of the day to work this area thoroughly.

Large numbers of birds concentrate on Ashton's Callows, a south-eastern extension of the main callows (and in Tipperary), and can be observed from an IWC hide which is reached by a track across a small bog south-west of New Bridge.

When both these parts have been fully checked, drive around to the Shannon at Lavagh and look across at Big Island and Friar's Island where large numbers of duck often settle when there is shooting.

Timing

This is a late autumn, winter and spring site. Visit from September to April. If a large number of birds is your target, visit in February or March. Try to avoid weekends as there is shooting in sections, and this causes disturbance. Part of the callows is a statutory wildfowl sanctuary.

Calendar

Autumn-winter-early spring: Mute Swan, Whooper Swan, Bewick's Swan, Greenland White-fronted Goose, Wigeon, Teal, Mallard, Shoveler, Pintail, Golden Plover, Lapwing, Dunlin, Black-tailed Godwit, Curlew, Redshank, Greenshank.

OTHER OFFALY SITE

101 BULLOCK ISLAND

OSI ½″ map: sheet 15
N01

Habitat and Species

Bullock Island is an area of about 40 hectares of traditional hay meadow south of Shannon Harbour on the east bank of the Shannon. It is separated from the mainland by a narrow creek on its western side. Access by tractors is over a small bridge. The island holds a number of pairs of breeding Corncrakes and a relatively high density of nesting Lapwings, Snipe, Curlews and Redshanks. Duck species nesting in the area include Mallard, Teal and Shoveler.

In winter, much of the meadow floods and large numbers of Wigeon and Teal feed on the island. In spring, Whimbrels stop off on migration.

Access

This is an area which should be approached with care as its main feature is breeding birds. Corncrakes can be heard easily but the other species are rather sensitive and, under no circumstances, should nests be sought out as this will cause quite unnecessary disturbance.

The island is approached by turning west off the road south from Shannon Harbour.

The Irish Wildbird Conservancy has purchased some of the land on the island as a reserve for Corncrakes, and research into the biology of the species is being carried out here in summer. There is no warden.

WESTMEATH

Introduction

Westmeath is a county of lakes, popular for fishing in summer and autumn, and with good numbers of ducks in winter. The underlying geology is undulating carboniferous limestone and there are only a few hills of over 250 m. Most of the county is cattle farming country, though the farms tend to be smaller than those of Meath to the east.

The western edge of the county is bounded by Lough Ree and the River Shannon. Towards the Shannon there are large expanses of bogland.

For the birdwatcher, the principal interest is in the birds of the large lakes. These are close enough together to be visited in one day and hold quite different bird populations. Lough Ree, part of which falls within this county, has been dealt with under the accounts for Roscommon.

Sites

102 LOUGH DERRAVARAGH   *Lake; wild swans; diving ducks; autumn waders.*

Other sites:

103 Lough Owel   *Lake; ducks, especially Shoveler.*
104 Lough Ennell   *Lake; ducks.*
105 Lough Iron   *Lake; Greenland White-fronted Geese; wild swans; ducks.*

102 LOUGH DERRAVARAGH

OSI ½" map: sheet 12
N36 N46

Habitat

Derravaragh is a large limestone lake on the River Inny system which drains eventually into the Shannon. To the north-west of the lake is a large area of raised bog, but the long arm which runs to the south-east extends between oak-covered limestone ridges which slope steeply to the lake. Drainage of the Inny over the years has reduced the water level at Derravaragh and extensive areas of the lake bed are exposed at the north-west end. These sand and mud banks once provided feeding for regular migrant waders, but are now overgrown and less attractive to shorebirds.

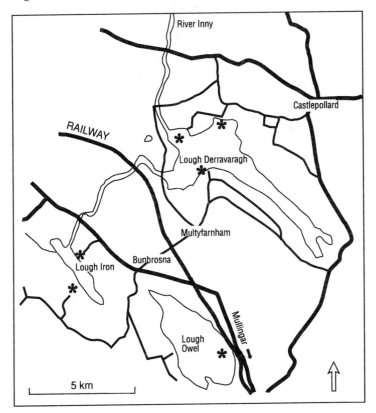

Loughs Derravaragh, Iron and Owel, Co Westmeath

Species

This is an excellent wildfowl site in autumn and winter. In August there is a large post-breeding congregation of Mallard and Pochard begin to appear. In September they peak but then disperse rapidly, and from October Tufted Duck numbers increase. Peak numbers of several hundred occur and a large flock of Coots also occurs at this time. Mallard, Wigeon, and Teal winter in relatively small numbers and other species, such as Shoveler and Pintail, can be seen as well. Whooper Swans are regular in winter, with a flock of up to 60 being usual.

Derravaragh has potential as an inland wader site. The sandy and muddy shore in the north-west corner attracts a few passage migrants in both spring and autumn. All the usual passage migrants have been seen in the past, including Wood Sandpiper, Ruff, Little Stint and Curlew Sandpiper, and a number of American waders also occurred, but numbers nowadays are much lower.

Skuas have been seen in autumn, and Sabine's Gull has been recorded. The lake is not watched with anything like the frequency of good wildfowl and wader spots on the coast and would repay regular visits.

Access

Lough Derravaragh lies to the north of Multyfarnham, a small town reached by turning right off the main road between Mullingar and Edgeworthstown. Follow the signpost for Multyfarnham about 9 km beyond Mullingar.

The north-west corner of the lake is approached by taking the road to the north-west from Multyfarnham, which curls around Derravaragh's western end. This narrow road crosses the Inny twice, once where it exits the lake, and again where it enters the lake. Turn right about 1 km after the first crossing of the Inny and follow the narrow road down to the lough. This point provides excellent viewing. Access to the northern corner is by following the road north-west from Multyfarnham, crossing the Inny river twice, before reaching a junction. At the junction, turn right and then take the first right again (after about 2 km). This lane leads to the lake edge and provides access at several points.

The south-western side can be reached from Multyfarnham by taking the road to the north-east bearing left at a fork after 1.5 km, then taking the first left hand turn down to the lake.

Timing

This is a good lake to visit at any time from August through to May. Autumn and spring, especially August and September, are the best time to search for migrant waders. September to November usually have the highest duck numbers. Later in winter could produce an unusual duck.

Calendar

Autumn: Pochard flocks, Redshank, Greenshank, Ruff, Wood Sandpiper, Curlew Sandpiper, possible American wader, possible skuas.

Winter: Whooper Swan, Tufted Duck and Coot flocks, Wigeon, Teal, Mallard, Shoveler, flocks of Lapwing and Golden Plover.

Spring: Migrant waders, late ducks.

OTHER WESTMEATH SITES

103 LOUGH OWEL

OSI ½" map: sheet 12
N36 N35 N45

Habitat and Species

Owel is another shallow lake on a limestone bed with marl deposits on the bottom. There are some reedbeds on the western side. The lake is the source of the water supply for the town of Mullingar and the water level fluctuates considerably. In late summer and early autumn it is often quite low and can be attractive for waders, especially around Church Island. This lake is a popular trout fishery.

Like most of the surrounding lakes, it has a sizeable population of Tufted Ducks, Pochard and Coots with up to 2,000 of each species occurring at times. The numbers of surface-feeding duck are much higher than those of the other lakes, with the numbers of Shoveler at times being well over 1,000, much the largest concentration in the country. There are also small numbers of Teal, Wigeon and Mallard.

Numbers can vary from day to day and it is probably best to see this lake as part of a complex with Derravaragh, Ennell, Iron and several smaller lakes. Depending on disturbance, birds move around from lake to lake.

The lake is well worth visiting in winter after storms. Great Northern Divers and Kittiwakes often occur and Long-tailed Ducks (up to four), Smew and Sabine's Gull have been seen.

Access

This lake lies on the left hand side of the main road from Dublin to Sligo. Pass through Mullingar and the lake comes into view after about 5 km. The road is higher than the lake and provides a good vantage point to see most of the birds. Access is possible on the south-west side of Owel, by turning left at Bunbrosna, and taking the lane to the left after about 5 km. This route leads right down to the edge of the lake.

104 LOUGH ENNELL

OSI ½" map: sheet 12
N34 N44

Habitat and Species

Lough Ennell, like the other lakes in this area, is a shallow limestone lake. Drainage has led to the exposure of a wide, stony margin. The lake is highly eutrophic.

Lake Farm on the west side of the lake is a traditional wintering White-fronted Goose site, but the flock appears to have moved away in recent years, perhaps to Lough Iron. The lake itself has flocks of several hundred Pochard, Tufted Ducks and Coots.

Access

Lake Farm and the adjoining Kilcooley House farm are the subject of a no-shooting Order. The land is private property and should not be entered upon without permission.

The lake itself can be viewed best from the south-west corner near Kilcooley House and from the main Mullingar-Kilbeggan road on the north-east side.

105 LOUGH IRON

OSI ½" map: sheet 12
N36

Habitat and Species

Lough Iron is smaller than Lough Owel and situated about 3 km to the north-west. It has large wintering populations of Tufted Duck and Pochard, but not so large as at Derravaragh or Owel. Up to 300 each of Wigeon, Teal and Mallard sometimes occur and, when there is disturbance at Lough Owel, substantial numbers of Shoveler visit the lake. Gadwall and Pintail are both regular in small numbers in winter. Like Derravaragh, this lake also has wintering Whooper Swans.

The principal feature of the lake for the birdwatcher is its wintering flock of Greenland White-fronted Geese which numbers over 200. The geese tend to feed on pasture fields on both the east and south sides of the lake. When disturbed, they fly out onto the water.

Occasional other geese occur, the most regular being Greylag Geese. There are also large flocks of Lapwings, Golden Plovers and Curlews.

Access

Although there is a no-shooting Order on some of the land around this lake, it is all on private property and public roads do not provide access directly to the shore. Permission should, therefore, be sought from landowners before venturing from the road to the edge. The lake lies less than 1 km south-west of the main road between Mullingar and Edgeworthstown.

LONGFORD

Introduction

Longford is another lowlying county like Westmeath with a number of lakes and its western edge bordered by Lough Ree and the River Shannon. The lakes here are even less often watched than those of Westmeath.

Lough Ree has been dealt with under the accounts for Roscommon so, while one of the best sites in the county, it is not considered here to save duplication.

The two sites described appear to be minor, but more intensive watching might show them to be more varied than they seem.

Minor Sites:

| 106 | Lough Kinale | *Ducks, Coots.* |
| 107 | Castleforbes | *White-fronted Geese.* |

MINOR LONGFORD SITES

106 LOUGH KINALE
OSI ½" map: sheet 12
N27 N38

Habitat and Species

This is a small lake adjacent to Lough Sheelin, famous for its trout fishing. Kinale also has trout but is not so popular as many of the other lakes in this region. The lake is surrounded by lowlying wet pasture and has large reedbeds around the margin.

The lake holds large numbers of Pochard, Tufted Ducks and Coots in winter. Great Crested Grebes breed in summer. It has rarely been visited by birdwatchers but looks an ideal place for unusual duck.

Access

Kinale is a small lake but rather difficult to work thoroughly because the road comes close at only one point and the reedbeds block views. The easiest way to see the birds is to take the first turn to the right on the road from Granard to Ballyjamesduff. The road leads to Abbeylara but runs close to the western side of the lake.

107 CASTLEFORBES

OSI ½" map: sheet 12
N08

Habitat and Species

Castleforbes Estate is private, forming the centre of a complex of areas where a large flock of Greenland White-fronted Geese winters. The estate includes well-fertilised pasture fields, but the area is private and access is not available. The geese, however, also use the surrounding bogs and the callows on the Camlin river.

Access

The best place to seek for the geese is on the callows between Ballykenny Bridge and Brianstown House, or to the north of Lough Forbes on marshy fields near Cloonart Bridge.

ULSTER

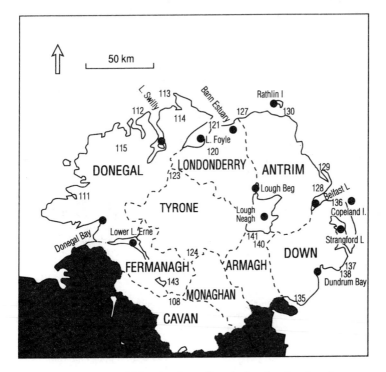

Ulster: counties, Major sites (named) and other sites (numbered)

Cavan
108. Lough Oughter
Monaghan
Donegal
109. DONEGAL BAY
110. LOUGH SWILLY
111. Sheskinmore Lough
112. Horn Head
113. Malin Head
114. Trawbreaga Bay
115. Glenveagh National Park
Londonderry
116. LOUGH FOYLE
117. BANN ESTUARY
118. LOUGH BEG
119. LOUGH NEAGH: NORTH-WEST SHORE
120. Roe Valley Country Park

121. Downhill
Tyrone
122. LOUGH NEAGH: WEST SHORE
123. Grange
124. Annaghroe
Antrim
125. RATHLIN ISLAND
126. SHANE'S CASTLE
127. Ramore Head
128. Belfast Lough: north shore
129. Larne Lough
130. Fair Head
Down
131. BELFAST LOUGH: SOUTH SHORE
132. STRANGFORD LOUGH
133. COPELAND BIRD OBSERVATORY

134. DUNDRUM BAY	**Armagh**
135. Carlingford Lough: north shore	139. LOUGH NEAGH: OXFORD ISLAND
136. Groomsport	140. Lurgan Park Lane
137. Strand Lough and Killough Harbour	141. Craigavon Lakes
138. St John's Point	**Fermanagh**
	142. LOWER LOUGH ERNE
	143. Upper Lough Erne

CAVAN

Introduction

Cavan is a county of numerous lakes but no coastline. It is far from Belfast and Dublin so tends not to be visited regularly by birdwatchers. However, the undulating drumlin landscape, with small lakes between the hills and a considerable extent of woodland on the rim of the lakes, provides habitat for a reasonable diversity of both breeding and wintering birds.

The centre of the county is dominated by the Lough Oughter system, formed by the broadening out of the River Erne among the drumlins. To the south and west are a number of smaller lakes, some of which are little more than ponds. As well as the Lough Oughter system, Lough Gowna and Lough Sheelin on the southern edge of the county appear likely to be of interest.

Only one study of the birds of the county has been published and that was a report on a census of breeding Great Crested Grebes, which covered 115 waters over three summers and estimated a total of 813 birds.

Sites

Minor site:
108   Lough Oughter   *Complex lake system; winter wildfowl.*

References

Lovatt, J.K. Great Crested Grebe Census in County Cavan, summers 1986–1988 (*Irish Birds* 3: 575–580, 1988).

MINOR SITE

108 LOUGH OUGHTER

OSI ½" map: sheet 8/
OSNI ½" map: sheet 3
H30 H31

Habitat and Species

Lough Oughter is a maze of islands and peninsulas separated by narrow channels and small lakes, all resulting from the submergence of drumlins. There are *Phragmites* beds on many parts of the system and the southern part is well wooded.

The area is better described as a lake system as it comprises a large number of interconnected lakes, many of which have their own names.

In summer this is an excellent area for breeding Great Crested Grebes, Little Grebes, Coots, Mallard and Tufted Ducks. It is very secluded so rarer species could occur as well.

In winter there are known to be large numbers of Whooper Swans and Mute Swans. Smaller numbers of Bewick's Swans have been seen. The lakes also hold between 100 and 200 Great Crested Grebes in winter.

The wooded areas in the south have nesting Blackcaps and should hold breeding Garden Warblers.

Access
Because these lakes have been so little watched, nobody really knows which is the best area. The visitor is best advised to move around the entire area from Belturbet in the north to Killeshandra in the west and around to Butler's Bridge in the east.

MONAGHAN

Introduction
Monaghan is a small, landlocked county with a number of lakes. These tend to be smaller than those in Cavan and are certainly less known. Many of the lakes hold populations of duck in winter and breeding Great Crested Grebes, Little Grebes and duck in summer.

Lough Egish appears to be the best lake for birds with a large colony of breeding gulls and wintering Whooper and Bewick's Swans and both surface feeding and diving ducks.

DONEGAL

Introduction
The most north-westerly county in Ireland, Donegal could be expected to attract a larger share of migrants from Iceland and Greenland than most other counties because of its position, and this is probably the case. Like so many of the western counties, however, Donegal has been relatively little watched and the untapped potential is clearly enormous.

The coastline of the county is very varied. Donegal Bay in the south is lowlying as far west as Killybegs, but then the landscape takes on a wilder and more rugged aspect. The coast of west Donegal is a mixture of sheer cliffs, narrow bays and wet bogland. Few trees grow and exposed hedges show the impact of the strong winds. The north coast, from Sheep Haven around to Lough Foyle, is slightly more sheltered and includes a number of long narrow inlets.

Inland, much of Donegal is mountainous and boggy. Many of the hollows are filled with small lakes and a few of these hold breeding Red-throated Divers, the only place where they can be found in Ireland. Black-throated Diver and Whooper Swan have been proved to breed in recent years but it is perhaps surprising that other rare northerly species have not been found breeding in the county as the county has ample habitat for occasional Goldeneyes, Greenshanks, Redwings or Bramblings to nest.

Sites

109	DONEGAL BAY	*Divers, wildfowl, waders, gulls.*
110	LOUGH SWILLY	*Divers, wildfowl, waders.*

Other sites:

111	Sheskinmore Lough	*Breeding waders, wintering wildfowl, especially Greenland White-fronted and Barnacle Geese.*
112	Horn Head	*Breeding seabirds.*
113	Malin Head	*Migrant seabirds and passerines.*
114	Trawbreaga Bay	*Barnacle and Brent Geese, estuary.*
115	Glenveagh National Park	
		Woodland and mountain birds.

References

MacLochlainn, C. Breeding and Wintering Bird Communities of Glenveagh National Park, Co Donegal (*Irish Birds* 2: 482–500, 1984).

Perry, Kenneth W. *The Birds of the Inishowen Peninsula* (Privately published and out of print, 1975).

Sheppard, J.R. Whooper and Bewick's Swans in North West Ireland (*Irish Birds* 2: 48–59, 1981).

Sheskinmore Lough IWC leaflet, IWC, Ruttledge House, 8 Longford Terrace, Monkstown, Co Dublin.

OSI ½" map: sheet 3/
OSNI ¼"map: sheet 3/
1:50,000 map: sheet 16
G86 G87 G77

109 DONEGAL BAY

Habitat

Donegal Bay is a very extensive area and comprises several quite distinct habitats. Taking the bay to mean, in its broadest terms, the entire area from Bundoran in the south round to Donegal town and west to Killybegs, incorporating Inver Bay, the most obvious habitat is the shallow waters off the coastline. These are ideal sea-duck and diver habitat. Less obvious are the small strips of inter-tidal mudflat at Ballyshannon and below Donegal town which attract waders and some wildfowl.

Durnish Lough to the north of Rossnowlagh is unquestionably the best area for surface-feeding wildfowl. It is a shallow freshwater lake impounded by sand dunes. There are extensive reedbeds around the margin and the area is surrounded by marshy fields. This lake has been called Birra Lough in the past, but is correctly named Durnish.

The principal economic activities of this area are farming and fishing. The main fishing port is Killybegs. Ireland's largest trawlers are based here and the resulting activity attracts large numbers of gulls.

Species

The shoreline is excellent for divers and scoters. Great Northern and Red-throated Divers are numerous. Up to 56 Great Northern and 95 Red-throated have been recorded. Black-throated Divers, normally rare on the Irish coast, appear to be regular off Mountcharles, and up to 13 have been counted in recent years.

Common Scoters are numerous, and up to 1,650 have been counted in the bay, though numbers fluctuate. Rossnowlagh is usually the best place for large numbers. The flocks should be checked carefully as both Surf Scoter and Velvet Scoter have been seen here. Indeed the records are so frequent that both species are probably annual here. Eiders, Red-breasted Mergansers and Long-tailed Ducks also winter in this bay. Indeed, there have been records in August of enormous flocks of Red-breasted Mergansers — over 500 at a time — off Ballyshannon, and these are believed to be moulting birds.

This is one of the best places in the country for Long-tailed Ducks, and there have been several counts of over 50, though numbers vary from year to year.

Durnish Lough, a separate habitat within the bay complex, is the best place for swans. Up to 100 Whoopers and 100 Mute Swans are regular in winter, and small numbers of Bewick's are very occasional. Mallard, Teal, Wigeon, Pochard and Tufted Ducks can all be seen.

The small inlets and bays at the head of Donegal Bay have inter-tidal flats which support a small flock of Brent Geese and about 1,000 waders. Oystercatchers, Curlews, Redshanks and Dunlin are the most

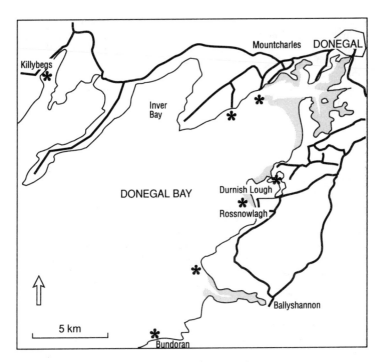

Donegal Bay, Co Donegal

widespread, but Lapwings, Turnstones and occasional Bar-tailed Godwits and Greenshanks should be seen on most winter visits.

The stony shores have small numbers of Purple Sandpipers and the sandier beaches have Ringed Plovers and Sanderlings.

Killybegs harbour is an essential port of call for the birdwatcher visiting this area. Glaucous and Iceland Gulls are virtually certain in winter and rarer gulls should be looked for. The American race of Herring Gull has been recorded, and rare Arctic gulls such as Ross's and Ivory must be expected, given the position of the fishing port.

Timing

Donegal Bay is a winter site, best visited between September and early April. The state of tide matters little, but coverage of the bay will require a full day.

Access

The bay is relatively easily watched, though the distances involved in a thorough search are substantial. The coast road from Ballyshannon north to Ballintra provides several access points to the shore for scanning the diver and scoter parties. Bundoran town is a good place to see Brent Geese and Purple Sandpipers in winter.

Durnish Lough is accessible from several points. The southern end of the lake can be seen from the road between Rossnowlagh and Ballintra. The northern end can be approached by taking the first turn on the right after passing the lake on the road from Ballintra to Rossnowlagh (ignoring the lane through the reedbeds). Park at the first junction on the right, after about 1 km.

Inner Donegal Bay can be explored by following the main road from Laghy to Donegal and around to Mountcharles, taking turns off to the left where suitable habitat is seen. Just before Mountcharles, take the left turn which runs along the north-western edge of the bay. This area is good for Black-throated Divers.

The road from Mountcharles to Killybegs skirts the top of Inver Bay, McSwyne's Bay and Killybegs Harbour. These inlets can be explored easily by taking the byroads which run along the edges of the bays. Killybegs itself is a bustling, busy harbour and gulls surround the port.

Species

All year: Mute Swan, Eider, Red-breasted Merganser, Oystercatcher, Ringed Plover, Curlew.

Autumn-winter-spring: Red-throated Diver, Great Northern Diver, Black-throated Diver, Whooper Swan, Bewick's Swan, Brent Goose, Mallard, Wigeon, Teal, Pochard, Tufted Duck, Scaup, Common Scoter, possibility of Velvet and Surf Scoter, Long-tailed Duck, Dunlin, Sanderling, Purple Sandpiper, Redshank, Greenshank, Glaucous Gull, Iceland Gull, possible rarer gulls.

110 LOUGH SWILLY

OSI ½" map: sheet 1/
OSNI ½" map: sheet 1/
1:50,000 sheets 6, 7
C21 C22 C23 C24 C31 C32 C33

Habitat

Lough Swilly is a long, deep sea lough with several areas of inter-tidal mudflat and a couple of brackish lagoons. The lough is about 50 km long and 4 km broad at its mid point. The upper part of the lough, from Letterkenny to Buncrana in the east and Rathmullan in the west, is much the most interesting for birds. Farther out, the lough is too deep for most diving birds and the shoreline is rocky.

The Swilly estuary at the head of the lough is a small area of inter-tidal flats formed where the Swilly river meanders into the bay below the town of Letterkenny.

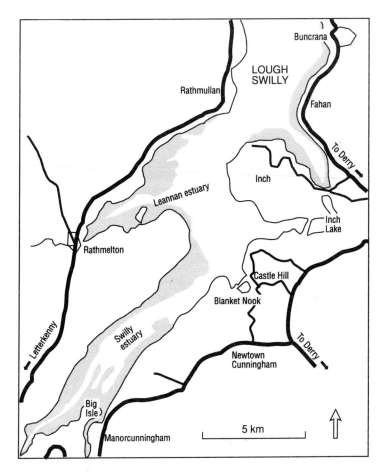

Lough Swilly, Co Donegal

The Leannan estuary is another area of mudflats to the east of the town of Rathmelton.

On the eastern side are the two areas of lagoon. Inch Lake, much the most important for birds, was formed by blocking off with dykes the two ends of a channel between Inch Island and the mainland. The resulting lake is brackish with extensive marshes which flood in winter. The water level at Inch is controlled by a sluice.

On the seaward side of Inch Island the shallow waters provide feeding for divers and grebes. There is also a small area of mudflat on the north and east of the island providing feeding for Brent Geese.

Blanket Nook, the other lagoon, is a small inlet which was cut off from the bay by the construction of a dyke across its mouth. The inlet is bordered by wet fields and by mudflats at low tide.

Species

Lough Swilly has a wide diversity of wintering wildfowl and waders and an excellent breeding bird site at Inch Lough.

In summer, Inch has nesting Great Crested Grebes and Little Grebes and a breeding colony of up to 70 pairs of Mute Swans. There is only one other colony of swans known in Ireland (at Lady's Island Lake in Wexford) so the assembly on the small island in the south-west corner of the lake is particularly interesting. Shelduck, Mallard, Tufted Ducks and Coots also nest as well as several hundred pairs of Black-headed Gulls, about 100 pairs of Sandwich and smaller numbers of Common Terns. Dunlin have bred in the surrounding area.

In winter the shallow waters off Inch Island and Buncrana attract Red-throated and Great Northern Divers, and occasional Black-throated Divers. Great Crested Grebes, Little Grebes and a few Slavonian Grebes are all regular as well. Indeed, this is one of the few places in Ireland where Slavonian Grebes can be found with certainty.

The area is excellent for swans and geese. Whooper Swans usually make their Irish landfall in autumn, on their return from Iceland, in the area between Lough Swilly and Derry. Up to 2,000 can be seen in the huge reclaimed fields opposite Inch or at Big Isle near Manorcunningham from late October onwards. Numbers usually decline somewhat from early November, presumably as the birds fan out to winter throughout Ireland. Bewick's Swans arrive a little later, normally in early November, and numbers are much lower.

Several species of geese can be seen. Brent Geese can be found along the north-eastern coast of Inch Island on the creek opposite Fahan. Greylag Geese winter at Inch Lake, Blanket Nook and Big Isle. White-fronted Geese concentrate at Big Isle, sometimes appear at Inch, but are rarely seen at Blanket Nook. A few Pink-footed Geese are sometimes among the other geese and Bean Goose has been recorded. The geese, like the swans, are very volatile, moving around the south-east side of Lough Swilly, across to Port Lough near Roosky and to the River Foyle between Carrigans and Saint Johnstown on the west side, and south to Grange on the east side.

The lough has a rich diversity of wintering duck species also. In the shallow waters of Lough Swilly itself there is a scattering of Red-breasted Mergansers, but the best places are the lagoons and estuaries. Shelduck, Wigeon, Teal, Mallard, Shoveler, Pintail, Tufted Duck, Pochard, Scaup and Goldeneye are all regular, and Inch Lake is the best place to see them. Gadwall are probably annual and rarities recorded at

Inch have included American Wigeon, Ring-necked Duck and Ferruginous Duck.

In absolute terms, Lough Swilly is not a great place for wader numbers, but it holds more birds than any other bay west of Lough Foyle in Londonderry. Oystercatchers, Lapwing, Golden Plover, Curlews, Redshanks and Dunlin are widespread where there is suitable habitat. At Inch and Blanket Nook there is the possibility of scarcer species. Inch, in recent years, has had Ruffs, Little Stints, Curlew Sandpiper and, on one occasion each, American Golden Plover and Semipalmated Sandpiper. Inch also holds a small winter population of Black-tailed Godwits.

The entire area is good for birds of prey. Peregrine and Buzzard are regular visitors to the lough and Short-eared Owls have wintered in the vicinity of Inch Lake.

In summer Corncrakes still breed in small numbers near Inch and in recent years Quail have been heard calling each summer. In winter there are large finch flocks at both Blanket Nook and Inch Lake and sometimes parties of Snow Buntings.

Timing

Inch is worth visiting at any time of year. Breeding grebes, ducks, Corncrakes and terns are present in summer. Migrant waders and wildfowl are likely in spring and autumn and large numbers of wintering wildfowl

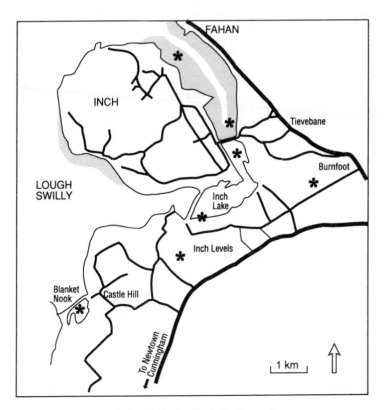

Inch and Blanket Nook, Co Donegal

are present in winter. Late October is the time to see the most spectacular numbers of Whooper Swans.

The other sites are best between September and April. The largest numbers of birds are present from November to March.

State of tide only matters at the Leannan and Swilly estuaries where low tide or a rising tide are best.

Access

The estuary of the Leannan is best watched from the main road between Rathmelton and Rathmullan.

The Swilly estuary can be viewed on the north-western side by taking the road from Letterkenny to Rathmelton and turning off to the right after 5 km. This road provides viewing at several points. On the south-eastern side, the road from Letterkenny to Manorcunningham runs along the southern side of extensive fields where Whooper Swans can be seen. Big Isle can be approached by taking the last left turn before the turn off to the left for Manorcunningham, but is best watched by telescope from the main road.

Blanket Nook is approached by turning left off the road from Newtown Cunningham to Buncrana, about 2 km after Newtown Cunningham. Follow the narrow road to Castle Hill and turn right, following the twisting road until the lake comes into view. At the lake pass through the old railway embankment and walk along it. The lake itself can be approached by following a rough track across a bridge over a stream to the pumping station. Good views can be had from this point.

Inch is reached by turning left off the main road from Derry to Fahan just beyond Burnfoot. The road leads onto a causeway which provides an ideal viewing point for many of the wildfowl in winter. The embankment on the south-eastern side, which once held a railway line, can be walked if necessary. Many of the swans are usually in the fields on the southern side of the lake and can be seen from the road. The southern side of the lake can be approached by driving along the road which leads to an old ford across the lake.

The road across Inch Island is worth following, as good views of Brent Geese can usually be obtained by looking across towards Fahan.

Calendar

All year: Great Crested Grebe, Little Grebe, Mute Swan, Shelduck, Mallard, Tufted Duck, Coot, Oystercatcher, Ringed Plover, Lapwing, possible Dunlin, Curlew, Redshank, Black-headed Gull, Stonechat.

Summer: Corncrake, Quail, Sandwich Tern, Common Tern.

Autumn: Red-throated Diver, Great Northern Diver, Whooper Swan, Brent Goose, Greylag Goose, Greenland White-fronted Goose, possible Pink-footed Goose, Wigeon, Teal, Pintail, Shoveler, Scaup, Pochard, Goldeneye, Golden Plover, Curlew Sandpiper, Little Stint, Ruff, Greenshank, Turnstone, possible American waders.

Winter-spring: Red-throated Diver, Great Northern Diver, possible Black-throated Diver, Slavonian Grebe, Whooper Swan, Bewick's Swan, Brent Goose, Greylag Goose, Greenland White-fronted Goose, possible Pink-footed Goose, Wigeon, Teal, Pintail, Shoveler, Scaup, Pochard, Goldeneye, Golden Plover, Grey Plover, Greenshank, Turnstone.

OTHER DONEGAL SITES

OSI ½" map: sheet 3/
OSNI ½" map: sheet 1/
1:50,000 map: sheet 10
G69 G79

111 SHESKINMORE LOUGH

Habitat and Species

Sheskinmore is a shallow lake, fringed to the north by reeds, and surrounded by marshland to the north and sandy grassland to the south, which eventually grades into sand dunes and, finally, beach. The area is important botanically as well as being of interest for birds. The marsh zone contains a number of orchid species including marsh helleborines and fragrant orchids. The rocky ground behind the marsh to the north has been grazed in traditional ways and also contains interesting plants.

In summer the lough has a number of species of breeding wader. Lapwing and Snipe are common and very obvious. Ringed Plover, Dunlin and Common Sandpiper also breed here. In addition to the waders, Mute Swans, Mallard, Teal and Water Rails nest. Corncrakes may still be heard in the surrounding hay meadows, but are disappearing fast.

In winter, the lough holds important flocks of Barnacle and Greenland White-fronted Geese. The White-fronted Geese roost on the lake and feed here when disturbance is at a low level, but they also feed at a number of surrounding lakes and bogs. As well as the geese, Sheskinmore has Mute Swans, Whooper Swans, Wigeon and Teal as well as occasional visits by Greylag and Pink-footed Geese.

Choughs feed in the surrounding grassland and Peregrines and Hen Harriers frequently quarter the lough.

Access

Sheskinmore is approached by turning left off the main road north from Ardara for Rosbeg. A footpath is signposted from the road and this leads to a public hide, situated on the northern edge of the lake. Part of the lake and surrounding marsh are a reserve owned by the Irish Wildbird Conservancy and the National Parks and Wildlife Service, but some of the land is private and should not be entered upon without prior permission of the owners.

OSI ½" map: sheet 1/
OSNI ½"map: sheet 1/
1:50,000 map: sheet 2
C04

112 HORN HEAD

Habitat and Species

Horn Head has some of the most spectacular cliffs in the country and they are certainly the highest on the north coast. The head has been known since the middle of the last century as a major breeding site for seabirds and, particularly, as the principal Irish breeding colony of the Razorbill.

The seabirds have been fully counted on very few occasions, but a count is a major exercise because of the extent of cliff. A recent documented count took two observers a week. In 1980 there were about 2,000 Fulmar sites, 4,500 Kittiwake nests, 5,550 Guillemots, 12,400 Razorbills, several hundred Puffins and small numbers of Shags, Common Gulls, Herring Gulls, Great Black-backed Gulls and Black Guillemots;

numbers in 1987 were down to 3,950 Kittiwakes, 4,056 Guillemots and 4,278 Razorbills.

Access

The Head is approached by driving north from Dunfanaghy along the scenic road. The road ends at a layby below Coastguard Hill. The largest numbers of Razorbills are about 2.5 km to the east of Coastguard Hill, but all the cliffs teem with nesting birds.

Dunfanaghy New Lake, just outside Dunfanaghy, is well worth looking at as well. It holds breeding Mallard and Tufted Ducks and wintering Wigeon and diving ducks.

OSI ½" map: sheet 1/
OSNI ½" map: sheet 1/
1:50,000 map: sheet 3
C35

113 MALIN HEAD

Habitat and Species

Malin is the most northerly point on the mainland of Ireland. Only the relatively inaccessible Inishtrahull island is farther north. A Bird Observatory operated here in the 1960s for several years but it closed owing to shortage of manpower. The promontory is rugged and bleak with relatively little cover. Nevertheless, its location is ideal for attracting migrants in late autumn.

The Observatory records show that seawatching could be quite spectacular at times and Little Auks, Great and Sooty Shearwaters and skuas were seen. Rarities included Black-browed Albatross. Whooper Swans, Greylag Geese, White-fronted Geese, Barnacle Geese, Fieldfares, Redwings, Lapland Buntings and Snow Buntings were all recorded in good numbers. Scarcer passerines recorded included Hoopoe, Red-breasted Flycatcher and Yellow-browed Warbler.

Seawatching is still done at Malin and remains excellent in the right conditions of north-westerly winds. Leach's Petrels, Sooty Shearwaters and Sabine's Gulls all turn up in these conditions in autumn. Visits

Hoopoe

in periods of south-easterly winds should produce a good variety of passerines.

Access

The road from Derry north to Carndonagh leads on to Malin and eventually right out to the head. The entire tip of the peninsula can hold birds. Seawatching is best from the cliffs just north of the signal tower.

114 TRAWBREAGA BAY

OSI ½" map: sheet 1/
OSNI ½" map: sheet 1/
1:50,000 map: sheet 3
C45 C44

Habitat and Species

Trawbreaga Bay is a muddy inlet lying between Malin village and the sea, but largely impounded by the Isle of Doagh, a wide area of sandhills and meadow. Eiders are common here in both summer and winter. Common, Arctic and Little Terns nest on the shingle bank on the north-west side of the Isle of Doagh along with Oystercatchers, Ringed Plovers and Common Gulls. Lapwings nest on the meadow behind the dunes.

In winter Brent Geese feed on the mudflats of Trawbreaga Bay and Barnacle Geese on the Isle of Doagh meadows. The open water at the mouth of the bay usually has Long-tailed Ducks and divers as well as Eiders. In winter the mudflats hold Shelduck, Mallard, Wigeon, Teal, Curlews, Oystercatchers and most of the common wader species. Spotted Redshanks and Curlew Sandpipers are probably near annual in autumn.

Access

The area is approached by driving north from Derry to Carndonagh and then north to Malin village. The estuary and the Isle of Doagh can be reached at a number of points.

Malin Bridge and the road along the north shore of Trawbreaga Bay are among the best vantage points for the estuary. The Isle of Doagh can be walked across if a car is left at the beach at Pollan Bay about 1 km north of Ballyliffin.

115 GLENVEAGH NATIONAL PARK

OSI ½" map: sheet 1/
OSNI ½"map: sheet 1/
1:50,000 map: sheet 3
C02 C91 C92

Habitat and Species

The Glenveagh National Park was privately owned up to 1975 and comprises 9,600 hectares in the mountainous centre of Donegal. Of this area, an enclosed deer forest covers 8,100 hectares. Lough Veagh, nearly 5.5 km long, lies in the narrow valley which bisects the park. The imposing pseudo-Gothic castle on the shore of Lough Veagh was the home of the owner of this Irish example of the classic sporting estate. There are over 500 red deer in the park.

The mountains are granite and the slopes are drained by numerous streams which run into small lakes. Most of the Park is covered by bog and moorland, but there are stands of sessile oak on the slopes and some planted woodland in the glen and around the castle.

The birds have been studied by staff of the Office of Public Works who operate the National Park and are very varied. In summer, one or two pairs of Red-throated Divers and Goosanders nest on the lakes, along with small numbers of Common Gulls. Peregrines, Ravens and Ring Ouzels nest on the rockier slopes and cliffs. Red Grouse, Curlews, Whinchats, Grasshopper Warblers and Wheatears nest on the moorland, with a few Golden Plovers on the plateaux. The woodland habitat holds as diverse a mixture of species as anywhere else in Ireland and has had Woodcock, Redstart, Wood Warbler, Pied Flycatcher, Tree Pipit and Crossbill recorded in summer in recent years.

In winter Snow Buntings frequent the more exposed parts. Fieldfares and Redwings are common lower down, particularly in early winter.

This must be a likely site for even more rare breeding birds. It has a range of habitats and is situated so far north that species like Whooper Swan, Black-throated Diver, Dotterel, Greenshank, Snow Bunting and Redwing might be hoped for.

Access

The national park is approached from Letterkenny by taking the road for Dunfanaghy and turning left at Termon, 3 km beyond Kilmacrenan. The entrance to the park is signposted on the left after another 9 km. There is a visitor centre at the entrance with impressive displays and, in summer, a mini-bus service between the centre and the castle. The park brochure has a 1:50,000 map with trails marked on it, and a booklet on the birds is available.

LONDONDERRY

Introduction

The coast of Londonderry is dominated by the huge inter-tidal mudflats of Lough Foyle, which run out to the open sea past Magilligan Point. Although the western side of the lough is in Donegal, virtually all the best birdwatching spots are in this county.

From Magilligan eastwards to Downhill is sandy beach backed by sand dunes, but at Downhill there are steep cliffs with breeding Fulmars. Beyond Downhill, along the coast, is the mouth of the Bann estuary and then a rocky stretch of coast around to Portrush.

The eastern side of the county is marked by the River Bann which runs from Lough Neagh through Lough Beg, and then along a broad flood plain to the sea north of Coleraine.

Inland, this is a hilly county with the Sperrin Mountains on the southern border with Tyrone the highest and most remote.

There are a number of wooded estates and country parks, some of which are open to the public, where woodland birds can be seen.

Sites

116	LOUGH FOYLE	*Estuary and sea lough.*
117	BANN ESTUARY	*Estuary.*
118	LOUGH BEG	*Freshwater lake.*
119	LOUGH NEAGH: NORTH-WEST SHORE	
		Large freshwater lake.

Other sites:

120   Roe Valley Country Park   *Woodland.*
121   Downhill   *Inland cliffs.*

References

Belfast RSPB Members' Group *Birds Beyond Belfast* (RSPB, Belfast, 1985).
D'Arcy, Gordon. *Birds at Lough Beg* (Blackstaff Press, Belfast, 1978).
Winfield, D.K., Davidson, R.D. & Winfield, I.J. Long-term Trends (1965–1988) in the Numbers of Waterfowl Overwintering on Lough Neagh and Lough Beg, Northern Ireland (*Irish Birds* 4: 19–42, 1989).

OSI ½″ **map: sheets 1, 2/**
OSNI ½″ **map: sheet 2/**
1:50,000 map: sheets 2, 4
C41 C51 C61 C62

116   LOUGH FOYLE

Habitat

This is the largest and broadest sea lough on the north coast. It runs for over 30 km from Derry to the open sea and is 12 km wide at its broadest, but little more than 1 km wide at its mouth. The north-west shore in Donegal is deep and there are virtually no mudflats exposed at low tide with the exception of a small section at Muff, just across the border from Derry.

The southern and eastern shores are very different with extensive inter-tidal flats backed by lowlying reclaimed land which was formerly famous for White-fronted Geese. Although there has been considerable drainage, the reclaimed farmland behind the embankment protecting it from inundation is still attractive for swans and smaller numbers of geese.

At the mouth, Magilligan Point is an 8-km long sandspit backed by extensive sand dunes.

Species

The most obvious birds in Lough Foyle are the enormous numbers of ducks and waders. This site holds varying numbers of Bewick's Swans (up to 200), over 1,000 Whooper Swans, up to 200 each of White-fronted and Greylag Geese, up to 6,000 Brent Geese, peaks of between 8,000 and 22,000 Wigeon, 2,000 Mallard, 125 Pintail and small numbers of other duck species. They have been counted regularly for many years so the pattern of their occurrence is well known. The best time to see wildfowl in numbers is October when most are at their peak. The large numbers of Wigeon are believed to be Icelandic birds making landfall before moving farther south to other sites. By mid-winter numbers of Wigeon are much reduced.

Brent Geese have increased enormously in recent years, mirroring the increase in the Pale-bellied Brent population generally. Not all the Brent

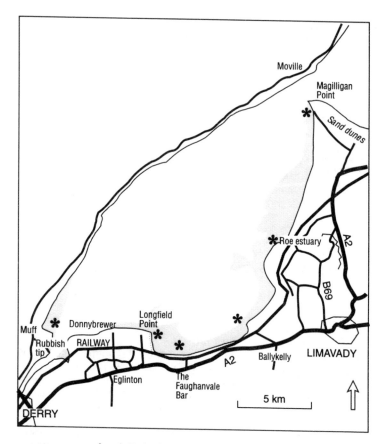

Lough Foyle, Cos Londonderry and Donegal

here are Pale-bellied, however, as there have been records of a single American Black Brant in most recent winters. Dark-bellied Brent may also occur occasionally, but doubt has been cast on records of these birds because of the possibility that birds may occur showing characters midway between the Pale-bellied and Black Brant, resulting from pairing of these two races.

Out in the deeper waters near Magilligan Point, divers and grebes can be seen throughout late autumn and winter. Great Northern and Red-throated Divers are common with up to about ten of each being regular. Occasional Black-throated Divers turn up and they may well be annual here. Great Crested Grebes also occur here, but Slavonian Grebes, which are annual visitors in small numbers, are most easily seen from Myroe where the River Roe enters the lough. As many as 50 have been seen here in winter.'

Wader numbers are high but not so spectacular as the wildfowl flocks. Up to 2,000 Oystercatchers, 3,000 Curlews, 2,000 Bar-tailed Godwits and over 1,000 each of Lapwing, Golden Plover and Dunlin are the most numerous, but Redshanks, Grey Plovers, Greenshanks and Turnstones also winter. In autumn scarcer migrant species turn up. Spotted Redshanks are annual and Curlew Sandpipers and Little Stints near annual. At Magilligan Point there is a wintering flock of Sanderlings on the beach.

Off Magilligan, passing seabirds, including skuas, can be seen in suitable weather conditions.

The stubble fields behind the embankment midway along the estuary are good for wintering finches and buntings, especially Snow Buntings. In 1986, there were about 1,000 Snow Buntings counted at Myroe, the largest flock ever recorded in Ireland, but this was quite exceptional. Up to 50 would be more usual. Lapland Buntings have been seen in some winters.

These fields are regularly quartered by Peregrines, Merlins and Buzzards.

Timing

Without question the best time to visit the Foyle is from late autumn to early spring and the real optimum is late October or early November. At this time, wildfowl numbers are at their highest and most of the winter visitors have arrived.

Most sections of the bay are best visited at or near high tide, when the water level forces waders and surface-feeding wildfowl onto the reclaimed land or its edge.

Access

From Derry eastwards on the Limavady road, access is possible at a number of points by turning left down minor roads.

Donnybrewer was once a famous goose haunt but has been much reduced in importance by drainage. It still holds good numbers of duck and is reached by turning left from the main Limavady road at the White Horse Inn, forking right after 500 m, taking the left turn after another 800 m and then continuing on for another 1.5 km to a level crossing where cars can be parked.

Eglinton Station to the east of Donnybrewer is reached by turning left off the main road opposite the turn to Eglinton. Continue to the station and cross the railway line. Check the fields on either side for wild swans and geese.

Longfield Point to the east of Donnybrewer is reached by turning left at the turn marked for Eglinton Flying Club. Cars can be parked at the Point where the road terminates.

At Ballykelly, about 10 km east of Eglinton, the shore and an excellent high tide roost at Ballykelly Marsh, can be reached by turning left at the Bridge House restaurant.

The Roe Estuary, where the river Roe finally turns westwards into Lough Foyle after meandering north from Limavady, is the next spot. In Limavady, take the B69 to the north, following the signposts for Downhill. After 3 km turn left for Limavady Junction railway station; at the T-junction reached after 3 km turn right and take the road to the estuary, ignoring the cul de sac sign on the way. Cars can be left at the end of the road and the estuary approached by crossing the railway line.

The north side of the Roe Estuary, Ball's Point, can be reached by driving north on the B69 until it joins the A2, then turning left along the A2. About 1.5 km from this junction, turn left just past a small school and follow the narrow road to the estuary.

Magilligan Point at the north-eastern extremity of Lough Foyle is reached by taking the A2 road from Limavady to Downhill. The left turn for Magilligan is signposted about 12 km from Limavady. The narrow road should be followed for about 5 km, past the prison, to a carpark. The army firing range behind the carpark should be avoided and a red flag flies when the range is in use. This is one of the best parts of the lough for divers in winter and for terns and skuas in summer and autumn.

Meadow Pipit

Calendar

Autumn-winter-spring: Red-throated Diver, Great Northern Diver, Great Crested Grebe, Slavonian Grebe, Whooper Swan, Bewick's Swan, Brent Goose, Greylag Goose, Greenland White-fronted Goose, Wigeon, Teal, Mallard, Pintail, Peregrine, Merlin, Sparrowhawk, Kestrel, Oystercatcher, Golden Plover, Lapwing, Dunlin, Sanderling, Knot, Curlew, Redshank, Linnet, Greenfinch, Chaffinch, Snow Bunting, Twite, Skylark, Meadow Pipit.

Autumn: Little Stint, Curlew Sandpiper, Ruff, Spotted Redshank.

Summer: Terns and gulls at Magilligan.

OSI ½" map: sheet 2/
OSNI ½" map: sheet 2/
1:50,000 map: sheet 4
C73 C83

117 BANN ESTUARY

Habitat

The estuary of the Bann has a diversity of habitat which has made it one of the prime sites for rare waders in Northern Ireland. The River Bann flows into the sea about 10 km west-north-west of Coleraine, broadening out into an estuary about 2 km before exiting at Castlerock strand.

The muddy estuary holds waders and ducks and is overlooked by a National Trust hide which provides an ideal viewing point when the tide is rising.

Castlerock strand is a popular sandy beach with a good dune system and a golf course. Near the mouth of the estuary is Barmouth Pier, a small pier which can be quite good for seawatching (though Ramore Head at Portrush in Antrim to the east is much better).

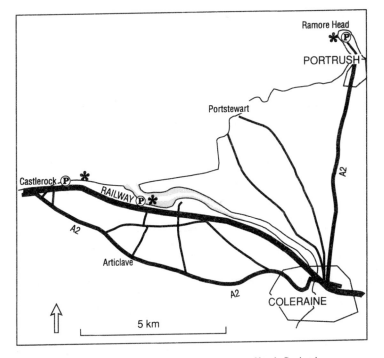

Bann Estuary, Co Londonderry, and Ramore Head, Co Antrim

Species

The Bann is an excellent autumn migration watch point. On the sea, onshore north-westerlies bring seabirds such as skuas, Gannets and auks close to shore. On the edge of the mud, Knots, Dunlins, Whimbrels, Curlew Sandpipers and occasional Little Stints can often be seen. Sanderlings and Ringed Plovers are common on the beach. Rarities seen here include Semipalmated Sandpiper, Long-billed Dowitcher, Gull-billed Tern and Forster's Tern.

Commoner waders such as Oystercatchers, Curlews and Redshanks are regular here from autumn through to spring.

Mallard, Teal, Wigeon, Shelduck and Goldeneye all winter on the estuary. At the mouth of the Bann, divers, Great Crested Grebes and Eiders are found from autumn through to the spring. The sand dunes frequently hold wintering Snow Buntings.

In summer, Common Terns nest at the estuary.

Timing

The Bann is best in September-October and in April-May. Autumn is very much the optimal time for a visit but spring migrant waders do turn up in some years. A winter visit can be productive — Ring-billed Gulls have been seen — but the numbers of wildfowl and waders are much lower than at the nearby Lough Foyle.

Access

Access to the estuary is from the A2 between Coleraine and Downhill. At Articlave turn right, after 1.5 km turn left at a T-junction, cross the bridge and turn right. Continue to the carpark just before the railway crossing. Cross the railway on foot and continue to the estuary.

There is a National Trust hide at the edge of the water which may be used. If it is locked, call for the key at the nearest of the row of cottages facing the river.

Castlerock is reached by following the signposts beyond Articlave. This is a small seaside village with a carpark at the shore. The beach and pier may be walked to from here.

Calendar

Autumn: Divers, Great Crested Grebes, Mallard, Teal, Wigeon, Goldeneye, Oystercatcher, Ringed Plover, Golden Plover, Lapwing, Knot, Dunlin, Sanderling, Curlew Sandpiper, Little Stint, Curlew, Spotted Redshank, Redshank, Greenshank, possibility of rare waders, skuas, terns, gulls.

Winter-spring: Divers, Great Crested Grebes, Mallard, Teal, Wigeon, Goldeneye, Oystercatcher, Ringed Plover, Golden Plover, Lapwing, Dunlin, Sanderling, Curlew, Redshank, Greenshank, gulls.

Summer: Breeding Common Tern.

118 LOUGH BEG

OSI ½″ map: sheet 4/
OSNI ½″ map: sheet 2/
1:50,000 map: sheets 8, 14
H99

Habitat

Lough Beg is a shallow lake at the north-west corner of Lough Neagh formed by the broadening out of the River Bann 3 km after leaving the larger lake. It is one of the prime birdwatching sites in Northern Ireland because of its mix of habitats and its position on the Bann valley, which acts as a flyway between the north coast and Lough Neagh. The lough itself is approximately 5 km long and about 1.5 km wide at its broadest. The lough is generally shallow but a deeper, narrow channel runs through the middle. In summer the area of water is approximately 500 hectares, but this can double with winter flooding.

Lough Beg was formerly much larger in extent. During the 1930s flood

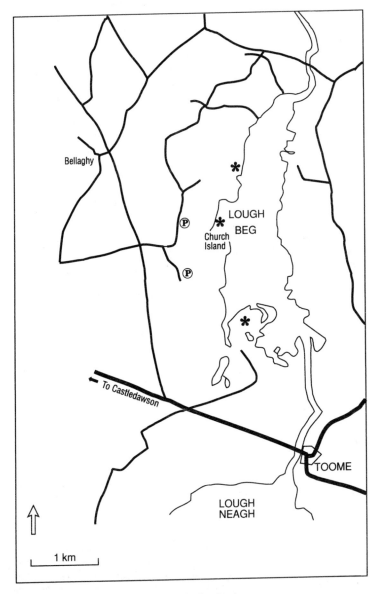

Lough Beg, Co Londonderry

gates were erected where the Bann exits from Lough Neagh and these lowered the water level of Lough Beg. The southern end of the lough has the remnants of what were once thriving sand pits at Toome. These have long been abandoned and this part now comprises a mix of small islands and lagoons. The eastern side has reedbeds and some areas of mixed woodland, mainly alder and willow. A much more extensive woody section is in the north-west corner where Ballyscullion Estate has a variety of planted trees, mainly deciduous. Most of the remainder of the western side is rough grazing pasture which floods in winter.

The vicinity of the lough is extremely interesting botanically. Marsh orchids are common and two rare species, Irish ladies tresses orchid and butterfly orchid, occur here.

Species

In his booklet on the birds of Lough Beg, published in 1978, Gordon D'Arcy recorded a total of 171 species up to the end of 1975 and aggregations of up to 10,000 ducks in a day. The species list has certainly expanded since then and is probably the largest recorded for anywhere in Ireland that does not directly adjoin the coast.

One of the reasons for the long list is the lough's attractiveness to passage waders in autumn. Small numbers of Black-tailed Godwits, Green Sandpipers, Wood Sandpipers, Common Sandpipers, Greenshanks, Knots, Little Stints, Curlew Sandpipers and Ruffs are annual. Pectoral Sandpipers occur in most years and other American species recorded include Long-billed Dowitcher, Greater Yellowlegs, Lesser Yellowlegs, Wilson's Phalarope, Baird's and White-rumped Sandpipers.

The wintering wildfowl and waders are among the highlights. Several hundred Whooper and smaller numbers of Bewick's Swans are present from late October to April. In hard weather, numbers can rise rapidly. A few Greylag Geese can often be seen in winter, but other goose species are rare. The duck numbers, however, are very rewarding. Up to 2,000 Wigeon, 1,200 Teal, 1,000 Mallard, 1,000 Pochard (though sometimes many more), 100 Goldeneye and small numbers of Shovelers, Tufted Ducks and occasional Pintail and Red-breasted Mergansers can be found from October to March. Coots are also numerous in winter. Large numbers of Lapwings and Golden Plover, and smaller numbers of Curlews, Redshanks, Snipe and Dunlins can be seen from September to March.

Passage in spring is particularly exciting as returning migrants can be seen in May flying into the lough from the south and often moving on to the north without stopping. Whimbrels and Black-tailed Godwits are especially notable in spring at Lough Beg, and Garganeys have been found in many years.

In summer Great Crested Grebes nest in the southern part of the lough. Mallard, Teal, Shoveler, Tufted Duck, Red-breasted Merganser and Shelduck are the breeding duck species. Lapwings, Snipe, Curlews, Redshanks and occasional Dunlins breed here. A pair of Ravens has nested recently.

There are two colonies of Black-headed Gulls on islands.

In autumn the lough acts as a focal point for hirundines to assemble before commencing migration. Some thousands of Swallows, House Martins and Sand Martins can be seen in August. Later on, in September and October, passage of Meadow Pipits, wagtails and Skylarks is noticeable.

The most frequent birds of prey are Kestrels, Peregrines, Sparrow-hawks and, in winter, Merlins. Hen Harriers and Short-eared Owls are occasionally seen in winter.

Timing

Lough Beg is worth visiting at any time of the year. In autumn, passage waders can be seen from August onwards. The main wildfowl arrival is from mid September and peak numbers are usually in December or January. Spring passage peaks in April and May, but can continue into June. A record of Broad-billed Sandpiper in June indicates how occasional rarities can turn up at the most unexpected time of the year.

In summer, there are lots of breeding birds and always the chance of something quite exotic.

Access

From Belfast, Lough Beg is approached by taking the M2 from Belfast and following the signposts for Toome. Toome is at the southern end of Lough Beg and access is best on the western side. From Toome drive west for Castledawson and turn right (following the signs for Bellaghy) after 3 km. Drive on for another 3 km until a crossroads is reached. Turn right here and then take the next right turn, following the narrow road down to a ruined farm at Annagh. The flood meadows can be crossed here and the lough approached.

Alternatively, do not take the last right turn, but continue on along the road across a narrow stream and park the car opposite Church Island, making sure to ask permission at the house adjacent to the road junction.

Male Reed Bunting

Calendar

All year: Great Crested Grebe, Grey Heron, Mute Swan, Teal, Mallard, Shoveler, Tufted Duck, Pochard, Kestrel, Sparrowhawk, Moorhen, Coot, Lapwing, Snipe, Curlew, Redshank, Dunlin, Common Gull, Black-headed Gull, Herring Gull, Lesser Black-backed Gull, Great Black-backed Gull, Kingfisher, Reed Bunting.

Autumn: Whooper Swan, Wigeon, Pintail, Golden Plover, Grey Plover, Curlew Sandpiper, Little Stint, Black-tailed Godwit, Spotted Redshank, Greenshank, Green Sandpiper, Common Sandpiper, possible American waders, hirundines. Possibility of Hen Harrier or Osprey.

Winter: Whooper Swan, Bewick's Swan, Wigeon, Pintail, Hen Harrier, Merlin, Short-eared Owl, Golden Plover, Grey Plover, Jack Snipe, Greenshank.

Spring: Lingering winter wildfowl and waders, Garganey, Black-tailed Godwit, Whimbrel.

119 LOUGH NEAGH: NORTH-WEST SHORE

OSI ½″ map: sheet 4/
OSNI ½″ map: sheet 4/
1:50,000 map: sheet 14
H98

Habitat

Lough Neagh is the largest freshwater lake in Britain and Ireland, covering an area of 387 km² and forming part of the borders of Tyrone, Antrim, Down and Armagh as well as Londonderry. In this section, only the shoreline which falls within county Londonderry is dealt with, though some general features of the lake are considered.

The lake has a total shoreline of 125 km, of which 77% is exposed and mainly rocky. The Lough is very shallow, with a mean depth of 8.9 m. In winter it is rarely covered with ice. Lough Neagh is very productive with an abundant invertebrate fauna. In addition, it is heavily polluted with nutrients, though its reputation in the 1970s as one of the most eutrophic water bodies in the world is no longer deserved.

The west shore is varied but has a great deal of alder wood on the edge. It is generally difficult to approach because few roads run close to the lake and most of the land adjoining the Lough is privately owned.

Species

Lough Neagh differs greatly from Lough Beg, even though the lakes are almost adjoining, because it is much more exposed, slightly deeper and has very little muddy or sandy shore. As a result, Lough Neagh holds few

Blackbird

waders and much smaller numbers of surface-feeding ducks. But it does hold far the largest concentrations of diving ducks in Britain and Ireland.

These concentrations have been counted since the 1960s in a mammoth series of monthly censuses conducted from the shoreline. In the recent past, peak counts of 20,000 Pochard, 18,000 Tufted Ducks, 1,500 Scaup, 11,000 Goldeneye and 4,000 Coots have been made. Surface-feeding duck peaks have included 1,500 Wigeon, 100 Gadwall, 1,700 Teal, 4,000 Mallard and 80 Shoveler. Rarer species such as Red-crested Pochard, Smew, Ring-necked Duck and Lesser Scaup have also been seen, but these are not usually recorded on the west side.

The Lough Neagh shoreline also holds large numbers of Mute, Whooper and Bewick's Swans, but these are strung out all along the edge of the lake and the visitor will usually see quite small numbers of each.

The north-west corner of Lough Neagh, around Ballyronan Point, is one of the best places for seeing Scaup. Pochard, Tufted Ducks and Goldeneye are also off the shore in good numbers. The road south of Ballyronan, which runs along the shore for about 1.5 km, and the disused airfield close to Toomebridge usually provide views of Whooper and Bewick's Swans.

Lapwings and Golden Plovers winter on fields in the area.

In summer, Great Crested Grebes, Shelducks, Mallard, Tufted Ducks, Moorhens and Coots breed near Ballyronan.

Timing

The best time for a visit is between September and April.

Access

Ballyronan Point, some 10 km from Toome, is the best place to approach the north-west side of the Lough. Drive west from Toome on the road to Castledawson. After 3 km, turn left for Ballyronan and follow the signposts to the village. Just before the village, the Marina can be seen on the left. Cars can be left at the carpark here and the birds of the Lough viewed from the piers.

The woodland, which runs northwards along the shoreline, has paths marked in it. This alder scrub holds most common woodland birds.

Calendar

Winter: Whooper Swan, Bewick's Swan, Wigeon, Teal, Mallard, Scaup, Pochard, Tufted Duck, Goldeneye, Coot, Golden Plover, Lapwing, Curlew, Redshank.

Summer: Great Crested Grebe, Shelduck, Mallard, Tufted Duck, Moorhen, Coot, Sedge Warbler, Redpoll.

OTHER LONDONDERRY SITES

120 ROE VALLEY COUNTRY PARK

OSI ½″ map: sheet 2/
OSNI ½″ map: sheet 2/
1:50,000 map: sheet 4
C62

Habitat and Species

This site is one of the finest and most accessible woodland habitats on the western edge of Northern Ireland. It comprises a mixture of old riverine valley woodland and modern, planted deciduous trees. The Park follows the banks of the River Roe for 5 km.

Breeding species include most of those one would hope to see in Irish woodland including Sparrowhawk, Kestrel, Chiffchaff, Willow Warbler and Siskin, but also Wood Warbler, a scarce Irish breeding species.

In winter, thrushes and finches can be seen in good numbers.

Access

From Derry take the A2 for Limavady and turn right, just before Limavady (0.5 km from the town), on the Dungiven road. Make sure to turn left for Dungiven along the B192 at the fork which is reached after 1 km. Drive along the road for 3 km, then turn left along Dogleap Road. Follow this road for 1.5 km until you reach the main carpark. There is an exhibition centre and small cafe. Trails are marked through the park and along the river.

Bullfinch

OSI ½" map: sheet 2/
OSNI ½" map: sheet 2/
1:50,000 map: sheet 4
C73

121   DOWNHILL

Habitat and Species

These cliffs are spectacular for their breeding Fulmars. The cliffs extend from close to the beach at Downhill itself and sweep south-westwards and inland to Binevenagh peak. The Fulmars nest all along the cliffs, following them away from the coast.

Although the Fulmars are the most obvious of the breeding birds, Peregrines, Buzzards and Ravens also nest here.

Access

There is a carpark at Downhill just below the cliffs. Downhill is on the coast road from Coleraine to Limavady, about 3 km beyond the turning to Castlerock. The Gortmore viewpoint, reached by taking the steep road up the gulley by the Downhill Hotel, has a cliff-edge carpark which provides views as far as Magilligan. It is 5 km from Downhill.

After Downhill, the road continues on below the cliffs and provides striking views of the Fulmars.

TYRONE

Introduction

Tyrone is a large inland county bordering the western shore of Lough Neagh between the Ballinderry and Blackwater rivers. The northern edge of the county is formed by the Sperrin Mountains; the south-eastern edge is bordered by the Blackwater; the south by moorlands and damp lake country on the fringe of the Lough Erne system, and the west by the Rivers Foyle and Finn.

The most obvious feature of the county is its extent of mountain and moorland and these habitats hold significant numbers of birds. The

Sperrin Mountains have breeding Curlews and a very few Golden Plovers. Peregrines and Ravens are widespread. In the wooded estates are Woodcock, Long-eared Owls, Kestrels, Blackcaps, Jays and Siskins as well as the other common woodland breeders. The small lakes hold breeding Mallard and Tufted Ducks and wintering Pochard together with, in some cases, Whooper Swans.

Sites

122 LOUGH NEAGH: WEST SHORE   *Largest Irish lake.*

Other sites:

123 Grange   *Swans and geese.*
124 Annaghroe   *Swans and geese.*

References

Belfast RSPB Members' Group. *Birds Beyond Belfast* (RSPB, Belfast, 1985).
Winfield, D.K., Davidson, R.D. & Winfield, I.J. Long-term Trends (1965–1988) in the Numbers of Waterfowl Overwintering on Lough Neagh and Lough Beg, Northern Ireland (*Irish Birds* 4: 19–42, 1989).

122 LOUGH NEAGH: WEST SHORE

OSI ½" map: sheet 4/
OSNI ½" map: sheet 4/
1:50,000 map: sheet 14
H96 H97 H98

Habitat

As already described in the account of the north-west shore, which forms part of the border of Londonderry, Lough Neagh is the largest freshwater lake in Britain and Ireland, covering an area of 387 km.

In this section, only the part which falls within county Tyrone is dealt with, though a visit to the Tyrone shore should ideally be combined with a visit to the Londonderry shore and to Lough Beg. For more information on the lough in general, see the account of the north-west corner.

The west shore has a considerable extent of alder wood on the edge and is difficult to approach because few roads run close to the lake and most of the land adjoining the lough is privately owned. Newport Trench and Ardboe Point are easily accessible, however, and provide good views over the lough.

Species

Small numbers of diving ducks can be seen off the pier at Newport Trench and from Ardboe Point. Tufted Ducks, Pochard, Goldeneyes and Scaup are usually present. Mallard, Wigeon and Teal are also regular.

The abandoned Kinrush airfield nearby is a haunt of Whooper and Bewick's Swans, Lapwings, Golden Plovers, thrushes, Skylarks and finches.

All the common gull species occur here in winter.

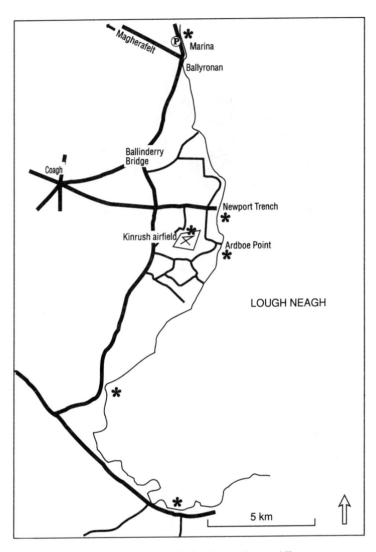

West shore of Lough Neagh, Cos Londonderry and Tyrone

Timing
The best time for a visit is between September and April.

Access
Driving south from Toome, pass through Ballyronan (or check the area for wildfowl *en route*) and keep on the B160 for Coagh until a left turn is reached, just after crossing the Ballinderry river. Take the left turn and drive for 3 km to a crossroads. Turn left here, following the signs for Battery, and follow the road to the edge of the Lough. This is Newport Trench. The small pier provides a vantage point for scanning the lough.

To reach Ardboe Point, retrace your journey from Newport Trench and take the first left, after about 500 m, and follow the signs for Ardboe

Mistle Thrush

High Cross. The old graveyard, where the monument is situated, provides excellent views of the lough.

The abandoned Kinrush airfield can be reached from the road which leads down to Ardboe Point.

Make sure to look at the tenth-century Ardboe High Cross in Ardboe graveyard.

Calendar

Winter: Whooper Swan, Bewick's Swan, Wigeon, Teal, Mallard, Scaup, Pochard, Tufted Duck, Goldeneye, Coot, Golden Plover, Lapwing, Curlew.

Summer: Great Crested Grebe, Shelduck, Mallard, Tufted Duck, Moorhen, Coot, Sedge Warbler.

OTHER TYRONE SITES

OSI ½″ map: sheet 1/
OSNI ½″ map: sheet 1/
1:50,000 map: sheet 7
C30

123 GRANGE

Habitat and Species

Grange is on the east bank of the River Foyle midway between Strabane and Derry. The large, open fields are frequented at times by Whooper and Bewick's Swans and by both Greylag and Greenland White-fronted

Geese in winter. These birds are part of the complex of sites which include Inch and Blanket Nook at Lough Swilly in Donegal (see map on page 193).

Access

The A5 from Strabane to Derry is the approach road for this site.

Scan the fields to the left from a point about 10 km north of Strabane. About 12 km north of Strabane, turn left along the narrow road which leads to Bready. The open fields can be viewed from the road.

OSI ½" map: sheet 8/
OSNI ½" map: sheet 4/
1: 50,000 map: sheet 19

124 ANNAGHROE
H74

Habitat and Species

The Blackwater river frequently floods near Caledon, and the resulting wet pastures attract a flock of up to 100 Greenland White-fronted Geese and some Whooper Swans. Although fairly widespread in the midlands and west of Ireland, White-fronted Geese are hard to find in Northern Ireland. This flock uses the flooded fields at Annaghroe as one of several sites in a series of haunts used in the area, so the birds are not always present.

Golden Plovers, Lapwings, Snipe and Curlews are usually present in winter.

Access

From Armagh, drive west along the A28 to Caledon. After passing through Caledon, take the B45, signposted for Monaghan, to the left. The road runs along the northern side of the Caledon estate before reaching the bridge over the Blackwater river and the border between Northern Ireland and the Republic. Look from the road to the west across the flooded meadows towards the ruined Annaghroe House.

ANTRIM

Introduction

This county comprises the north-east corner of the country. The north and north-east coasts are spectacularly beautiful and the islands such as Muck, Carrick-a-Rede, Sheep, Skerries and Rathlin, provide breeding sites for seabirds in summer. The mainland coast from Portrush around to Larne is mostly a wall of cliff, but some sandy bays interrupt it at places like Whitepark Bay, Ballycastle and Murlough Bay. Much of the coast is owned by the National Trust, and the Ulster Way, a long-distance footpath of some 800 km, follows the edge of the sea from Portrush around to Glenarm before turning inland. The enthusiastic birdwatcher can, therefore, walk most of this coast without much difficulty, though it will take three or four days.

The eastern coast of the county terminates at Larne Lough and Belfast Lough, both of which have significant inter-tidal mudflats with wildfowl and wader populations.

Inland, the principal feature of the county is the Antrim plateau where

Golden Plovers, Curlews and Red Grouse nest. This is a wild and bleak area but of immense value for breeding birds. There are some small lakes where Black-headed Gulls nest and small numbers of Redshanks also breed. The nesting waders are declining, however, and there are probably fewer than a dozen pairs of Golden Plovers nesting now.

The western edge of the county is formed largely by the River Bann and Lough Neagh. The Bann valley is an important migration route and has already been considered in the accounts of the Bann Estuary and Lough Beg (see under Londonderry). The Antrim side of Lough Neagh is accessible at a number of points.

Sites

125	RATHLIN ISLAND	*Island seabird breeding colony.*
126	SHANE'S CASTLE	*East shore of Lough Neagh; woodland.*

Other sites:

127	Ramore Head	*Seawatching point.*
128	Belfast Lough: north shore	*Sea lough and mudflats.*
129	Larne Lough	*Estuary.*
130	Fair Head	*Coastal cliffs.*

References

Belfast RSPB Members' Group. *Birds Beyond Belfast* (RSPB, Belfast, 1985).

Belfast RSPB Members' Group. *Birds Around Belfast* (2nd edition, RSPB, Belfast, 1989).

Bond, Gerry. *Birds of Rathlin Island* (Privately published, no date).

125 RATHLIN ISLAND

OSI ½" map: sheet 2/
OSNI ½" map: sheet 2/
1:50,000 map: sheet 5
D05 D15 D14

Habitat

Rathlin is shaped like an inverted letter 'L'. A long arm runs from east to west and is surrounded by high cliffs where large numbers of seabirds breed. Another arm runs from north to south but is much lower as the ground falls away to sea level at the South Lighthouse at Rue Point.

The cliffs are a mixture of basalt and chalk. The southern cliffs are chalk, but from Bull Point at the western end around the entire northern coast, the cliffs and stacks are dark basalt. Inland, the most widespread habitat is moorland and rough pasture. There are several small lakes scattered around the island. Craigmacagan, midway along the southern arm, has an extensive reedbed.

In summer the grasslands are carpeted with orchids: heath spotted, common spotted and early purple.

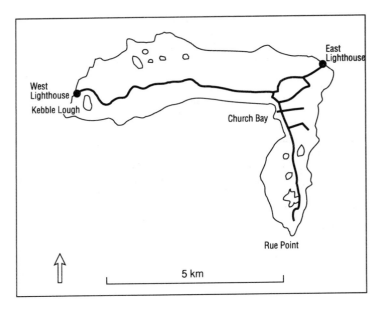

Rathlin Island, Co Antrim

Species

The highlight of a visit to Rathlin for the birdwatcher must be the great numbers of seabirds. The main colonies are at the Kebble National Nature Reserve near the West Lighthouse and at the RSPB Rathlin Cliffs Reserve which runs along about 4 km of cliff. The most numerous birds are Guillemots and Razorbills of which there are about 40,000 and 9,000 birds respectively. Black Guillemots also nest, though in relatively miniscule numbers, with about 50 pairs. Perhaps 2,000 pairs of Puffin nest. Fulmars are quite common with about 800 nest sites. A small colony of Manx Shearwaters numbers several hundred birds. Great Black-backed Gulls, Lesser Black-backed Gulls and Kittiwakes (up to 8,000 nests) breed on the cliffs and both Common and Black-headed Gulls nest on the lakes.

These numbers are really spectacular, but among the seabirds are up to ten pairs of Buzzards and several pairs of Peregrines and Ravens. Golden Eagles have been seen on occasion, but Choughs unfortunately no longer breed.

On the land, Eiders nest on the southern arm leading out to Rue Point. Skylarks, Wheatears, Stonechats, Sedge Warblers, Meadow Pipits, Rock Pipits, Linnets, Reed Buntings and one or two pairs of Whinchats also breed. Twites breed in some years. The wet areas hold breeding Mallard, Tufted Ducks, Moorhens and Coots. Nesting waders include Oystercatchers and Ringed Plovers on the shingle beaches, Lapwing on the rougher grazing land, and Snipe on the marshy areas.

Timing

Rathlin is best in summer when the weather is fine and the birds are on the cliffs. The period from mid-May to early July is optimal.

Access

Boats leave Ballycastle regularly during the summer, but advance booking is advisable. Rathlin Ferry Company (telephone 02657–63917, 63977 and 63934) operates the *M.V. Rathlin Venture* and Rathlin Ferries (telephone 02657–63907 and 63915) operates the *M. V. Iona Isle*. At times when the weather is rough, the boats will not run.

Accommodation is available at the guesthouse operated by Kay McCurdy (telephone 02657–63917) in the Activity Centre operated by Tom Cecil (telephone 02657–63915) and in the Manor House (telephone 02657–63920). Camping is permitted and there are limited facilities in the field beside the pub to the south of the harbour.

Birdwatching trips by boat are available from Liam McFaul (telephone 02657–63935) and bus tours of the island from Noel McCurdy (telephone 02657–63943), Kathryn McFaul (telephone 02657–63939) and Gusty McCurdy (telephone 02657–63909). The bus operators will take visitors to the West Lighthouse, about 8 km from the harbour at Church Bay. A bus saves time, but the walk provides a much better feel for the island and good views of cliffs where Buzzards should be seen. At the West Lighthouse, most of the breeding seabird species can be seen, but Black Guillemots should be looked for below the chalk cliffs. Access to the Lighthouse platform is only by escort with the RSPB Warden, Liam McFaul (telephone 02657–63935).

The road to Rue Point provides access to moorland on the way out where Twites are a possibility and eventually to the Point itself where Eiders and Oystercatchers nest.

An excellent booklet on the island, its geology, fauna and flora is available for purchase.

Starlings (autumn)

Calendar

Summer: Little Grebe, Fulmar, Manx Shearwater (visible from the boat to and from the island), Gannet (also visible from the boat), Shag, Shelduck, Mallard, Tufted Duck, Eider, Buzzard, Peregrine, Kestrel, Coot, Oystercatcher, Ringed Plover, Lapwing, Snipe, Redshank, Common

Gull, Black-headed Gull, Herring Gull, Lesser Black-backed Gull, Great Black-backed Gull, Kittiwake, Razorbill, Guillemot, Black Guillemot, Puffin, Rock Dove, Skylark, Raven, Hooded Crow, Wheatear, Stonechat, Whinchat, Sedge Warbler, Meadow Pipit, Rock Pipit, Linnet, Reed Bunting, occasional Twite.

126 SHANE'S CASTLE

OSNI ½" map: sheet 4/
OSNI 1:50,000 map: sheet 14
G18

Habitat

Shane's Castle Park is located on the estate of the O'Neills and co-exists with a steam railway which attracts large numbers of visitors. The castle is ruined but is surrounded by fine mixed woodland. The entire estate is a popular place for outings from Belfast, only 29 km away.

The Park is bordered on the west side by Lough Neagh and is one of the prime access points for viewing the wintering wildfowl there.

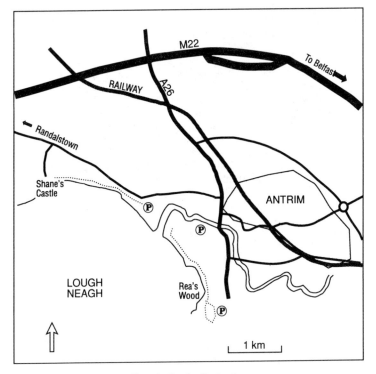

Shane's Castle, Co Antrim

221

Species

From the battlements of the old castle large flocks of wildfowl can be seen in winter and this is probably as good a place as any to see a representative selection of the birds of Lough Neagh. Great rafts of Tufted Ducks and Pochard, together with Wigeon, Mallard, Teal, Scaup and Goldeneye and, at times, Gadwall, Pintail and Red-breasted Mergansers. Rarer ducks seen here include American Wigeon, Red-crested Pochard, Goosander and Smew. These are mainly winter species but in summer Great Crested Grebes nest and their fabulous courtship display can be seen in April and May.

Whooper and Bewick's Swans can also be seen very occasionally along this shoreline.

Large numbers of gulls roost off Shane's Castle in winter. Little and Ring-billed Gulls have been recorded among the commoner species.

The wooded area is good for small birds. Use the well marked nature trails. In summer Blackcaps and Woodcock nest but all the common woodland birds, such as Chiffchaffs, Spotted Flycatchers, Treecreepers and Long-tailed Tits, breed as well.

The reedbeds which fringe the lake shore hold breeding Sedge Warblers and Reed Buntings. The Milburn stream has Grey Wagtails, Dippers, Kingfishers and Moorhens.

This is a good place to see mammals. Fallow deer, badgers, otters and pine martins all occur here.

Timing

In winter the numbers of wildfowl on the lough are at their highest and the chances of a rarity greatest. Summer, however, provides views of nesting Great Crested Grebes and woodland birds.

Access

Shane's Castle is reached from Belfast by heading west on the M2 and leaving the motorway at the A26 exit where the main signs indicate the exit for Ballymena and Coleraine. The first left turn at the roundabout is signposted for Shane's Castle. Take the road towards Antrim and turn right after 5 km along the road for Randalstown. The entrance to the reserve is 1 km along this road on the left.

There is an admittance fee payable at Shane's Castle. The reserve is open to the public on certain days between Easter and mid-September from mid-day to 7 p.m. At other times the gateman should be contacted in advance (telephone 08494–63380).

Calendar

All year: Great Crested Grebe, Mute Swan, Teal, Mallard, Tufted Duck, Pochard, Moorhen, Coot, Black-headed Gull, Common Gull, Herring Gull, Great Black-backed Gull, Dipper, Kingfisher, Grey Wagtail, Goldcrest, Long-tailed Tit, Redpoll, Reed Bunting.

Winter: Whooper Swan, Bewick's Swan, Wigeon, Gadwall, Pintail, Scaup, Goldeneye. Possibility of rare ducks, Lapwing, Curlew, Redwing, Fieldfare, Siskin.

Summer: Blackcap, Sedge Warbler, Chiffchaff, Willow Warbler.

Long-tailed Tits

OTHER ANTRIM SITES

127 RAMORE HEAD

OSI ½″ map: sheet 2/
OSNI ½″ map: sheet 2/
1:50,000 map: sheets 4, 5
C84

Habitat and Species

Ramore Head is at the tip of the promontory which extends to the north from the town of Portrush. The low cliffs are basaltic and grass topped, but the principal feature for the birdwatcher is the head's suitability for autumn seawatching.

In north-westerly winds a great diversity of birds can be seen. Red-throated and Great Northern Divers, Fulmars, Manx and Sooty Shear-waters, Storm Petrels, Leach's Petrels, Gannets and the three common skua species are regular. Mediterranean Shearwaters are near annual and Sabine's Gulls are seen every year. Long-tailed Skuas have been annual in recent years. Mediterranean, Little, Glaucous and Iceland Gulls occur in some years and Ross's has been seen.

As well as seabirds, Barnacle Geese can be seen on the Skerries islands offshore and Eiders, Purple Sandpipers and Turnstones on the rocks below.

Access

Follow the traffic through Portrush to the harbour. Continue onwards, fork right, then turn left at the top of the hill and continue to the carpark at Lansdown. Park the car and walk to the coastguard look-out on the cliff.

128 BELFAST LOUGH: NORTH SHORE

OSNI ½" map: sheets 2, 4/
1:50,000 map: sheet 15
J48 J38 J37

Habitat and Species

The north coast of Belfast Lough from Newtownabbey to Carrickfergus has a number of viewing points for seeing the ducks and grebes wintering on the sheltered waters of the lough and the waders using the rather limited inter-tidal mudflats. As the breeding population of Great Crested Grebes has expanded in recent years on Lough Neagh, so the winter numbers on Belfast Lough have increased and close to 1,000 are now counted each year. Occasional Slavonian Grebes occur among them.

Large numbers of Tufted Ducks, Goldeneye and Red-breasted Mergansers flock on the open water and a few Scaup occur. Although the numbers of Goldeneyes at 300–400 are far less than the thousands which occur on Lough Neagh, this is still a very important wintering site for the species. Eiders, Long-tailed Ducks and Common Scoters are more often found at the mouth of Carrickfergus Harbour.

The waders of the inter-tidal zone include Oystercatchers, Ringed Plovers, Golden Plovers, Lapwings, Curlews, Bar-tailed Godwits, Redshanks, Greenshanks, Dunlins, Purple Sandpipers and Turnstones.

All the common gull species occur throughout much of the year and Iceland, Glaucous, Ring-billed, Little and Mediterranean Gulls have been seen.

Access

From Belfast take the M2 and then the M5 for Carrickfergus. At the roundabout at the end of the M5 take the right-hand turn for Hazelbank Park. Park the car and walk along the path which runs along the shore to Macedon Point and beyond.

The A2 leads on to Whiteabbey, Loughshore Park and Carrickfergus. The lough can be scanned with a telescope from several points along here.

Carrickfergus has an impressive Norman castle, well worthy of inspection, even if your priority is birds. About 2 km before the town, there is a carpark on the left of the dual carriageway with a long pipeline running out to sea from the shore on the other side of the road. This is a good place for gulls.

At Carrickfergus itself, the bay can be scanned from the harbour. Fisherman's Quay, about 1 km beyond the Castle, is an excellent vantage point for sea-ducks.

129 LARNE LOUGH

OSNI ½" map: sheet 2/
1:50,000 map: sheet 9
J49 D40

Habitat and Species

Larne Lough is a sheltered sea lough impounded behind the long arm of Islandmagee with mudflats, saltmarsh and some reedbeds. Whooper Swans, Brent Geese, Wigeon, Teal and Mallard winter here and occasional rare waders turn up in autumn.

Great Crested Grebes winter in small numbers.

In summer Swan Island, an RSPB reserve, is an important tern colony with breeding Arctic, Common, Sandwich and, at the time of writing, one or two pairs of Roseate Terns still hanging on. Red-breasted Mergansers and Black-headed Gulls also nest on the island.

Access
Larne Lough can be seen well from the A2 road. Leave Belfast on the M2 and head north onto the M5 and then the A2. The southern end of the lough is 25 km from Belfast.

Suitable places for viewing the lough include Ballycarry causeway at the southern end, laybys on the A2 and the village of Glynn.

Access to Swan Island is prohibited at all times. However, the feeding terns can be seen well from the shore of the lough.

OSI ½″ map: sheet 2/
OSNI ½″ map: sheet 2/
1:50,000 map: sheet 1
D14

130   FAIR HEAD

Habitat and Species
Fair Head is a magnificent headland with sheer basalt cliffs rising nearly 200 m from the sea. It is famous among ornithologists as the site where a pair of Golden Eagles bred in the 1950s.

Nowadays, the largest raptors to be found here are Buzzards, which are quite numerous, and Peregrines, but Sparrowhawks and Kestrels are both common. Rock Doves, Cuckoos, Meadow Pipits, Stonechats, Wheatears, Choughs and Ravens can also be seen on the top of the head which has a surface of heather and rough pasture.

There are also three small lakes which hold Tufted Ducks and Black-headed Gulls.

Cuckoo

225

Just around the corner to the east is Murlough Bay where Oyster-catchers, Curlews and Redshanks can be seen on the shore and Fulmars, Gannets, Eiders, gulls and auks on the sea.

Access

One of the great scenic sights of Northern Ireland, Fair Head is on the north Antrim coast, about 8 km to the east of Ballycastle. From Ballycastle, drive east for Cushendun. After 4 km turn left, following the signs for Fair Head and Murlough. There are well signposted carparks at both locations.

The top of the cliff has marked paths. The enthusiastic walker can follow trails around the head and back to Ballycastle.

DOWN

Introduction

County Down has two of the finest Irish wetland sites, the great sea loughs of Belfast Lough and Strangford Lough. The coastline is lowlying, even though the Mourne Mountains come close to part of it, and has several promontories which are good for seabirds. The Copeland Islands, lying off the north of the Ards Peninsula, include the oldest extant bird observatory in the country and the longest studied seabird colony. The Ards Peninsula, the arm which encloses Strangford Lough, has fishing ports, such as Portavogie, which attract gulls and occasional rarities, and a rocky shoreline which has been found by regular censuses to be extremely important for waders.

The largest inlets by far are Belfast and Strangford Loughs. Both are well watched and have fine bird populations. But Killough Harbour and Dundrum Bay, slightly further south, and Carlingford Lough, which divides Down in Northern Ireland from Louth in the Republic, should not be overlooked as good birding sites where the unexpected can at times turn up.

While the north-eastern, eastern and southern boundaries of the county are entirely coastal, the western side follows the Newry Canal for much of its length. This county and Fermanagh, far to the west, are the only two of Northern Ireland's counties which do not share portion of Lough Neagh.

Inland, the county has a number of small reed-fringed lakes, many of which hold small numbers of both breeding and wintering wildfowl, and the south-eastern corner is dominated by the Mourne Mountains. The Mournes are not particularly rich in birds, but their wildness and the presence of Ravens, Peregrines and, in summer, Ring Ouzels, are attractions for the visitor who wants to leave the coast.

Sites

131 BELFAST LOUGH: SOUTH SHORE
Estuary and sea lough.
132 STRANGFORD LOUGH   *Estuary and sea lough.*
133 COPELAND BIRD OBSERVATORY
Bird Observatory.
134 DUNDRUM BAY   *Estuary, shallow coast.*

Other sites:
135 Carlingford Lough: north shore
Sea lough.
136 Groomsport *Beach, harbour, mudflats.*
137 Strand Lough and Killough Harbour
Lake, harbour, muddy creeks.
138 St John's Point *Seawatching and passerine watchpoint.*

References

Belfast RSPB Members' Group. *Birds Beyond Belfast* (RSPB, Belfast, 1985).
Belfast RSPB Members' Group. *Birds Around Belfast* (2nd edition, RSPB, Belfast, 1989).
Brown, Robert. *Strangford Lough — the Wildlife of an Irish Sea Lough* (The Institute of Irish Studies, Queen's University, Belfast, 1990).
Copeland Bird Observatory Annual Reports.
Marr, B.A.E. Groomsport and its Birds (*Northern Ireland Bird Report 1986–90*: 121–124, 1991).

131 BELFAST LOUGH: SOUTH SHORE

OSNI ½" map: sheet 4/
1:50,000 map: sheet 15
J37 J48

Habitat

Belfast Lough is a large and rather broad sea lough with the heavily industrialised city of Belfast at its head. The northern shore is in Antrim and is dealt with under that county. The southern shore still has quite extensive mudflats though these have been steadily reduced by land reclamation over the past 150 years. Because of industrial encroachment and the needs of security, the Lough cannot be reached by the birdwatcher all along this shore. Instead, only certain points can be visited.

Working from Belfast city centre out along the coastline are a number of sites where the birds can be seen. Victoria Park is right at the head of the lough and has a small lake which is dry in winter and acts as a roost for waders. The park adjoins Belfast Lough and is separated from the inter-tidal flats by an embankment. The area has many sports pitches and is thronged with people at weekends.

Some 5 km north-east of Belfast are Kinnegar and Belfast Harbour Estate, where extensive sand and mudflats are backed by brackish lagoons, patches of scrub, rough pasture and a sewage works. This is a rich and relatively undisturbed patchwork of habitats right on the edge of industrialised Belfast. The lagoons, situated between an oil terminal and the Lough, are important roosting sites for the birds which feed on

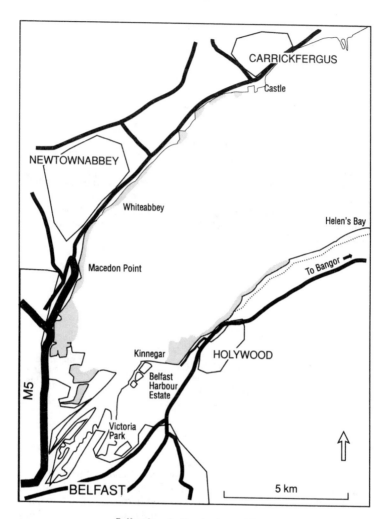

Belfast Lough, Cos Antrim and Down

the muddy estuary at low tide. The area is private and access to the pools (known as the BP Pools) at Belfast Harbour Estate is by permit from the Harbour Police.

Continuing land claim at the Lough culminating in plans to drain the three BP Pools led to a campaign to save at least one of them and the mudflats. This has resulted in the declaration of the mudflats as an Area of Special Scientific Interest and in agreement not just to restore degraded habitat but to create new wildlife habitat as well.

Farther on, from Holywood, the shoreline is more accessible to the birdwatcher as it runs out to Cultra, Helen's Bay and, eventually, Bangor at the mouth of Belfast Lough. The shoreline is a mixture of rocky, sandy and muddy coast. A coastal path runs from Holywood to Bangor and the surrounding land includes grassland and scrub with some wooded areas.

Species

The south side of the Lough has Great Crested Grebes, divers, Scaup, Goldeneyes, Red-breasted Mergansers, Common Scoters, Eiders and a few Long-tailed Ducks much like the northern side. The mouth of the Lough tends to be best for most sea-duck though they can be seen at any point.

Large numbers of Shelduck, Wigeon, Teal and Mallard winter, with smaller numbers of Shovelers and Pochards and a small flock of Brent Geese. The lagoons at Belfast Harbour Estate are the best place to see them. This is also the best place for large wader flocks which in recent years have included peaks of 10,000 Oystercatchers and 2,000 Redshanks in autumn and 4,000 Lapwings, 2,000 Curlews and 2,000 Dunlins in winter. Victoria Park is also a good spot for each of these wader species at high tide. For birds which prefer rockier shores, such as Turnstones and Purple Sandpipers, the best places are near the mouth of the lough.

The Lough is an excellent place for seeing scarcer migrant wildfowl and waders. Green-winged Teals have been seen at the BP Pools in winter, Black-winged Stilt in spring and Little Ringed Plover and several species of American wader is autumn. Garganeys are annual in spring and Curlew Sandpipers, Little Stints, Ruffs and Spotted Redshanks are regular autumn migrants.

In autumn and winter Peregrines hunt the area regularly. Large numbers of gulls are present for most of the year and rarities such as Ring-billed, Iceland, Glaucous and Mediterranean are annual, with as many as six Ring-billed Gulls at the Belfast Harbour Pools at times. In spring, summer and autumn, terns and skuas visit the Lough. They are usually better seen from near the mouth of the lough but Black and White-winged Black Terns have been seen at Belfast Harbour Pools.

The unkempt vicinity of the Belfast Harbour Estate is not only attractive for birds in autumn, winter and spring. Its diversity of habitat also provides nesting sites for Shelducks, Mallard, Coots, Moorhens, Lapwings, Ringed Plovers, Redshanks, Snipe and Black-headed Gulls as well as one or two Shovelers.

Further out along the shore of the lough, most common woodland birds can be seen from the path between Holywood and Bangor.

Timing

The wonderful point about Belfast Lough is that rewarding visits can be made at any time of the year. In autumn and winter, wildfowl and waders are most numerous; in spring there is obvious passage migration and by the summer breeding birds are on their territories. Rarities are more likely in autumn than at other seasons, but Black-winged Stilt was seen in May and White-winged Black Tern in June and July. So, a visit always holds out the real possibility of the unexpected.

As with most estuarine areas, a visit within three hours either side of high tide is best.

Access

Working from Belfast out along the coast, each of the sites dealt with is reached as follows:

Victoria Park lies between the Sydenham Bypass and Belfast Lough, but is approached by following the signs from Holywood Road to Connsbrook Avenue. Turn left off Connsbrook Avenue down Park

Avenue and drive to the right and under the Sydenham Bypass to Victoria Park. The park can also be reached by parking at Inverary Drive and crossing over the footbridge.

Kinnegar and Belfast Harbour Estate are reached by taking the A2 from Belfast for Holywood and Bangor. At the second set of traffic lights, turn left and follow the road under the railway and around to the left. Drive along the shore road to the barrier by the Army Depot. Cars are permitted through the barrier up to 5 p.m., but pedestrians can pass at any time. If the barrier is closed, turn right and park down by the shore. Parking by the Army Depot is usually not permitted. The foreshore at Kinnegar can be viewed from the road beyond the barrier, but there is a gate at the entrance to Belfast Harbour Estate which is only opened for those with permits.

The outer part of Belfast Lough is far more accessible. A footpath runs the 17 km from Holywood to Bangor and can be accessed at a number of points. At Holywood, the path commences on the shore opposite the Army Depot near Kinnegar, but it can be reached by turning left at Cultra, Sea Park, or St Helen's Bay. The path terminates at Pickie Pool at Bangor.

Calendar

All year: Great Crested Grebe, Cormorant, Shag, Mute Swan, Shelduck, Teal, Mallard, Shoveler, Eider, Red-breasted Merganser, Moorhen, Coot, Peregrine, Kestrel, Sparrowhawk, Oystercatcher, Lapwing, Curlew, Snipe, Redshank, Turnstone, Black-headed Gull, Common Gull, Herring Gull, Lesser Black-backed Gull, Great Black-backed Gull, Stonechat, Linnet.

Autumn: Divers, Wigeon, Teal, Goldeneye, Scaup, Long-tailed Duck, Common Scoter, Golden Plover, Grey Plover, Knot, Dunlin, Curlew Sandpiper, Little Stint, Purple Sandpiper, Ruff, Black-tailed Godwit, Bar-tailed Godwit, Spotted Redshank, Greenshank, Common Sandpiper, vagrant waders from North America, Ring-billed Gull, Mediterranean Gull.

Winter: Divers, Brent Goose, Wigeon, Teal, Goldeneye, Scaup, Long-tailed Duck, Common Scoter, Golden Plover, Grey Plover, Dunlin, Purple Sandpiper, Jack Snipe, Bar-tailed Godwit, Greenshank, occasional Ruff, Glaucous Gull, Iceland Gull, Ring-billed Gull,

Spring: Late-staying wildfowl and waders. Annual Garganey. Whimbrel and Common Sandpiper, Terns. Possibility of exotic vagrants.

Summer: Breeding wildfowl and waders.

132 STRANGFORD LOUGH

OSI ½" map: sheet 9 (southern half)/
OSNI ½" map: sheet 4/
1:50,000 map: sheet 21
J47 J46 J57 J56 J55 J54

Habitat

Strangford is an enormous sea lough encompassing a range of habitats. Much of it has been managed by the National Trust for many years and wildfowl and wader counts have been carried out for over 25 years so quite a lot is known of the distribution of its birds. Indeed, a book on the wildlife of the Lough by Bob Brown, a former National Trust Warden and now the Northern Ireland RSPB Regional Officer, is an indispensable companion to anybody making an extended visit to the area.

Strangford is more than 30 km long and has an area in excess of 150 km². The lough varies in depth but, at its deepest, reaches 60 m. It connects with the Irish Sea at the 'Narrows', between Portaferry and the village of Strangford, where the exit channel is 30 m deep and only 800 m wide. The main body of the lough is much broader, varying up to 8 km from side to side.

There are more than 120 islands in the lough and many more reefs and rocks. Most of them are on the west side. Most of the islands are partly submerged drumlins created by glaciers which deposited soil and gravel in a mosaic of rounded hills. The shoreline is extremely indented and extends for about 240 km, more than a third of the entire coastline of Northern Ireland.

Although the sea and the islands are important for some bird species, the really vital habitat for the birdwatcher is the enormous area of inter-tidal mudflats, estimated to cover 40% of the area of the lough. The inter-tidal zone at the Narrows comprises rocky shore. Further into the lough there are shores where large boulders lie on sand and coarse mud. This habitat is widespread on the east side of the lough and on the west side south of Killyleagh. From Greyabbey north, however, fine grained mudflats extend across the northern end of the Lough and around to Mahee Island on the western side.

The northern end of Strangford has large areas of eel-grass *Zostera*, which provide rich feeding for Brent Geese on their arrival from the Canadian Arctic. The mudflats surrounding the shallow bays at this end have a green appearance in early autumn as the plants develop, but by the end of November they have been so heavily grazed by geese that the mudflats revert to their usual hue.

Above the tideline there are areas of saltmarsh in the north-west corner of the lough, especially at the Comber river estuary near Castle Espie. Behind the shoreline, the land is lowlying with drumlins to the north and west. Most of the land to the north is farmed intensively for cereals and vegetables and many of the old hedges and ditches in the fields between Newtownards and Comber have been removed. Farther south, there are smaller fields and, around the exit from the lough, the fields are smaller still and divided by dry stone walls. There are some areas of scrubland and a scattering of woodland clumps.

Around the edge of the lough are a number of small marshes and freshwater lakes surrounded by reeds, willows and alders. These small lakes provide feeding for some wildfowl, which fly to and from the mudflats on the lough when the tides rise or they are disturbed. The Quoile Pondage, a freshwater lagoon formed by the impounding of the River Quoile by a barrage in 1957, is much the most important fresh-water habitat on the fringe of the lough. The estuary was once backed by the floodmeadows of the Downpatrick Marshes, famous for geese and ducks in the first half of the century, but now largely drained and almost devoid of wildfowl. Despite the Quoile Pondage now being almost entirely freshwater, there are still flood meadows which attract Greylag Geese and Wigeon. This particular area is a National Nature Reserve.

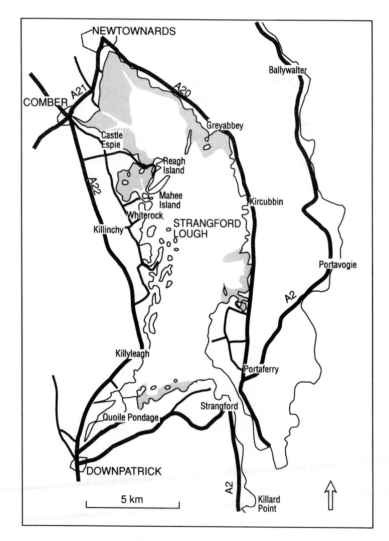

Strangford Lough, Co Down

Species

Strangford holds peak numbers of nearly 25,000 wildfowl and about 45,000 waders, making it one of the most important wetlands in the country. Its particular attraction is that many of these birds can be seen within 20 km of Belfast.

The dominant feature of Strangford's wintering wildfowl is its great flocks of Brent Geese. The first birds arrive from northern Canada in late August and flocks pile in during September and October to reach an October peak of 10,000–12,000 birds. They feed voraciously and, having grazed the *Zostera*, many move on to sites further south and the remainder turn to other food such as green algae *Enteromorpha*. Some birds move on quite quickly, so the Lough is a vitally important staging point for the species. Among the Pale-bellied Brent Geese are one or two Black Brant, which usually winter on the Pacific coast of North America. The same individuals appear to return annually to Strangford, and Greyabbey is probably the best place to start a search for them. Dark-bellied Brent have been recorded as well, but seem to be even rarer than Black Brant, and there are indications that birds with mixed Pale-bellied Brent/Black Brant parentage are occurring.

Most of the other geese to be seen at the lough are feral. Greylag, Barnacle and Canada Geese have all been released here. A few wild Greenland White-fronts sometimes occur and occasional Pink-footed Geese have been seen. The common swan of the Lough is the Mute Swan, but a small number of Whooper Swans do winter. The stubble fields between Strabo and Comber are a good place to look for them.

Strangford was once famous for its huge wintering flocks of Wigeon. As recently as the 1970s there were over 20,000, but nowadays the peak is only 2,000. Research is being carried out into the reasons for this decline, and in particular to find out why it has happened during a period when Brent Goose numbers have increased.

Shelduck and Mallard occur in similar numbers to Wigeon, Teal in somewhat smaller numbers and there are a few hundred each of Pintail, Shovelers, Pochard, Tufted Ducks, Goldeneye and Red-breasted Mergansers. Gadwall and Scaup also occur in small numbers. A few Slavonian Grebes and one or two Black-throated Divers winter as well.

Wader numbers are very impressive. The lough is internationally important for its Knot and Redshank numbers. Up to 5,000 Oyster-catchers, 9,000 Golden Plovers, 14,000 Lapwings, 10,000 Knots, 6,000 Dunlins, 1,000 Bar-tailed Godwits, 2,000 Curlews and 3,000 Redshanks occur each autumn and winter. All the other common wader species occur as well. Passage migrants, such as Ruffs and Spotted Redshanks, sometimes appear on the lagoons at the Castle Espie Conservation Centre or the river nearby and at the Quoile Pondage.

The southern end of the Lough holds substantial numbers of Turn-stones on the rocky shores. Smaller numbers of Purple Sandpipers can be found among them.

In summer, the Lough is an important breeding area for wildfowl, waders and terns. A few pairs of feral Greylag, Barnacle and Canada Geese breed, mainly on islands. Shelducks, Mallard, Gadwall, Tufted Ducks, Red-breasted Mergansers and one or two Eiders nest on the Lough. The breeding waders include Oystercatchers, Ringed Plovers, Lapwings and a couple of pairs of Redshanks.

Large numbers of gulls and terns nest on the islands of the lough. Over 5,000 pairs of Black-headed Gulls, 60 pairs of Common Gulls, 80 pairs of

Lesser Black-backed Gulls, 70 pairs of Great Black-backed and 600 pairs of Herring Gulls breed. The most numerous terns are Sandwich with 700 nesting pairs; about 500 pairs of Common and 100 pairs of Arctic Terns nest as well. Roseate Terns once bred here, but now only occur as non-breeding visitors.

Cormorants, Black Guillemots and Herons also breed.

Although the area of the lough is enormous and the birds widely distributed, most of them can be seen at a small number of sites where viewing conditions are excellent. The Wildfowl and Wetlands Trust has a reserve at Castle Espie and the Department of the Environment (NI) has a reserve at the Quoile Pondage. Both these sites have visitor centres. The islands where the gulls and terns nest are, for obvious reasons, closed to the public, though Swan Island, close to the quay at Strangford village, provides excellent viewing opportunities because of its proximity to the mainland.

The Lough is so extensive that parts of it attract seabirds. Gannets feed in the Narrows at the southern end and Manx Shearwaters, Fulmars and occasional Storm Petrels can be seen in the same area. Razorbills and Guillemots feed in the Lough at all times of the year.

Around the edge of the Lough, the shoreline hedge and gorse scrub provide excellent habitat for Stonechats, Linnets, Twites, Reed Buntings and Tree Sparrows. Birds of prey quarter the saltmarshes and Short-eared Owls are regular.

Timing

Strangford is at its best for wildfowl in September and October when the Brent Geese peak. Wader diversity is probably at its highest at the same time. Peak numbers are later for some species.

The best time for visiting is within three hours of high tide when the birds are within relatively close range of the shore.

The breeding terns and gulls can best be seen from May to July, though the Sandwich Terns arrive earlier.

Access

There are numerous access points as the road system runs around the entire Lough. Bob Brown's book on Strangford (see references under the list of Down sites) includes a gazetteer which takes a tour around the complete shoreline and also a tour by boat through the centre of the Lough. This account must necessarily concentrate on the most prominent access points. On the western side the following are among the best places to see a variety of species:

Island Hill is close to Comber, the starting point for a tour of the west side of Strangford. From Comber take the road for Newtownards (the A21). After 1.5 km take the right turn onto Ringcreevy Road. This links with Island Hill Road and terminates at the shore, where there is a public carpark. This section of the Lough is excellent for Brent Geese and for wintering waders.

Castle Espie is a Wildfowl and Wetlands Trust reserve and has an impressive wildfowl collection, an art gallery, a restaurant and shop, an education room and woodland walks. Leave Comber on the A22 heading south for Killyleagh. After less than 500 m turn left at the sign-post for Mahee Island. Follow the road for about 4 km until you see the signpost to the reserve on the left. Drive in and park. There are lagoons here where scarce waders such as Ruffs and Black-tailed Godwits are

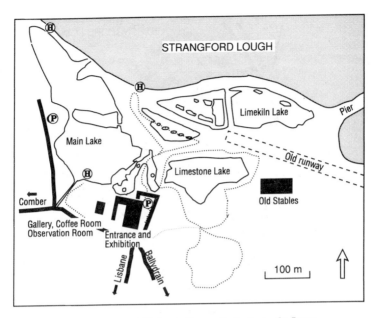

The Wildfowl and Wetlands Centre, Castle Espie, Co Down

sometimes seen in autumn. These lagoons are the remnants of lime-stone and clay quarries. To see the wildfowl on the mudflats, walk from the Centre buildings towards the shore or take the lane down to the shore immediately before the Reserve (on the Comber side). The Montgomery Hide is situated on the edge of the Lough and provides good views of Brent Geese, Shelducks, Wigeon and waders. It really is essential to be here within two hours of high tide as otherwise the birds are very distant. The Curator is James Orr, Wildfowl and Wetlands Trust, Castle Espie, Ballydrain Road, Comber, Co Down BT23 6EA, (telephone 0247–874146).

Island Reagh is another access point to the mudflats. Continue on beyond Castle Espie in the direction of Mahee Island. At Ballydrain turn left onto Ringneill Road and follow the signs for Nendrum. The road crosses a causeway onto Island Reagh. About 1 km after the causeway, a small carpark is reached. A National Trust hide has facilities for the disabled. This section of mudflats has fewer Brent Geese but is good for Pintails, Shovelers and Black-tailed Godwits.

Whiterock Bay is further south. Take the A22 road from Comber for Killyleagh and turn left at Balloo, following the signpost to Whiterock. This is a popular sailing centre but it holds Brent Geese, Teal and waders on the mudflats opposite the saltmarsh north of the yacht club. The marsh itself is a good place to get excellent views of Snipe. Farther out, near Hen Island, Goldeneyes and occasional Slavonian Grebes feed in winter.

Quoile Pondage National Nature Reserve, a reserve operated by the Environment Service of the Department of the Environment, is at the southern end of the west side of the Lough. Follow the A22 through Killyleagh and on to the Quoile Bridge. Turn left over the bridge and then left again, following the signs for Strangford. The Quoile Country-

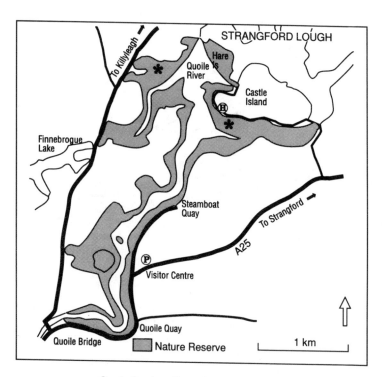

Quoile Pondage Nature Reserve, Co Down

side Centre is well signposted and has an exhibition centre illustrating how the area has been changed by the barrage. This is an excellent breeding area for a number of species including Great Crested Grebe, Grey Heron, Shelduck, Mallard, Gadwall and Tufted Duck. Terns feed here in summer. In winter, the Pondage has hundreds of Greylag Geese, mostly feral, Mallard, Wigeon, Teal, Tufted Ducks, Pochards and Goldeneyes. Smaller numbers of Gadwall, Pintail, Shovelers and Scaup also occur. Wader numbers are not very large, but diversity is high. Spotted Redshanks are regular and Wood and Green Sandpipers occasional in autumn. Access to most of the reserve is restricted to prevent disturbance. Visitors should contact the Warden for advice on open access areas for viewing the birds. There is a hide at Castle Island which overlooks the largest concentrations of birds. The Warden is Dr Shaun D'Arcy-Burt, Quoile Countryside Centre, 5 Quay Road, Downpatrick, Co Down, BT30 7JB, (telephone 0396–615520).

On the east side of the Lough are a number of additional points where access is straightforward.

Tidebank is on the southern side of Newtownards. Leave Newtownards on the A20 for Portaferry. Just outside the town, there is a small carpark where the road meets the shore of the Lough. Look for the square sewage pumping station building on the right; the parking area is just beyond the entrance. From here it is possible to walk along the embankment and see flocks of Brent Geese and waders.

The Maltings at Ballyreagh is about 1 km further along the A20. There is a layby which gives good views of massive flocks of Golden Plovers and Knots as well as the other common wader species. Brent Geese also congregate here, and Whooper Swans can sometimes be seen.

The old Gasworks are farther on along the A20 towards Greyabbey. There is a National Trust carpark on the right hand side about 300 m beyond the entrance to Mount Stewart. The gasworks at one stage manufactured gas for the estate, but now provide an excellent vantage point for scanning the mudflats with binoculars and telescopes. The offshore islands can be seen well from this point.

Greyabbey is a small village on the A20 about 12 km south-east of Newtownards. The carpark on the right hand side, just beyond the village, overlooks the Lough. This part of Strangford does not hold so many birds as the mudflats to the north, but it has held one or two Black Brant in the recent past.

Between Greyabbey and Kircubbin, farther south again, the coastline is good for Slavonian Grebes, and both Black-throated Diver and Red-necked Grebe have been reported in recent years. Access is difficult along much of the shore. The best viewing point is from the shoreline at Kircubbin.

Calendar

All year: Great Crested Grebe, Little Grebe, Cormorant, Heron, Mute Swan, Greylag Goose, Barnacle Goose, Canada Goose, Shelduck, Mallard, Gadwall, Shoveler, Tufted Duck, Pochard, Eider, Red-breasted Merganser, Coot, Moorhen, Oystercatcher, Ringed Plover, Lapwing, Snipe, Curlew, Redshank, gulls. Black Guillemot.

Winter: Whooper Swan, Brent Goose, Wigeon, Teal, Pintail, Scaup, Goldeneye, Golden Plover, Grey Plover, Knot, Dunlin, Purple Sandpiper, Black-tailed Godwit, Bar-tailed Godwit, Snipe, Jack Snipe, Greenshank.

Summer: Common Sandpiper, Common Tern, Arctic Tern, Sandwich Tern, possibility of Roseate Tern.

Autumn: Wintering wildfowl and waders, plus Whimbrel, Common Sandpiper. Spotted Redshank, Ruff, possible Little Stint, terns.

Spring: Wintering wildfowl and waders, plus Whimbrel, Common Sandpiper and terns.

Note: The map for Castle Espie is redrawn from The Wildfowl and Wetlands Trust reserve map; the map for Quoile Pondage Nature Reserve is redrawn from the Department of the Environment's reserve map.

133 COPELAND BIRD OBSERVATORY

OSNI ½" map: sheet 4/
1:50,000 map: sheet 15
J58 J68

Habitat

The Bird Observatory on John's Island, one of the three islands of the Copeland group, is the oldest in Ireland, having been founded in 1954. The islands are located off the north coast of Down, about 7 km from Donaghadee. John's Island is small, oval shaped and quite high, with small cliffs on its east side and gentle slopes on the other sides. The area is only 16 hectares and the highest point is 30 m above sea level. The island is covered with grass, but there are elders, willows and sycamores in sheltered parts. The Observatory itself is based in the old lighthouse buildings, which have been restored to provide accommodation and ringing facilities.

Species

Copeland has a breeding colony of some 500 pairs of Manx Shearwaters; this has been the subject of a ringing study for nearly 40 years. Birds first ringed in the early 1950s are still occasionally retrapped, so some are clearly very long-lived. The most distant recoveries have been of several birds in South America. There are also breeding Great Black-backed, Lesser Black-backed, Herring and Common Gulls and small numbers of Fulmars and Black Guillemots. A few pairs of Eiders, Red-breasted Mergansers, Oystercatchers, Water Rails and Stock Doves also nest. Storm Petrels are caught and ringed at night in late summer, but do not breed on the island.

Passerine migration in spring and autumn is not as varied as in south coast counties, and rarities are much less frequent. However, good numbers of Wheatears, Willow Warblers, Chiffchaffs and Goldcrests are recorded together with small numbers of Whinchats, Redstarts and other warbler species. Numbers of migrants in spring are usually higher than in autumn.

Rare birds do turn up, however, and the island has had such extreme rarities as Scarlet Tanager and Fox Sparrow.

Timing

As the island is uninhabited, visits must be made by prior arrangement with the Observatory bookings secretary, and are easiest if a party of regular visitors is joined. The islands is manned most weekends between April and October and there are day visits in June.

Access

The island is private and access is by prior arrangement with the Bookings Secretary, Neville McKee, 67 Temple Rise, Templepatrick, Antrim BT39 0AG (telephone 08494–33068). The boat leaves from Donaghadee.

Calendar

Summer: Manx Shearwater, Storm Petrel, Fulmar, Eider, Water Rail, gulls, terns, Black Guillemot.

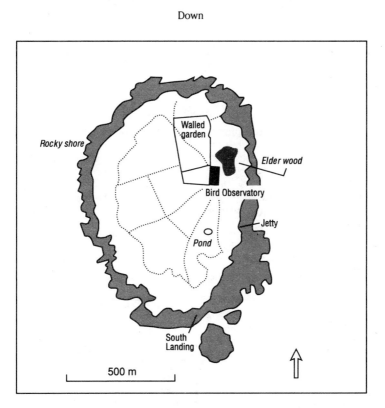

Copeland Bird Observatory, Co Down

Spring: Wheatear, Willow Warbler, Chiffchaff, Grasshopper Warbler, Blackcap, Garden Warbler, Whitethroat, Goldcrest, Redstart, Spotted Flycatcher, Meadow Pipit, Tree Pipit.

Autumn: Great Skua, Arctic Skua, Sedge Warbler, Chiffchaff, Willow Warbler, Whitethroat, Blackcap, Goldcrest, Spotted Flycatcher, Meadow Pipit, Skylark, possibility of Pied Flycatcher, Redstart and Tree Pipit.

Note: The map for the site is redrawn from the Copeland Bird Observatory Report map.

Down

OSI ½" map: sheet 9/
OSNI ½" map: sheet 4/
1:50,000 map: sheet 21
J43

134 DUNDRUM BAY

Habitat

Dundrum Bay comprises the inner bay and Murlough National Nature Reserve, an area of heath and dune between the estuarine inner bay and the sea. The inner bay is an extremely sheltered estuary with extensive inter-tidal mudflats.

The Nature Reserve is vegetated with heath in the north, grassland in the centre and dense sea buckthorn in the south. The seaward side of the Reserve is bounded with sand dunes backing onto a long sandy beach.

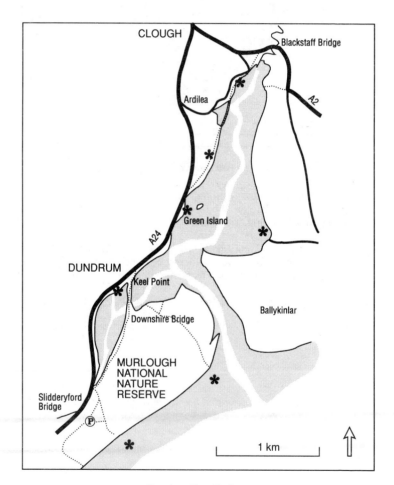

Dundrum Bay, Co Down

Species

The inner bay holds good numbers of Shelduck, Wigeon, Mallard, Teal, Goldeneye and Red-breasted Mergansers, together with several thousand waders. Outside the bay, large rafts of Common Scoters winter off Newcastle beach. Occasional Velvet Scoters are usually among them, and Surf Scoters have been found. Great Northern and Red-throated Divers, Great Crested Grebes, Goldeneyes, Scaup and one or two Long-tailed Ducks also winter in the outer bay.

The entire area holds up to 9,000 waders in winter, mostly on the mudflats of the inner bay. This section is an excellent place for autumn passage waders, especially Spotted Redshanks, Curlew Sandpipers and Little Stints.

The sand dune system holds a varied population of breeding birds including Cuckoo, Stonechat, Grasshopper Warbler and Blackcap.

Timing

Autumn is the best time for passage waders, winter for wildfowl and larger flocks of waders on the inner bay and sea-ducks and grebes off the beach. In summer, the sand dune system has its breeding birds.

Access

Dundrum is 40 km south of Belfast and about 5 km north of Newcastle. The inner bay is accessible by road at a number of points along its north-west shore. Blackstaff Bridge on the A2 between Clough and Ardglass is at the northern head of the estuary. From here the National Trust Coastal Footpath runs along the edge of the estuary to Green Island where the A24 road is picked up again near Dundrum village. The A24 runs south from Dundrum and provides views of the southern arm of the inner bay. Murlough Nature Reserve can be reached by turning left off the A24 at Slidderyford Bridge or by turning into the National Trust carpark about 1 km further on along the same road.

The Warden can be contacted at the Reserve (telephone 039–675467).

Calendar

All year: Grey Heron, Mute Swan, Shelduck, Mallard, Red-breasted Merganser, Kestrel, Sparrowhawk, Oystercatcher, Ringed Plover, Collared Dove, Long-eared Owl, Skylark, Meadow Pipit, Kingfisher, Goldfinch, Linnet, Reed Bunting.

Autumn: Passage waders including Curlew Sandpiper, Little Stint, Black-tailed Godwit, Whimbrel, Spotted Redshank, Greenshank, possibility of Nearctic waders.

Winter: Red-throated Diver, Great Northern Diver, Great Crested Grebe, Whooper Swan, Bewick's Swan, Brent Goose, Wigeon, Teal, Goldeneye, Long-tailed Duck, Common Scoter, possible Velvet Scoter and Surf Scoter, Golden Plover, Grey Plover, Lapwing, Dunlin, Curlew, Redshank, Redwing, Fieldfare, Twite.

Summer: Sand Martin, Wheatear, Grasshopper Warbler, Whitethroat, Blackcap, Spotted Flycatcher.

Note: The map for this site is redrawn from the National Trust Nature Reserve map.

OTHER DOWN SITES

135 CARLINGFORD LOUGH: NORTH SHORE

OSI ½" map: sheet 9/
OSNI ½" map: sheet 4/
1:50,000 map: sheet 29
J11 J21

Habitat and Species

Carlingford is a long and deep sea lough which straddles the border between Northern Ireland and the Republic. The southern side, which is backed by the Carlingford Mountains on the Cooley peninsula, is dealt with under the accounts for Louth in the province of Leinster. The northern side, which concerns us here, has the more extensive mudflats and important seabird breeding islands, and is also backed by mountains, in this case the Mournes. With mountains on both sides, a tour of the lough shore is a very attractive scenic drive.

The Lough has flocks of several hundred sea-duck, mostly Scaup but also Goldeneyes, Red-breasted Mergansers and a few Long-tailed Ducks. Great Crested Grebes and both Red-throated and Great Northern Divers also occur, and one or two Slavonian Grebes usually winter. On the mudflats Brent Geese, Shelduck, Wigeon, Teal, Mallard and the common wader species can all be seen in winter.

In summer, Green Island and Greencastle Point Islands, which are RSPB reserves, have breeding Common, Arctic and Sandwich Terns and perhaps one or two pairs of Roseate Terns. These islands are closed to visitors but the terns can be seen well from the shore.

Access

Carlingford is a long lough. The best spots are near the mouth at Greencastle Point and near the head at Rostrevor Bay. Greencastle is best for terns in summer, but Rostrevor Bay is better for Scaup and the possibility of Slavonian Grebes and Long-tailed Ducks.

Greencastle is approached from Kilkeel by following the road south towards Cranfield, turning right after 4 km and following the signs for Greencastle. Rostrevor is a village on the A2 midway between Kilkeel and Newry.

136 GROOMSPORT

OSNI ½" map: sheet 4/
1:50,000 map: sheet 15
J58

Habitat and Species

A small village on the coast about 5 km north-east of Bangor, Groomsport has a harbour, muddy and rocky shoreline and a small island offshore which provide a range of habitats. In addition, the location of the village at the mouth of Belfast Lough provides views of seabirds moving in and out of the Lough as well as along the coast. A birdwatcher who spent just over a year and a half in the village, Tony Marr, compiled a list of 139 species seen in the area in that period. The list included rarities such as Red-necked Grebe, Sabine's Gull, White-winged Black Tern and Forster's Tern. The records probably reflect as much the regularity of observation as the excellence of the habitats, but they show the potential of many similar places around the Irish coastline.

Dunnock

Cockle Island, the grassy island in the harbour, has breeding Ringed Plovers and Arctic Terns.

Access

Groomsport is reached by taking the B511 out of Bangor for Groomsport. Cars can be parked at the harbour.

137 STRAND LOUGH AND KILLOUGH HARBOUR

OSI ½″ map: sheet 9/
OSNI ½″ map: sheet 4/
1:50,000 map: sheet 29
J53

Habitat and Species

Strand Lough is a small freshwater lough which drains into a narrow muddy creek at the head of the open expanse of Killough Harbour. The lake has quite extensive reedbeds where Little Grebes, Mallard, Moorhens, Water Rails, Coots, Sedge Warblers and Reed Buntings nest. In winter Wigeon, Teal, Mallard, Pochard, Tufted Duck and Goldeneye can all be seen and there are occasional visits by Whooper and Bewick's Swans, Pintail and Shoveler. Wader numbers are low but diversity is high and Ruffs are regular. Green and Wood Sandpipers turn up occasionally in autumn. Rarities recorded here include Lesser Yellowlegs and White-winged Black Tern.

Killough Harbour is an open muddy bay with good numbers of Mute Swans, Shelducks, Mallard and Wigeon, and at times a party of Brent Geese. The common estuarine wader species can all be seen and occasional Glaucous Gulls turn up among the other gull species.

Access

Killough Harbour can be viewed from the A2 between Ardglass and Killough. The road runs around the harbour to Killough village, where there is a carpark to the left of the main street and close to the pier.

Strand Lough is best watched from Killough Bridge on the road between Ardglass and Killough. Parking by the roadside is not easy and care should be exercised.

138 ST JOHN'S POINT

OSI ½" map: sheet 9/
OSNI ½" map: sheet 4/
1:50,000 map: sheet 29
J53

Habitat and Species

This is a rocky headland, which projects southwards into the Irish Sea, giving excellent views of the sea. It is a popular seawatching point and can be attractive for passerine migrants. It tends to be better in autumn than spring.

Divers, Manx Shearwaters, occasional Sooty and Mediterranean Shearwaters, Storm Petrels, Fulmars, Great Skuas, Arctic Skuas, Pomarine Skuas and terns all pass. Wheatears, warblers and hirundines can be seen in suitable conditions. For both seabirds and passerines, the best conditions are in south-easterly winds.

Access

The headland is reached by driving south from Ardglass through Killough. At the end of Killough village, follow the signposts to the lighthouse and park at the point.

ARMAGH

Introduction

This inland county is small and largely agricultural, with gardens and scattered wooded estates providing cover for breeding passerines. Although not having direct access to the sea, the northern boundary is the next best thing to coastal, being formed by the lake edge of the southern shore of Lough Neagh.

The north-western boundary of the county is formed by the slow-moving River Blackwater, which holds breeding wildfowl and Snipe along its margins. The centre of the county is hilly. The eastern edge is marked by the Newry Canal, which joins Lough Neagh to Newry and eventually the sea at Carlingford Lough. The south is an area of small farms and villages adjoining the counties of Monaghan and Louth in the Republic.

Sites

139   LOUGH NEAGH: OXFORD ISLAND
Large freshwater lough,islands.

Other sites:

140   Lurgan Park Lake   *Freshwater lake.*
141   Craigavon Lakes   *Freshwater lakes.*

244

Reference

Belfast RSPB Members Group. *Birds Beyond Belfast* (RSPB, Belfast, 1985).

139 LOUGH NEAGH: OXFORD ISLAND

OSNI ½″ map: sheet 4/
1:50,000 map: sheet 20
J06

Habitat

The south-east corner of Lough Neagh is one of the best sections of the lake for diversity of wintering birds. Like much of the rest of the lough shoreline, the edge is backed by pasture and scrub of willow and alder. The peninsula, not really an island, projects out into Lough Neagh and is owned and managed by Craigavon Borough Council and is a National Nature Reserve. On either side are shallow, reed-fringed bays, full of ducks in winter.

There are hides on each side of the peninsula from which most of the birds can be seen.

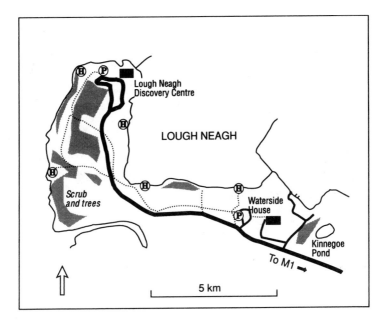

Oxford Island Nature Reserve, Co Armagh

Species

Large numbers of diving duck and smaller numbers of surface-feeding duck and wild swans winter in the area. Whooper and Bewick's Swans are found on the fields nearby, but the principal features for the bird-watcher are the flocks of Pochards, Tufted Ducks and Goldeneyes, together with parties of Great Crested Grebes, Teal, Mallard and Scaup, which feed around the peninsula. Rarer species occur among these ducks each winter. In recent years, Red-crested Pochards and Smew have been annual and Ferruginous Ducks, Ring-necked Ducks and Goosanders have occurred. The only Irish record of Lesser Scaup is of a bird which has returned annually for several winters, and there have been several records of White-winged Black Tern in recent years.

In summer the reedbeds and offshore islands support over 150 pairs of Great Crested Grebes and smaller numbers of Mallard and Tufted Ducks as well as a handful of pairs of Gadwall and Pochard. Black-headed Gulls and Common Terns nest on the small islands visible from the peninsula.

The scrub around the edge of the peninsula attracts a variety of breeding and wintering passerines. Reed Buntings, Grasshopper Warblers and Sedge Warblers nest, flocks of thrushes and finches winter.

Timing

Oxford Island is at its best in winter between November and April when the chances of scarcer ducks species are highest. However, in summer the nesting grebes and duck are an attraction as well. Autumn is the best time for migrant terns and waders.

Being so close to Craigavon, the area gets very crowded on Saturday and Sunday afternoons.

Access

The reserve is located close to the M1 about 7 km from Lurgan. Driving along the M1 from Belfast, turn off at junction 10 and take the third exit at the roundabout. The signposts point the way to Oxford Island. The Lough Neagh Discovery Centre is located at the reserve and comprises an exhibition centre, cafe and shop. The permanent exhibition includes graphic and multi-media displays covering most aspects of Lough Neagh from its history to its wildlife. Birdwatching trips by boat are also available.

There are five hides and a network of paths runs around the Reserve. Admission is £2 for adults, with lower rates for children and groups.

For information, contact The Lough Neagh Discovery Centre, Oxford Island National Nature Reserve, Craigavon, Co Armagh, BT66 6NJ (telephone 0762–322205).

Calendar

Winter: Great Crested Grebe, Little Grebe, Whooper Swan, Bewick's Swan, rafts of Tufted Duck, Pochard and Goldeneye, Teal, Mallard, Scaup, Ruddy Duck, Water Rail, Golden Plover, occasional rarities such as Smew, Goosander, even Lesser Scaup.

Summer: Breeding Great Crested Grebe, Little Grebe, Mallard, Gadwall, Tufted Duck, Pochard, Ruddy Duck, Black-headed Gull, Common Tern, Willow Warbler, Sedge Warbler, Grasshopper Warbler, Reed Bunting.

Autumn: Black Tern, occasional Little Gull

Note: The map for this site is redrawn from Craigavon Borough Council's map of the reserve.

OTHER ARMAGH SITES

140 LURGAN PARK LAKE

OSNI ½″ map: sheet 4/
1:50,000 map: sheet 20
J05

Habitat and Species

The public park in the centre of Lurgan has a broad reed-fringed lake, which holds a good variety of species of duck and has held rarities. Because it is located so close to Lough Neagh and to the Craigavon Lakes, many duck move between the three areas. If a rare duck has been found at Oxford Island, it may well turn up again at Lurgan Park or the Craigavon Lakes.

The commonest wintering ducks are Mallard, Tufted Ducks and Pochard, together with smaller numbers of Teal, Shoveler and Ruddy Ducks. The last species breeds at Lough Neagh and up to 30 winter at

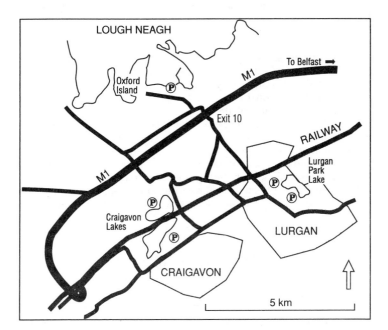

*Oxford Island Nature Reserve, Craigavon Lakes and
Lurgan Park Lake, Co Armagh*

Lurgan Park. They have colonised Northern Ireland from Britain within the last two decades. Rarities recorded here include Ring-necked Ducks and Ferruginous Ducks.

A Ring-billed Gull has wintered here in most years since 1983.

A few pairs of Great Crested Grebes, Little Grebes, Moorhens and Coots nest on the lake.

Access
Coming from Belfast on the M1 turn off at junction 10 and follow the signs for Lurgan. Drive into the centre of the town and turn left down Windsor Avenue. Park your car at the entrance to the park.

141 CRAIGAVON LAKES

OSNI ½" map: sheet 4/
1:50,000 map: sheet 20
J05

Habitat and Species
These lakes share with Lurgan Park Lake the advantage of being close to Lough Neagh. There are two artificial lakes, with three islands, and they have a shallow edge backed by open grassy areas and some scrub.

The lakes have similar wildfowl species to Oxford Island and Lurgan Park Lake: Pochard, Tufted Ducks and Goldeneyes are most common and Mallard also occur. Smews are annual, though they move between here and Oxford Island, and Ring-necked Duck, Red-crested Pochard, Ferruginous Duck and Goosander have been seen in recent years. Flocks of Golden Plovers and Lapwings are regular in winter on the open ground near the lakes.

Little Grebes, Mallard, Tufted Ducks, Coots and Moorhens nest on the lakes.

Access
Coming from Belfast on the M1, these lakes are approached from the same exit as are Oxford Island and Lurgan Park. Turn off at junction 10 and take the A76 towards Craigavon. Turn right after 1 km, following the sign for the Craigavon Centre. Take the right turn at the T-junction reached in 1.5 km and at the next roundabout follow the signs for Tannaghmore Gardens. There is a carpark here and a footpath leads to the northern lake.

The southern and larger lake is reached by driving on along the A76 into Lurgan and turning right onto the A3 for Portadown. Cross the next two roundabouts, following the signs for the Craigavon Centre, and at the third roundabout take the right exit to Craigavon Lakes. There is a carpark at the lake. This lake is popular for watersports at weekends.

FERMANAGH

Introduction
A county of lakes and woodland, Fermanagh is relatively underwatched by birdwatchers, probably because of its distance from Belfast, where most birders live. Yet as well as its lakes and woods, Fermanagh also

holds traditional pastures and damp meadows, which provide breeding areas for the majority of the remaining Corncrakes in Northern Ireland and for waders such as Lapwings and Snipe.

Upper and Lower Lough Erne split the county into two halves and are the most prominent birdwatching sites in the county. Yet there are a number of other lakes holding wildfowl in winter, and a number of forest parks which are open to the public and hold a good number of breeding bird species. Fermanagh is probably the centre of the Irish Garden Warbler breeding population.

This is another county without direct access to the sea, so seabird numbers are low, but terns and gulls breed on Lough Erne.

Sites

142   LOWER LOUGH ERNE   *Freshwater lough.*

Other site:
143   Upper Lough Erne   *Complex freshwater lough system.*

Reference
Belfast RSPB Members Group. *Birds Beyond Belfast* (RSPB, Belfast, 1985).

142   LOWER LOUGH ERNE

OSI ½" map: sheets 3, 7/
OSNI ½" map: sheet 3/
1:50,000 map: sheets 17, 18
H06 H07 H16 H17

Habitat
This is a broad, open, triangular shaped lough downstream of Enniskillen and very different in character to the Upper Lough. The water levels are controlled by the Ballyshannon Hydroelectric Scheme, so they fluctuate. Levels in winter are lower than in summer. The edge of the lough has been colonised by scrub, which provides breeding habitat for a number of breeding birds, and there are woodland areas at Castle Archdale on the east shore, Lough Navar on the west side and Castlecaldwell in the north-west corner, which support a number of passerine species in both summer and winter.

Species
The Lower Lough has fewer wildfowl in winter than the more sheltered Upper Lough, but it does have Great Crested Grebes, Little Grebes, Whooper Swans, Mallard, Teal, Tufted Duck, Pochard and Goldeneye.

In summer this lake has an interesting breeding wildfowl population. For many years this was the centre of the Irish Common Scoter breeding population and over 100 pairs nested, mostly at Castlecaldwell. In recent year numbers have reduced drastically to only a handful of pairs. Competition with roach for food and the impact of predatory mink on

Lower Lough Erne, Co Fermanagh

nesting females have been suggested as reasons for the decline. Roach were either deliberately introduced or released by fishermen who brought them as live bait for fishing, and the mink are descended from animals which escaped from mink farms.

One can never predict which species may occur at an inland lake like this. Both Velvet and Surf Scoter, for example, have been seen on Lower Lough Erne in summer, though breeding has not been suspected.

Great Crested Grebes, Mallard, Teal, Tufted Ducks and Red-breasted Mergansers all breed on Lower Lough Erne. The scrub around the fringe of the lake is very attractive for warblers in summer: Sedge Warbler, Grasshopper Warbler, Willow Warbler, Chiffchaff, Blackcap and Garden Warbler all nest. This area is the headquarters of the Irish Garden Warbler breeding population. Crossbills have bred at Castlecaldwell and Siskins and Redpolls also breed.

On the shoreline a scattering of Lapwings, Snipe, Curlews and Redshanks breed, and a tiny handful of Dunlins.

Great Black-backed, Lesser Black-backed and Black-headed Gulls as well as Sandwich and Common Terns nest on the islands.

Timing

Summer is much the best time to see Common Scoters and Garden Warblers, the specialities of Lower Lough Erne. The scoters return from the coast in April, lay eggs in late May, hatch in July and leave the lough during August.

Access

The shore of Lower Lough Erne is ringed by a road which runs close to the water's edge for most of its length.

Castlecaldwell is an RSPB Reserve in the north-west corner of the lough and has wooded islands, where most of the remaining Common Scoters nest. The old estate is owned by the Forest Service but operated by the RSPB under a management agreement. Access is off the main road from Kesh to Belleek and is signposted from both small towns. It is about 8 km from Belleek. The Warden is Joe Magee, c/o Leggs Post Office, Belleek, Co Fermanagh (telephone 0365–328).

Castle Archdale is another old estate and includes a group of islands on the east side of the lough. It also has nesting Common Scoters and Garden Warblers. Leave Enniskillen on the Pettigoe road and turn left onto the B82 about 6 km beyond the town. The Country Park is on the left hand side about 5 km along this road. This is a National Nature Reserve. The Warden is Hugh McCann, Castle Archdale Country Park, Lisnarick, Irvinestown, Co Fermanagh (telephone 0365–621588).

Calendar

Summer: Great Crested Grebe, Little Grebe, Mallard, Teal, Tufted Duck, Common Scoter, Red-breasted Merganser, Coot, Moorhen, Lapwing,

Magpie

Curlew, Snipe, Redshank, Dunlin, Black-headed Gull, Common Gull, Herring Gull, Lesser Black-backed Gull, Great Black-backed Gull, Sandwich Tern, Common Tern, Blackcap, Garden Warbler.

Winter: Great Crested Grebe, Whooper Swan, Wigeon, Mallard, Teal, Tufted Duck, Pochard, Goldeneye, Red-breasted Merganser, Golden Plover, Lapwing, Curlew.

OTHER FERMANAGH SITE

143 UPPER LOUGH ERNE

OSI ½″ map: sheet 8/
OSNI ½″ map: sheet 3/
1:50,000 map: sheets 27
H23 H33 H32

Habitat and Species

This is a much more complex habitat than the Lower Lough. It is a continuation of the Lough Oughter system in Co Cavan, and the mixture of drumlins, small bays and lagoons and extensive reedbeds is very similar. The shore is shallow and sheltered and very attractive for wintering wildfowl.

Winter wildfowl counts have shown that Upper Lough Erne holds over 400 Great Crested Grebes, over 400 Mute Swans and about 800 Whooper Swans in winter. These totals are very impressive, and these species are accompanied by large flocks of Wigeon, Teal and Mallard, and smaller numbers of Tufted Ducks, Pochard and Goldeneyes.

Some of the islands hold heronries and Cormorants are common non-breeding visitors. Moorhens and Coots are widespread in both winter and summer.

The marshy land around the lough holds the remnants of Northern Ireland's breeding Corncrake population and the largest concentrations of nesting waders. Lapwings, Snipe, Curlews and Redshanks all breed.

Access

The Upper Lough has a very indented shoreline, which is difficult to reach. A number of small roads lead down to the edge of many of the bays and the visitor should use the 1:50,000 map to check out which to follow. The main road between Lisnaskea and Derrylin crosses the lough and provides good viewing.

Kilmore Lough, Ross Lough and Moorlough on the east side of the lough are accessible from Lisnaskea and have a good cross-section of the birds of the area.

INDEX TO SPECIES AND SUBSPECIES

The species and, where relevant, subspecies are listed against the reference numbers of the sites. Those mentioned in the introductory chapters are also included.

253

Index to species and sub species